Understanding Scripture

Understanding Scripture

Forty Things to Know about the Christian Bible

Robert P. Vande Kappelle

WIPF & STOCK · Eugene, Oregon

UNDERSTANDING SCRIPTURE
Forty Things to Know about the Christian Bible

Copyright © 2020 Robert P. Vande Kappelle. All rights reserved. Except for brief quotations in critical publications or reviews, no part of this book may be reproduced in any manner without prior written permission from the publisher. Write: Permissions, Wipf and Stock Publishers, 199 W. 8th Ave., Suite 3, Eugene, OR 97401.

Unless otherwise noted, Bible quotations are from the *New Revised Standard Version of the Bible*, copyright © 1989 by the Division of Christian Education of the National Council of the Churches of Christ in the United States of America. Used by permission.

Wipf & Stock
An Imprint of Wipf and Stock Publishers
199 W. 8th Ave., Suite 3
Eugene, OR 97401

www.wipfandstock.com

PAPERBACK ISBN: 978-1-7252-9161-4
HARDCOVER ISBN: 978-1-7252-9162-1
EBOOK ISBN: 978-1-7252-9163-8

Manufactured in the U.S.A.   12/07/20

Contents

Preface		vii
Chapter 1	Two Things to Know about the Bible	1
Chapter 2	Three Things to Know about the Interpretation of Scripture	11
Chapter 3	Two Things to Know about the Inspiration of Scripture	21
Chapter 4	Three Things to Know about the Old Testament	32
Chapter 5	Three Things to Know about the Pentateuch	42
Chapter 6	Three Things to Know about the Historical Books	53
Chapter 7	Three Things to Know about the Poetic and Wisdom Books	67
Chapter 8	Three Things to Know about the Prophetic Books	85
Chapter 9	Three Things to Know about the New Testament	104
Chapter 10	Three Things to Know about the Gospels	116
Chapter 11	Three Things to Know about the Book of Acts	133
Chapter 12	Three Things to Know about the Epistles of Paul	148
Chapter 13	Three Things to Know about the General Epistles	160
Chapter 14	Three Things to Know about the Book of Revelation	173
Chapter 15	The Application of Scripture	189
Bibliography		193
Index		197

Preface

Utilizing the contributions of three disciplines—biblical introduction, biblical theology, and biblical interpretation—*Understanding Scripture* provides a sequel to my 2016 volume, *Securing Life*. Described as "a novel yet timely approach to reading and understanding the Bible," *Securing Life* uses three motifs to describe the enduring message of the Bible: Covenant, Community, and Creation to summarize the Old Testament message, and New Covenant, New Community, and New Creation to summarize the New Testament message. While *Understanding Scripture* can be read as a continuation of *Securing Life*, it can also be read independently, as a stand-alone volume.

Whereas *Securing Life* approaches the Bible broadly and comprehensively, *Understanding Scripture* is more of a handbook or study guide, focusing on the genres and units of biblical literature and concerned primarily with interpretation and application. To this end, it provides assignments and forty practical guidelines to make your reading of the Bible more useful and your understanding clearer.

The number forty is biblically symbolic, representing a spiritual time of testing, growth, and transformation. In the Bible, whenever God prepared someone for a spiritual purpose, it took forty days. We are told that the Deluge lasted forty days upon the earth (Gen. 7:4); Moses spent forty days on the Mount awaiting Torah (Exod. 24:18); the twelve spies, each representing one tribe of Israel, spent forty days investigating the Promised Land (Num. 13:25); Elijah took a forty-day sojourn to Horeb (Sinai), where he stood "before the Lord" (1 Kgs. 19:8, 11); Jonah called on Nineveh to repent within forty days (Jon. 3:4); Jesus fasted forty days and nights in the wilderness (Matt. 4:2), one day for every year the Israelites wandered in the wilderness, and he remained on earth forty days after his resurrection (Acts 1:3).

Forty years, the biblical length of life and hence a generation of time, represents not only the interim the Israelites spent wandering through the wilderness, a transitional period between their liberation from Egypt and the conquest of the Promised Land characterized by testing and transformation, but all indeterminate periods of spiritual growth and transformation.

Since not all Bibles are the same, we limit our study to sixty-six books, thirty-nine in the Old Testament and twenty-seven in the New Testament, the number and order found in Protestant Bibles, disregarding the apocryphal/deuterocanonical books.[1]

Understanding Scripture is useful for individual or group study. Each chapter concludes with questions suitable for discussion or reflection. As you read this book, consider journaling as a way to learn and understand. As you reflect and write, be honest with your thoughts and hopes, without ignoring your fears. In addition to the questions provided, individuals and group leaders are encouraged to add or substitute their own questions. The point of the reading is not to finish the assigned chapter or task, but rather to maintain momentum, that is, to keep the discussion fresh and vital and therefore open and ongoing. Upon concluding each chapter or session, readers and participants will profit by asking the question, "What is the primary insight I/we gained from this chapter or session?"

---

1. I examine these writings in two earlier volumes, *Wisdom Revealed* (2014) and *Response to the Other* (2020).

Chapter 1
_____

Two Things to Know about the Bible

CHRISTIANITY, THE PREDOMINANT, MOST accessible, and most diffuse of the world's religions, has arguably inspired the world's greatest art, music, and architecture. It has also inspired its most memorable speeches, sermons, and lectures; its most elevated theology and philosophy; and its most elegant rhetoric and prose. At the heart of this movement that has captured the imagination of people around the globe is its scripture, known as the Holy Bible, a library of books divided into testaments, one Jewish and the other Christian.

The Bible, the all-time best-selling book, is the most read, best known, most published, and most widely disseminated book in the world. Its value is inestimable, for it has single-handedly changed the course of world history, guiding empires, influencing legal systems, and impacting the lives of untold millions around the globe. Columbus took a copy to the New World, Charles Lindbergh stowed a copy in the cramped quarters of the Spirit of St. Louis on his epic trans-Atlantic flight, and astronaut James Irwin, who carried a copy on his moon walk, became the first person to quote from the Bible while on the moon: "I will lift up my eyes unto the hills, from whence cometh my help" (Ps. 121:1, KJV).

1. The Bible is not "sacred" or "holy" because of its origin or content.

For two thousand years the Bible, in part or in whole, has been viewed as sacred by generations of believers. At the time of their composition, however, the books of the Bible were not considered to be part of scripture.

Rather, the various parts of the Bible became sacred through canonization, a process that took several centuries. For Christians, the status of the Bible as sacred scripture means it is the primary collection of writings they know, definitive for faith and practice. The sacredness of scripture is validated by its ability to inspire believers in every age, thereby authenticating its enduring message.

The Jewish Bible (known to Christians as the Old Testament) and the Christian New Testament are ancient. Some portions of the Old Testament may have been written around three thousand years ago, while the books of the New Testament are about two thousand years old. In the twenty-first century, why should we study such archaic writings?

Many people, of course, read the Bible as scripture, meaning it is fundamental to their identity. They consider the Bible the Word of God and are committed to living their lives on the basis of the values they find therein. They read the Bible weekly in worship and live liturgically, their lives impacted deeply by ritual observances based on stories found in these texts, such as the Jewish Passover and Yom Kippur or the Christian Easter and Christmas.

There are other less religious reasons the Bible should be studied today. These are particularly relevant for readers who have little or no connection with the Bible as sacred text, but are important for those who are guided by its spiritual values and moral teachings. In addition to its spiritual and religious significance, the Bible continues to have a profound cultural influence on the Western world, including artistic, literary, political, and legal influence. The Bible, after all, is great literature, and those who ignore it cannot be considered educated.

The word "Bible" derives from the Greek *biblia*, which means "books." The Bible is not a single book but rather a collection of writings. It is a library of diverse pieces of literature that were collected together as scripture by Jewish and Christian communities. In the ancient world "book" really meant "scroll." With the development of the codex (a book with leaves or pages), a collection of books could be bound together in a single volume, and the Bible represents such a format.

2. *Christian Bibles are not all the same.*

The Jewish Bible (known as the Hebrew scriptures or to Jews simply as Tanakh) and the Christian Old Testament are similar but not identical.

For the Jewish community, the Bible is composed of twenty-four books divided into three sections: Torah (Law), Nebiim (Prophets), and Kethubim (Writings). While these books, written almost entirely in Hebrew, are fundamentally the same as the Christian Old Testament, the arrangement differs. To understand the Hebrew Bible, imagine three concentric circles. The inner circle, the Torah, presents the basic story of the people and includes laws for everyday life. The next circle, the Prophets, is a commentary on the life of the people to whom the Torah is given. The outer circle, the Writings, is a diverse collection that extends outward from Israel's worship and festivals to wisdom reflection.

The Christian Bible, after the first five books (known as the Books of Moses or the Pentateuch), displays a different order and adds up differently, making thirty-nine distinct books, in contrast to the twenty-four of the Tanakh. The differences are partly accounted for by the fact that the early Christians were a Greek-speaking community who read the Hebrew Bible in Greek, particularly in a translation begun in the third century BCE called the Septuagint. The Septuagint placed the prophetic writings last, while the Hebrew Bible concludes with the Writings (ending with 1–2 Chronicles). Traditionally, Christians prefer the Greek order because the prophetic books look ahead to a new beginning for Israel, creating a more effective transition to the New Testament. In addition, these books provide a prophetic bridge between the testaments, directly connecting Old Testament prophecy with New Testament fulfillment. For example, Matthew's opening narrative regularly references how the birth of Jesus fulfills Old Testament prophecy: "All this took place to fulfill what had been spoken by the Lord through the prophet" (Matt. 1:22; see also 2:5, 15, 17, 23). The Septuagint also includes a number of works that are not part of the Hebrew Bible, though these works once enjoyed considerable favor in Jewish circles.

Some Christian churches, including Roman Catholic, Eastern Orthodox, and a few Protestant groups, add six or seven additional books (plus additions to existing books) to the twenty-four books of the Tanakh. These additional works are called "deuterocanonical" (lit. "second canon," meaning that they came into the biblical canon at a later time than the books of the Hebrew Bible) by these groups and the "Apocrypha" by most Protestant groups, whose Old Testament has the same books as the Tanakh, although arranged somewhat differently. The following table illustrates these differences.

The Hebrew Bible (Tanakh)

The Torah (five books): Genesis, Exodus, Leviticus, Numbers, Deuteronomy

The Prophets (eight books):

- Former Prophets: Joshua, Judges, Samuel (counts as one book), Kings (counts as one book)
- Latter Prophets: Isaiah, Jeremiah, Ezekiel, the Twelve (counts as one book: Hosea, Joel, Amos, Obadiah, Jonah, Micah, Nahum, Habakkuk, Zephaniah, Haggai, Zechariah, Malachi)

The Writings (eleven books): Job, Psalms, Proverbs, Ruth, Song of Songs (also known as Song of Solomon), Ecclesiastes, Lamentations, Esther, Daniel, Ezra-Nehemiah (counts as one book), Chronicles (counts as one book)

The Christian Old Testament

The Pentateuch: (five books): Genesis, Exodus, Leviticus, Numbers, Deuteronomy

Historical Books (twelve books): Joshua, Judges, Ruth, 1 and 2 Samuel, 1 and 2 Kings, 1 and 2 Chronicles, Ezra, Nehemiah, Esther

Poetry and Wisdom Books (five books): Job, Psalms, Proverbs, Ecclesiastes, Song of Solomon

Prophetic Books (seventeen books)

- Major Prophets: Isaiah, Jeremiah, Lamentations, Ezekiel, Daniel
- Minor Prophets: Hosea, Joel, Amos, Obadiah, Jonah, Micah, Nahum, Habakkuk, Zephaniah, Haggai, Zechariah, Malachi

The Deuterocanonical (or Apocryphal) Books

Historical Books: Tobit, Judith, Additions to Esther; 1 and 2 Maccabees
Poetry and Wisdom: Wisdom of Solomon, Ecclesiasticus
Prophets: Additions to Daniel

The first fourteen books of the Old Testament (the first ten books of the Tanakh) have a narrative framework, recounting a story that begins with the creation of the heavens and the earth by God in Genesis and continues with the formation and flourishing of the nation Israel, and concludes with the chaos of the destruction of ancient Israel. The Pentateuch begins with prehistory (Genesis 1–11), including accounts of cosmic origins, the first humans, a disastrous flood, restoration after the flood, and the spread of humanity. The central historical narrative features ancestral stories (Genesis 12–50), beginning with the journey of Abraham and Sarah to the land of Canaan and eventually into Egypt, where they become slaves to Pharaoh. Eventually Moses leads the Israelites out of Egypt (Exodus 1–18), climaxing in a dramatic encounter with God at Mount Sinai, where they enter into a covenant with Yahweh (Exodus 19:1—Numbers 10:10). At the end of a forty-year sojourn through the wilderness, the tribes of Israel stand on the east bank of the Jordan River, ready to enter the land of promise. The account of wandering is accompanied by extensive ritual and legal legislation (such as the Book of the Covenant in Exodus 20:22—23:33 and the Holiness Code in Leviticus 17–26).

The final book of the Torah (Deuteronomy) marks a transition to the next section of the Bible (known as the Historical Books or to Jews as the Former Prophets), as Moses recounts to the people the journey on which God has led them, exhorts them to keep the law given by God, and prepares them for life in the land they are about to enter.

The Historical Books recount the dramatic story of the conquest and settling of the land of Canaan by the tribes of Israel under the leadership of Joshua (Joshua 1–Judges 2); the exploits of leaders known as judges who emerge to defend the tribes when they are threatened (Judges 3–21); the capture of Jerusalem and the creation of the nation of Israel under King David and his son Solomon, the building of the temple in Jerusalem, the division of the nation into the kingdoms of Israel (in the North) and Judah (in the South), and finally the conquest of the two kingdoms by the Assyrian and Babylonian empires, culminating in the destruction of the temple and the beginning of the exile in Babylon (1 and 2 Samuel, 1 and 2 Kings). The story throughout the Historical Books is told from the perspective introduced in the book of Deuteronomy, that the nation prospers when leaders and people are faithful to the law God revealed to them at Sinai. Hence, scholars often call this section the Deuteronomistic History.

In the Jewish canon narrative books are treated as prophecy because they are said to contain accurate and reliable lessons about history. A prophet, in Israel's religious tradition, was not a predictor of the future, but a reader of the present. That is to say, a prophet was one who could look at society critically and discern the will of God for the present time, then speak that will to the people. The authors of these Historical Books were prophets in this sense. They looked at Hebrew society of their time and judged that a particular lesson from Israel's history was needed to insure God's blessing.

The books of the Latter Prophets include collections of oracles and writings of the prophets, usually in poetic form, as well as stories about the prophets. The first three are called the major prophets because they are longer in length, while the shortest are called minor prophets.

The remaining books, a diverse collection of literature known as the Writings in the Tanakh, include religious poetry (Psalms and Lamentations), love poetry (Song of Solomon), conventional wisdom sayings (Proverbs), and skeptical wisdom (Ecclesiastes and Job). In addition, the Writings include a group of historical writings (Ezra, Nehemiah, and 1 and 2 Chronicles), called by scholars the Chronicler's History. These books revisit the story of the formation and collapse of the nation Israel, already introduced in the Former Prophets, and extends it to the return following the Babylonian Exile, focusing on the rebuilding of the Jerusalem temple, the walls of the city, and the renewal of the covenant with God. The Writings also include Ruth and Esther, short stories about heroic women who play crucial roles in the life of Israel. In Jewish tradition, five of the books in the Writings (Ruth, Esther, Song of Songs, Ecclesiastes, and Lamentations) are grouped together as the Megilloth or festival scrolls and assigned to be read at specific religious holidays.

Daniel, the remaining book in the Writings, is the only fully apocalyptic book in the Tanakh. It includes visions of a dramatic time in history known as the Maccabean period and hopes for a new age, the kingdom of God. In the Christian Old Testament this book is included with the prophetic books.

The deuterocanonical (or apocryphal) books reflect the same literary variety as the Old Testament. Tobit and Judith are short stories, recounting the exploits of heroic figures. Maccabees extends the historical narrative begun in the Historical Books. Edifying tales (Susanna and Bel and the Dragon) and poems (The Prayer of Azariah and the Song of the Three Men) are added to Daniel in the Deuterocanon.

An offshoot of Judaism, the early Christian community added twenty-seven early Christian writings to the Jewish Bible, which they formerly called simply "scripture." The addition became known as the New Testament. Considerably shorter than the Old Testament and written entirely in Greek, the New Testament can be grouped into five divisions, as the following chart shows.

The New Testament

Gospels (four books): Matthew, Mark, Luke, John

Historical (one book): Acts

Epistles (Letters) of Paul (thirteen books): Romans, 1 and 2 Corinthians, Galatians, Ephesians, Philippians, Colossians, 1 and 2 Thessalonians, 1 and 2 Timothy, Titus, Philemon

General (Catholic) Epistles (eight books): Hebrews, James, 1 and 2 Peter, 1, 2, and 3 John, Jude

Prophetic (1 book): Revelation

The books of the New Testament are not arranged according to chronology, that is, according to the order in which they were written, but rather according to the order in which the material they report happened.

- Gospels—deal with the life of Jesus
- Acts—deals with the birth of the church
- Epistles of Paul—deal with the growth of the church
- General Epistles—deal with the general nature of the church
- Revelation—deals with the immediate and distant future of the church

The New Testament begins with four works known as gospels. Each is a narrative of the life and teachings of Jesus of Nazareth, proclaiming him to be the Christ, which means the Messiah, the one anointed by God to fulfill the promises made to Israel. What began as a largely oral tradition, handed down in no particular order, gradually became a set of texts. The first three gospels, similar in structure and content, are known collectively as the Synoptics, whereas John, the last to be written and distinct in structure and point of view, is known as the Fourth Gospel.

The gospels are followed in the New Testament by Acts of the Apostles, a historical narrative that recounts a geographic shift—the spread of the Christian message from Jerusalem to Rome—and an ethnic shift—from a church predominantly Jewish to one predominantly Gentile in nature. Acts focuses on the role of two prominent individuals: Peter, an apostle of Jesus, and Paul, commissioned apostle by the risen Christ. Modern scholarship supports the view that the gospel of Luke and the Acts of the Apostles share authorship and purpose, joint volumes in a connected historical narrative of the birth of Christianity.

Thirteen of the twenty-seven books of the New Testament are letters attributed to Paul, who helped shape Christian belief, practice, and ethics and was instrumental in the spread of Christianity across the Mediterranean world. Paul's letters typically follow epistolary correspondence common in the Greek-speaking world of the first century. Most of these letters are addressed to Christian communities in the northern Mediterranean world, churches Paul visited during his three missionary journeys. The author gives thanks for the people's faithfulness, chastises them for their failings, exhorts them to live as disciples of Jesus Christ, and clarifies his understanding of the meaning of the Christian gospel.

Like other New Testament documents, the Pauline letters are not arranged chronologically, that is, in the order in which they were written, but rather according to two criteria: length and audience. The first nine letters, written to churches, precede the last four, written to individuals; Romans, the longest letter written to a community, appears first, and Philemon, the shortest letter written to an individual, appears last.

The other New Testament letters, called General or Catholic Epistles because their message is universal and intended for the church at large, are general tracts on Christian themes. The book of Hebrews appears not to be a letter but an early Christian sermon. These epistles are named either for the type of audience (Hebrews) or the claimed author (James; 1 and 2 Peter; 1, 2, and 3 John; Jude). The authors of the letters of James and Jude have been traditionally identified as brothers of Jesus and early Christian leaders. Peter is an apostle of Jesus prominent in the gospels and Acts. It is generally assumed that the "John" of the first epistle is not "the elder" identified in the other two letters of John.

The final book of the New Testament, written by a prophet named John and aptly named the book of Revelation, is, like the Old Testament book of Daniel, an apocalyptic work. It features visions of the end, describing the course of future events leading up to the defeat of evil and, with the triumphant return of Jesus Christ, the beginning of a new age. It is principally concerned with faithfulness, both of Christians and of God.

The Bible: A Narrative Drama in Five Acts

Since the Jewish and Christian Bibles are not single books but collections of works, they have a variety of themes and conflicting points of view. However, read canonically, the Bible contains a unified story. Biblical theologians see the Bible as a narrative drama, with God as the main character. While scholars disagree on the number of episodes in the biblical drama or on what to call them, the following headings adequately describe the plot: Creation, Covenant, Christ, Church, and Consummation.

The Bible focuses on the involvement of the Creator of the universe in the unfolding story of life. The book of Genesis begins with the origins of the cosmos and quickly moves to a story revolving around God's special relationship with human beings, particularly with the nation of Israel. It is the story of God's faithfulness and of the fulfillment humans enjoy when they respond with obedience to the way of life to which God calls them. A central theme in the Old Testament is God's special relationship with the people of Israel, founded on God's promise made to a couple named Abraham and Sarah that their descendants would become a great nation, with a land of their own, and that through this nation (which became known as Israel) all the peoples of the earth would be blessed. Because of this special relationship, the people of Israel are expected to follow the path God reveals to them through Torah, God's law given through Moses and reaffirmed by prophets, priests, and kings at various points in the story of the nation. However, Israel's leaders and people fail to keep these expectations and the Old Testament recounts the tragic story of God's judgment as Israel breaks up. Nevertheless, the underlying theme of God's faithfulness reappears in a variety of contexts, such as in Isaiah's Suffering Servant poems (Isa. 42:1–4, 49:1–6, 50:4–11, and 52:13—53:12), Jeremiah's promise of a new covenant (Jer. 31:31–34), and Daniel's Son of Man vision (Dan. 7:13–14). These references would become vital to the fledgling Christian community's self-understanding, creating a sense of hope that all God's promises were being fulfilled in Jesus Christ (see 2 Cor. 1:20).

The Christian Bible reorganizes the books of the Tanakh so that the focus is on the hope that God is acting in a new and decisive way to redeem Israel. From that perspective, the New Testament is the story of the church, a "new Israel" that includes not only physical descendants of Abraham but all people who respond faithfully to God's new revelation (Gal. 3:6–9, Rom. 4:16–25) in Jesus Christ. Therefore, the New Testament begins with the story of the life, death, and resurrection of Jesus in the gospels and follows with the account of the formation of a new community of faith founded on faith in Jesus, through whom all humans are brought back to a right relationship with the Creator. The New Testament ends by looking to the return of Jesus and the creation of a "new heaven and new earth" (Rev. 21:1, 5), a consummation in which the harmony God intended at the beginning will finally be realized.

The books of the Old and New Testament constitute the Christian canon, for Christians the authoritative Word of God. The reasons for its authoritative nature and the process of its canonization is explored in the following chapter.

Assignment

Having read chapter 1, answer the following questions, writing the answers in your journal. [If you are in a study group, be prepared to share your views with others in the class.]

1. In your estimation, why should we read the Bible? Does our motivation matter?

2. What do Christians generally mean when they say that the Bible is "holy"? Does the word "sacred" necessarily imply anything supernatural about the origin or nature of scripture? Explain your answer.

3. In your estimation, should the apocryphal/deuterocanonical books be read as scripture and be included in all Christian Bibles? Explain your answer.

4. Assess the merits of reading the Bible canonically, that is, as having a unified story. Where does Jesus Christ belong in the biblical drama, at the beginning, the middle, the end, or as central to all these periods? Explain your answer.

5. What is the primary insight I/we gained from this chapter or session?

Chapter 2

Three Things to Know about the Interpretation of Scripture

ALL LITERATURE INVITES INTERPRETATION; all important literature demands it. This is particularly true of scripture, its truth claims fraught with meaning and therefore open to investigation. As my colleague, Dan Stinson, notes, "Every passage of scripture begs for interpretation."

3. All reading of the Bible is interpretive.

Reading the stories of creation or the stories of Jesus' birth literally involves an interpretive decision equally as much as does the decision to read them metaphorically. When we speak of meaning in relation to a biblical text, five levels come to mind: (1) what the divine author intended (while this concern is primary for conservative readers, it applies indirectly to all who read the Bible as scripture); (2) what the human author intended (this concern should be important to all readers, conservative, moderate, and liberal alike); (3) how biblical scholars and theologians interpret a particular passage or verse (their views, both ancient and modern, are readily available in commentaries, handbooks, Study Bibles, and other interpretive aids. While it is important to recognize the bias or perspective of one's resources, those interested in breadth of insight should consult works from across the denominational and theological spectrum); (4) how leaders in one's church or denomination interpret a particular passage or verse; and finally, (5) what the text means to you. This final level, while indispensable, should not be arrived at quickly.

Without the corrective of the other levels, this approach to the Bible can result in as many meanings as it has readers. This postmodern approach, based on the belief that "the meaning of a text is what it means to me," lacks hermeneutical validity.

In the conversation between Philip and the Ethiopian official found in Acts 8, we read these words: "So Philip ran up to (the chariot) and heard (the Ethiopian) reading the prophet Isaiah. Philip asked, 'Do you understand what you are reading?' The Ethiopian replied, 'How can I, unless someone guides me?'" There is a reason why we have commentaries on the books of the Bible: these books are not always easy to understand without help. To understand these books is not just a question of satisfying intellectual curiosity; they have unique importance from both a religious and a spiritual significance. Furthermore, they are very ancient books, much older than other books most modern people ever read. Reading and interpreting any book is a complicated and subtle process. However, when we read straightforward texts written by our contemporaries, we often fail to notice the complications, because of their familiarity. Reading and interpreting the Bible is only a special case of a general problem, the problem of how one human being understands words written by another. The study of this problem is called hermeneutics, a discipline that involves three processes: understanding (grasping the meaning of a book or passage), exposition (stating the meaning of a text or passage in one's own words), and application (applying the meaning of a text or passage to one's own life).

To understand the Bible we must first know the biblical languages (Hebrew, Aramaic, and Greek) or have access to good translations and competent commentaries (preferably scholarly and theologically unbiased ones). It is also necessary to understand what kind of literature we are reading. To understand the Psalms, for example, we have to realize that they are poems and hymns, and that we should not read them as though they are statements of doctrine, though they certainly reflect theological points of view. To understand the writings of Paul, it is essential to know that they are letters, written to a particular set of readers whose problems and questions the writer was addressing. An important part of the task of biblical study is to classify the books of the Bible into different types or genres and thus to help modern readers understand the intentions of the writers.

4. In interpreting scripture, genre matters.

Whenever you read a book, whether you are aware of it or not, you make certain judgments even before you start reading. If you pick up a romance novel, you expect to read about broken hearts or extramarital affairs, but you certainly do not expect to read an enduring literary work. If you read a book on the Vietnam War or the Iraq War, you expect to read about historical events that led to the conflict or the political maneuverings that brought it to conclusion. You would not expect a tourist guide of places to visit in Saigon or Baghdad.

When you make judgments about different types of literature, you are making decisions about the genre of the work. The same holds true in other artistic endeavors, such as art or music. For example, most people can distinguish between impressionism or realism in art, or jazz from folk music. Painters, composers, and performers know that there are certain rules that govern their work. Sometimes they deviate from these rules in order to create interest or excitement, but when they go too far, they find themselves working in a different genre or possibly even creating a new genre. The same holds true for literature. Knowing whether the genre of a work is a novel, a biography, or science fiction is an important step in understanding how to interpret it.

The same holds true for the New Testament books; knowing their genre can dramatically impact interpretation. Some people look at the gospels, for example, and think of them as histories (in the modern sense of the word) or eyewitness accounts of the life of Jesus. However, scholarly research into the gospel writers and their intended audiences shows that they were intended as faith proclamations for communities committed to belief in Jesus as the Christ. Similarly, some people read the book of Revelation and think it will give them a timetable of the events that must take place before the end of the world. However, without a proper understanding of the apocalyptic genre, they will miss the intended message of Revelation. The book is highly symbolic, and while it appears to be about the end time, its real message is pastoral, hopeful, and timely.

5. To read scripture "literally" misses much of its meaning and can lead to misunderstanding its message.

People read the Bible for many reasons: literarily (as great literature), philosophically (as a guide for moral and reflective thought), theologically (as a compendium of truth), or devotionally (as a resource for meditation and a source of comfort). Despite the Bible's widespread scriptural use, most devout people read it only occasionally, and superficially. How people read it is perhaps more important than why they read it. For those who wish to engage with scripture seriously and in depth, I recommend that you find a method of study that works for you, whether individually or with others, and commit to it. Of many valid ways of reading scripture, the following are recommended:

- Reading for *information*—to learn as much as possible about the setting of the authors and their primary audience in order to discover the original meaning of a particular passage of scripture and its potential application.
- Reading for *formation*—to establish one's identity, values, and beliefs in order to live meaningfully, joyously, and securely.
- Reading for *transformation*—to provide resources for developing soulcentrically rather than egocentrically, aligning more deeply with one's powers of nurturing and creating, presence and wonder.

Of course, it is quite possible for these approaches to overlap, due to the complexity of our intellectual, theological, and spiritual needs. It is equally possible that biblical passages convey messages appropriate to our varied abilities and needs. Scripture is multivalent, meaning that it's message allows for multiple interpretations. While one text might strike terror in the heart of an unrepentant person, the same passage might exhort devout believers to greater faithfulness and even greater freedom. When you read any book or section of the Bible, particularly in a group setting, keep in mind the possibility that biblical passages contain multiple messages, depending on one's needs, temperament, and spiritual journey. Scripture, like a good smorgasbord, provides healthy options for different appetites. And you don't always have to eat the same food; sometimes a change of diet can be helpful.

As Paul showed in 1 Corinthians, the important thing is to keep growing spiritually. Paul's concern with the Corinthians was that they were in a state of spiritual immaturity, unable to eat solid food. It takes time—and conscious effort—to grow spiritually, from egocentrism to soulcentrism. How people hear and read scripture (eat spiritually) reflects their spiritual maturity.

Perhaps you have heard it said that the modern age has problems with authority in general, and with the authority of scripture in particular. However, according to 2 Timothy 3:16, the Bible should not be considered as an authority in the modern sense of the word; in other words, the Bible does not exist for its own sake. Note that this passage does not say, "All scripture is inspired by God and is *authoritative*." It says that all scripture is inspired and *useful*—useful to teach, rebuke, correct, instruct, and equip us for our mission as the people of God. For too long we have read the Bible as if it were God's encyclopedia, God's rule book, God's answer book, God's scientific text, God's easy-steps instruction book, God's little book of morals for all occasions. In Jesus' day, the only people who would have had anything close to these expectations of the Bible would have been the scribes and Pharisees. And Jesus certainly disapproved of their attitudes and methodology regarding scripture.

While the Hebraic scriptures (the Old Testament) provide codes of behavior and belief that can be systematized into groups of tens or twelves, the canonical writings of Christianity intentionally fail to do so, even for religious matters. To the question, "What does the New Testament teach on X or Y?" the proper answer seems, "What did you read last in the New Testament?" The New Testament is not a collection of books that provides a system of law for personal or public behavior, but rather a way of life based on discernment and wisdom, subjecting morality under fuzzy topics such as "love," "mercy," and "forgiveness."

When you let go of the Bible as God's answer book, you get it back as something so much better. It becomes the family story—the story of the people who have been called by the one true God to be his agents in the world, to be his servants to the rest of the world. So I suggest we stop reading the Bible as a "modern" answer book. But that doesn't mean we should discard it. Just the opposite! When we let it go as a modern answer book, we get to rediscover it for what it really is: an ancient book of incredible spiritual value for us, a kind of universal and cosmic history, a book that tells us who we are and what story we find ourselves in so that we know what to do and how to live. Of course, the Bible is even more than a book of wisdom and wisdom development. It is a book that calls together and helps create a community, a community that is a catalyst for God's work in our world.

In his intriguing fable, *A New Kind of Christian*, Brian McLaren criticizes modern liberals and conservatives alike for reading the Bible in very modern ways. Modern conservatives treat the Bible as if it were a modern book. They are used to reading modern history texts, modern encyclopedias, modern science articles, and modern legal codes, and so they assume that the Bible will yield its resources if they approach it like one of those texts. However, none of those categories even existed when the Bible was written. Sure, there was history, but not with all of the modern trimmings like a concern for factual accuracy, corroborating evidence, or absolute objectivity. There was law, but surely not a one-to-one correspondence between ancient Near Eastern concepts of law and our modern concept. The conservatives seem somewhat blind to these kinds of differences. Modern liberals seem to make a corresponding mistake. Acknowledging that the Bible is a different kind of text from our modern texts, they still judge it by modern standards. If something doesn't fit in with a modern Western mindset that reveres objectivity, science, democracy, individualism, and the like, they dismiss it as primitive and irrelevant.[1]

There is a third option: instead of reading the Bible, what if you let the Bible read you? If that sounds a bit ethereal, perhaps even mystical, think of it this way. Think of a scientist preparing to dissect a frog, or think of a detective at a crime scene. How would you describe their attitude or approach? Now think of a teenage girl meeting a boy at the mall. Surely her attitude differs from the scientist's or the detective's. Her approach wouldn't be so analytical or objective. And there would be some fun in it, a sense of personal investment, a feeling of adventure. In one sense, there's less caution, less holding back. Yet in another way, there is holding back, because she wants to make her move and then leave room for him to respond. This approach is less aggressive, less controlling, and more relational. We need to approach the Bible that way; we need to flirt with it, romance it—or possibly let its message romance us.[2]

Our modern age has predisposed us to only a limited range of postures with the Bible, like the objective analysis of a scientist or like forensic science, always trying to prove something. It's all about conquering the text, reducing it to something explainable by our preconceptions, turning it into moralisms, principles, outlines, conclusions, or proofs. What would happen if we approached the text less aggressively but even more energetically and passionately? What would happen if we honestly listened to the story and put ourselves under its spell, so to speak, not using

---

1. McLaren, *New Kind of Christian*, 55–56.
2. McLaren, *New Kind of Christian*, 56–57.

it to get all of our questions about God answered but instead trusting it to pose questions about us. What would happen if we simply trusted ourselves to it—the way we fall in love, or fall asleep?

Christianity is centered in the Bible. Of course, it is ultimately centered in God, but it is the God of whom the Bible speaks and to whom it points. God may be known in other ways and through other religions, but to be Christian is to be centered in the God of the Bible. This is not a mark of Christian exclusion, but of Christian identity. The Bible is for Christians their sacred scripture, their sacred story.[3]

Yet the Bible has become a stumbling block for many. In the last half century, many Christians have left the church because of the Bible. More precisely, they left because the traditional literal way of interpreting the Bible, with its emphasis on biblical infallibility, historical factuality, and moral and doctrinal absolutes, became intolerable. In his writings, biblical scholar Marcus Borg provides an alternative to biblical literalism. Utilizing three adjectives—*historical*, *metaphorical*, and *sacramental*—he describes how scripture, creeds, and other normative Christian teachings should be understood.[4]

To speak of *the Bible as a historical product* is to see that it is a human product, not a divine product. Not "absolute truth" but relatively and culturally conditioned, the Bible uses the language and concepts of the cultures in which it took shape. It tells us how our spiritual ancestors saw things, not how God sees things. The Bible is not verbally inspired, since the emphasis is not upon words inspired by God but on people moved by their experience of God.

For modern Christians, describing the Bible as sacred scripture and therefore as "holy" is to value the historical process known as canonization. The documents that make up the Bible were not "sacred" when they were written, but over time were declared sacred, meaning that they became the most important documents for that community, providing its foundation and shaping its identity.

Much of the language of the Bible is metaphorical: one third of the Old Testament is poetry or semi-poetical literature. To speak of *the Bible as metaphor* is to emphasize that this language should not be interpreted literally. Metaphor does not mean that the Bible is not true, but rather that it is not primarily concerned with facticity. The Bible does contain

---

3. Borg, *Heart of Christianity*, 43.

4. This segment appears in many of my commentaries and I use it again here because of its usefulness. It is adapted from Borg's *Heart of Christianity*, 43–60.

history, but even when a text contains historical memory, its meaning is more than (not less than) literal. For example, although the exile in Babylon in the sixth century BCE really happened, the way the story is told gives it a more than historical meaning. It became a metaphorical narrative of exile and return, providing images of the human condition and its remedy. In other cases, as the Genesis stories of creation, there may be little or no historical factuality. Though these stories are not literally factual, they are profoundly true.

Because the gospels combine memory and metaphor, some of these accounts, when literalized, become literally incredible. The story of Jesus walking on water illustrates the point. A literal reading of the story emphasizes the spectacular event as a sign of Jesus's identity, "proof" that he was divine. A metaphorical reading of this story yields a different meaning. It seems to be a way of saying: "Here in a nutshell is what the story of Jesus is about."

Historically speaking, the gospel accounts do not begin with what Jesus said and did before his death. Christianity begins with the experience of Jesus after his death by his followers. They write of him as one resurrected from the dead and exalted to God's presence. Accounts of his birth and transfiguration, of his feeding the multitudes, restoring sight to the blind, turning water into wine, raising the dead, and walking on the water, all are resurrection stories! The gospel accounts are all told from the perspective of resurrection, of victory over death. The evangelists are not writing about an ordinary human, but rather about one who is already viewed as Lord, Messiah, and preexistent Christ.

A metaphorical reading of the gospels provides rich meaning for Christians in all times and places; a literal reading misses all of this, emphasizing belief in the miraculous elements rather than on its meaning for a life of faith. Metaphorical language is *a way of seeing*. To apply this to the Bible means that in addition to its metaphorical language and metaphorical narratives, the Bible as a whole may be thought of as a "giant" metaphor. "Thus the point is not to believe in the Bible—but to see our lives with God through it."[5]

To speak of *the Bible as sacrament* is to say that it mediates the sacred. If a sacrament is a physical vehicle or vessel for the Spirit, the Bible is sacrament in the sense that it is a visible human product whereby God becomes present to us.

---

5. Borg, *Heart of Christianity*, 57.

For modern Christians, "the Bible—human in origin, sacred in status and function—is both metaphor and sacrament. As metaphor, it is a way of seeing—a way of seeing God and our life with God. As sacrament, it is a way that God speaks to us and comes to us."[6] The Bible is a two-way bridge, a path to the divine and a way to connect to our deepest self. Like a backboard in the game of basketball, scripture is a means to an end, not an end in itself.

A Method for Studying the Bible

When we read scripture, we encounter historical, linguistic, social, and cultural gaps between the ancient and modern worlds, barriers we must overcome if we are to understanding the original meaning of the text. In addition, each of us approaches the text with some preunderstanding of the subject. Those who read the Bible only from the perspective of their immediate personal circumstances, who forget that the passage was originally written for someone else, can easily misunderstand what the text says. We all do this on occasion, but some, seemingly unaware, do so to an extreme.

The Bible, viewed as God's Word, is said to provide unchanging values and eternal commandments. As scripture, the Bible holds answers to life's toughest questions: "Where did we come from? "Why are we here?" and "How will everything end?" Yet the Bible is also a book of bizarre events and strange mysteries, with references to angels and demons, giants and dragons, rivers turning to blood, fire and brimstone raining down on cities, ax-heads floating, people walking on water, and dead people coming back to life.

Also strange are certain commands in the Bible, such as offering animal sacrifices to the Lord, not eating foods like pork and shellfish, not wearing clothing made of more than one material, not tattooing one's body, and doing no work on Saturday. Even in the New Testament people are told to wash one another's feet, to sell everything they have and give the money to the poor, and to pluck out their eye or cut off their hand if they cause you to sin. Women are told to cover their heads with a veil, not to cut their hair or wear pearls or gold jewelry, and to keep quiet in church. Are these cultural matters that no longer apply? If so, what about passages that promote celibacy, discourage marriage, or forbid greed

---

6. Borg, *Heart of Christianity*, 59.

and homosexual behavior? Are these cultural as well? To navigate these challenging waters we need a method (a consistent approach that can be used on any passage), hermeneutical principles, and regular practice. The process of interpreting the Bible involves building a bridge over a chasm. We are separated from the biblical audience by linguistic, historical, social, and cultural gaps, differences that separate us from the text and that often prohibit us from grasping the meaning of the text. To span this chasm we must erect two pylons, one on either side of the gorge. The first pylon represents *the descriptive task* (discerning what a text *meant* to the original audience), and the second pylon represents *the application task* (discerning what a text *means* to me, in my current situation).

Assignment

Having read chapter 2, answer the following questions, writing the answers in your journal. [If you are in a study group, be prepared to share your views with others in the class.]

1. Evaluate the author's statement, "All reading of the Bible is interpretive."

2. How important is genre to your reading of the Bible? What difference should genre make in our study of scripture?

3. Do you read the Bible primarily for information, formation, or transformation? Explain your answer.

4. Assess the merits of Brian McLaren's view that rather than us reading the Bible, we should let the Bible read us? Have you had this experience with the Bible? If so, provide an example.

5. Assess Marcus Borg's three alternatives to biblical literalism, that is, his emphasis on reading the Bible historically, metaphorically, and sacramentally. Which of these do you consider most important or appealing? Explain your answer.

6. What is the primary insight I/we gained from this chapter or session?

Chapter 3

Two Things to Know about the Inspiration of Scripture

CHRISTIANS HAVE ALWAYS AFFIRMED a close relationship between the Bible and God, just as other religions affirm a close connection between the sacred and their holy scriptures. Foundational to reading the Bible is a decision about how to view its origin. Is it a divine product, a human product, or somehow both?

Building on the conviction that divine revelation and man-made religion are fundamentally irreconcilable, many Christians believe that the only choice a person can make about the Bible is to view it either as the infallible, inerrant word of God or as a collection of fairy tales with little or no value for modern people. Since the latter is what unbelievers think, fundamentalist Christians believe they must view the Bible as God's very word of truth, defending it in all respects, even on historical and scientific matters. For many, the Bible's reliability is so critical that they will argue, "If I can't believe the Bible when it speaks about creation or history, then how can I believe it about Jesus Christ and salvation?" To frame the question of the inspiration and authority of the Bible in this manner, however, is to do an injustice to the traditional doctrines of the inspiration and authority of scripture.

Acknowledging the obvious human element in the Bible, modern Christians generally take a both/and stance regarding biblical authorship: the Bible is both divine and human. However, this approach is also problematic. Viewing the Bible as both divine and human leaves us two options. One option is to say that it is all divine and all human. That may sound good, but no one maintains such an unworkable tension. The other, more typical option is to attempt to separate the divine parts from the human parts—as if some come from God and others are human. The parts that come from God are then given greater authority. However, who is to say which parts are divine and which human? The Bible does not come with footnotes that say, "This passage reflects the will of God; the next passage does not." Therefore, those who take the entire Bible as divine are consistent, but they might be consistently wrong.

How, for instance, does one understand the Ten Commandments? Most Christians who think of the Bible as both divine and human would say that the commandments come from God. Does that mean that they are equally authoritative? If so, all Christians should worship God on Saturday, since that is the day clearly in mind as the day of worship. There is biblical evidence that the sanctity of the Sabbath was in effect among the Israelites prior to the revelation of the commandments to Moses on Mount Sinai (cf. Exod. 16:22–30). And if the Ten Commandments are divinely inspired, why are they written from a male point of view (for instance, they prohibit coveting your neighbor's wife but say nothing about coveting your neighbor's husband)? Furthermore, the commandments against stealing, adultery, murder, bearing false witness, and so forth are simply rules that make it possible for humans to live together in community. Biblical scholarship affirms that the pattern upon which these commandments are based is a treaty pattern devised by the Hittites, a powerful empire that predated Moses and ended prior to the time of Moses. Divine genius is not required to come up with rules like these. This is not to say that the Ten Commandments are unimportant, but rather that their origin is human.[1]

6. *The Bible is the product of two faith communities, each responding uniquely to divine revelation.*

The Bible contains ancient Israel's perceptions and misperceptions, just as it contains the early Christian movement's perceptions and misperceptions. Likewise, the gospels, which record the account of Jesus, reflect not static truths but rather changing theological perspectives. Moreover, these texts are not the words of eyewitnesses, as is often claimed, but were shaped by the events of the second half of the first

---

1. Borg, *Reading the Bible*, 26–27.

century, perhaps even more dramatically than by the events of the time in which Jesus actually lived.

As important as biblical inspiration is to most Christians, when pressed to define the concept, some might reply with a shrug of the shoulders, others with a vague reference to the divine origin of the Bible, and still others might allude to 2 Timothy 3:16–17: "All scripture is inspired by God and is useful for teaching, for reproof, for correction, and for training in righteousness, so that everyone who belongs to God may be proficient, equipped for every good work." Conservative scholars note that the Greek word translated as "inspired" here literally means "God-breathed," a reference traditionally taken to mean that the authors were directed by God to produce documents that accurately reflected God's message to humanity. While many understand the term inspiration to describe something that happened to the authors, literalists note that this verse bypasses the authors and their humanity, speaking only of the written product as inspired.

Another passage often cited by conservative Christians is 2 Peter 1:20–21: "First of all you must understand this, that no prophecy of scripture is a matter of one's own interpretation, because no prophecy ever came by human will, but men and women moved by the Holy Spirit spoke from God." Verse 21 describes the inspiration process as one in which the human authors were "moved" by the Holy Spirit. In biblical times, the Greek verb used here referred to the moving of a ship's sails by the wind, an apt biblical metaphor for the role of the Holy Spirit.

While such a view of biblical authorship may be inaccurate, having a Bible inspired in this manner is foundational for first-half-of-life living and thinking (that is, for believers concerned with establishing identity, creating boundary markers, and seeking security). The implications of such an inspired Bible for theology are enormous: God exists, God is benevolent, and God communicates directly with us, endowing us with providential resources and values to safeguard our dignity and identity. Those who view scripture this way refer to the Bible as anchor, compass, and shelter in the time of storm. Such inspiration implies biblical reliability, down to tiniest details. Of course, when conservative Christians quote scripture to authenticate its own inspiration, they practice circular reasoning, always questionable.

Theories of Inspiration

Christians who look to the Bible as a source of religious teaching or for guidance concerning how to live bring to their reading presuppositions that affect interpretation. These presuppositions influence their understanding of inspiration and the authority of the Bible. Some church traditions say that God is the author of the Bible in the sense that God actually dictated the words of the Bible to human writers who recorded the words verbatim. This approach is called a *literalist view* of inspiration. Other church traditions hold that the human authors of the Bible are real authors in every sense, but that the words of scripture are still somehow what God wanted to communicate to humanity. This approach, called a *contextualist view* of inspiration, allows that God is the author of the Bible without specifying how the Bible is inspired, except to emphasize that the freedom, individuality, and creativity of the human authors are preserved. Of course, actual understandings of inspiration are often subtler and more complex than these approaches might suggest.

This book takes as its starting point an understanding of inspiration that accepts the full and free involvement of the Bible's human authors. This approach is called contextualist because it emphasizes that to understand scripture readers need to take into account the historical, political, cultural, literary, and religious contexts in which the documents were written. This approach is compatible with contemporary historical and literary methods of studying the Bible.

Concerning the authority of the Bible, communities and individuals that hold a contextualist approach to inspiration might say that the Bible is best described as compelling and persuasive. This means that the Bible has authority insofar as it compels us to respond with faith, hope, and love. Further, it does not legislate a particular moral action in response to specific situations, but it provides a series of guidelines upon which Christians can reflect on modern issues and concerns. William Countryman, a theologian and professor of the New Testament, explains the authority of scripture in this way: While the church participated in creating the Bible and acts as its interpreter, the Bible functions as the church's judge, constantly calling it to conversion.[2] Therefore, the authority of the Bible is closely connected to its power to transform.

Biblical scholars suggest three broad possibilities regarding the inspiration of the Bible:

---

2. Countryman, *Biblical Authority or Biblical Tyranny?*, 52–57.

- *verbal inspiration*—the view that every word of the Bible is divinely inspired and therefore inerrant;
- *human response to inspiration*—the view that biblical writers were witnesses to divine revelation; their words and experiences may be human but they serve as vehicles to a higher voice and a deeper reality;
- *inspired imagination*—the view that the Bible is great literature, designed to capture the imagination; though the books of the Bible contain heightened insight, their message is conditioned by historical, sociological, and cultural factors. When the Bible is studied academically, it is this view that scholars espouse.

The first view, simple, clear, and unambiguous, lends itself well to the perspectives and tasks of the first-half-of-life journey; the second and third views to the perspectives and tasks of the second-half-of-life-journey (to those who, sensing new spiritual urges and vision, are ready to risk letting go of old patterns and securities for the promise of the future). To these options we add as corollary *inspired process*, the view that scripture requires ongoing interpretation. This assertion, flowing naturally from the preceding options, recognizes that the sacredness of scripture is validated by its ability to inspire Christians in every age. Scripture, defined and finalized by the canonical process, has an open-ended quality in that it is dynamic and alive, thereby extending the revelatory process to the present. Viewing scripture as "inspired process" safeguards the original revelation while authenticating its ongoing meaning.

7. *The Bible is not inspired words of God but "inspired process."*

Most Christians, when they think about biblical inspiration, come to conclusions based on three assumptions: (1) God is the source and origin of scripture; (2) God is truth; and (3) humans can know God's truth. In my opinion, each of these assumptions is flawed and ultimately false. For instance, what do people have in mind when they affirm that all scripture comes from God or somehow reflects God's will? In order to make such affirmations, they are assuming that God is personal as humans are personal.

Of course, there is nothing wrong with personifying God or addressing God as personal, for it is hard to relate to a God that is abstract or impersonal. However, to think of God in personal terms presents insuperable problems, particularly when we take personifications of God literally. For example, when we speak of God's "right" hand, are we saying God is like us, human, and therefore limited to human physicality? Likewise, when we address God as male—or even as female—are we saying God has sex organs? At this point, most of us recognize that when we speak this way, we are thinking metaphorically and not literally. Why, then, when we speak of the Bible as God's Word, do we suddenly think literally, as if God speaks directly to humans, whether verbally or through images or suggestions? Does God have a larynx or a prefrontal cortex?

These problems don't go away when we substitute the Holy Spirit as the agency of inspiration. By so doing, are we saying that God's Spirit can manipulate or override human reason or willpower? If so, we wonder, what other unseen forces exist to control our human impulses? Are humans not free? If we are free, can our freedom be relinquished to unseen powers? If so, how can we know when it is us acting, thinking, and wishing, and not some invisible agent forcing action on our behalf? As you can imagine, similar problems arise when we imagine we can think God's thoughts or conceptualize God's eternal truths.

On the other hand, if the Bible does not reflect God's words or will—whether directly or indirectly—does this nullify the concept of biblical inspiration, or make it irrelevant? To the contrary, this approach makes the concept of inspiration more relevant and understandable and less contentious. By way of analogy, let us think of the United States Constitution. Americans don't consider it inerrant, for it can be amended and updated; and yet it remains authoritative for all citizens of the United States. Like one's national constitution defines what it means to be a citizen, so the Bible defines what it means to be a Christian. It guides the beliefs, values, and behavior of Christians not because it is inerrant, but because it shapes their identity. Its interpretation can—and must—adjust to changing personal, social, and cultural contexts and situations. In this respect, its influence is subjective, not objective. Its subjective nature makes it possible to be quoted affirmatively by people of differing theological persuasions. No matter what institution or communities might claim about its objective meaning and nature, practice shows that scripture is meaningful when it is individually interpreted and subjectively applied.

When scripture works this way, it is true to its origin and nature. As informed Christians now know, the formation of the Bible was gradual, complex, and somewhat haphazard. A close reading of most individual books of the Bible shows that they were composed over time from earlier traditions and authors, in many cases developed from oral accounts. In the transmission of these traditions, a theological meaning became combined with the original historical account, resulting in material that was now primarily theological in meaning. Such accounts were retold for the theological point they helped to make. In the transmission of those traditions as well as in their combination, theological reflection and appropriation continued to occur. The resultant scripture reflects the dynamic process at work in its formation and preservation, initially in the nations of Israel and Judah and later in the communities that shaped early Christianity.

Careful analysis of individual books of the Bible provides clear indication that they were assembled from traditions that had been worked and reworked over time by various authors, editors, and redactors. The book of Judges is a clear example of such a process. From older traditions about various heroes of the tribes of Israel, a recurring pattern was constructed. The theme, that the neglect of the true God has fearsome consequences for God's covenant people, is set out in 2:16–23. There we find a pattern of disobedience, disaster, repentance, and rescue, a cycle repeated seven times throughout the book. From this pattern, evidence emerges that individual tribal stories were collected and arranged to illustrate two truths, the first theological (obedience to God ensures blessing) and the second political (kings ensure stability).

One can observe the same process at work in the book of Exodus, where a series of regulations found in chapters 21 to 23 create two sets of complementary laws. The first set of regulations, tied to cultural stability, reflect traditional values regarding property rights and the status of women and slaves. The second set of regulations, advocating the humane treatment of aliens, widows, orphans, the poor, and domestic animals, transcends traditional societal regulations and locates the basis of society in compassion and mercy. The clash of divine mercy with conventional societal values highlights not a static scripture based on eternal unchanging laws, but rather a process whereby compassion overrides business as usual. The same process is found in Israel's prophetic literature.

In some cases, books were rewritten from other biblical books, produced to support a new theological or political perspective. The books of Chronicles, for example, are a recasting of 1 and 2 Kings, written to emphasize the centrality of the temple in Jerusalem, and to affirm Judah's priority over the northern tribe in religious matters. In a similar way,

Matthew and Luke can be viewed as commentaries on Mark's gospel, since they not only add to Mark's content but also reorder and in some cases recast the Markan material. The prophetic books, such as those attributed to Isaiah and Zechariah, consist of collected traditions associated with a given prophet, but often reflecting changing or differing points of view. Likewise, the books associated with Solomon (Proverbs, Ecclesiastes, Song of Solomon, and the deuterocanonical Wisdom of Solomon) were produced by sages long after the time of Solomon, and the books in the New Testament bearing the names of Paul, John, James, Jude, or Peter were in some cases produced by later authors who identified with those individuals, or who simply sought authority for their writings of points of view. Such pseudepigraphic writing continued well into the third century CE and even beyond.

As is now clear, biblical authors were by no means enslaved to their tradition. As new situations developed, old traditions were put to new use. For example, the tradition concerning the selection and blessing of Abraham (Gen. 12:1–3; 17:1–8), whose descendants became great and possessed the land of Canaan, is cited both in Ezekiel (33:23–29) and in Isaiah (51:1–3), yet for diametrically opposed reasons. While Isaiah reaffirms the promise to Abraham and uses it as the basis for the promise of restoration to the Babylonian exiles, in Ezekiel the promise is denied and the people are told not to cite such traditions as a basis for hope and comfort.

Similarly, Matthew and Luke make different use of Jesus' teachings, such as the parable of the lost sheep. In Matthew, believers are exhorted to make every effort to return errant believers to the church (18:10–17), whereas in Luke the author understands the point to be the need to reach out to sinners and other socially unacceptable non-believers (15:1–10). As is clear from this and other examples, not even the sayings of Jesus were regarded as immutable by the authors of the gospels. Far from having one fixed meaning, the sayings of Jesus were evidently regarded as capable of quite different meanings in different situations, and the authors who collected those traditions used them to make the theological point they thought necessary for their intended audience. If the composition of the gospels proceeded along the lines of collecting and interpreting traditions rather than of accurately narrating the events of Jesus' life, then this emphasizes their purpose to be primarily theological rather than chronological or historiographic.

Using traditions for different purposes than they originally possessed is a feature common to both testaments, and particularly normative when the Old Testament is used in the New. For example, when Paul quotes Deuteronomy 30:12–13 in his effort to show that faith in Christ rather than performance of the Mosaic legislation is now the way God wishes human beings to pursue righteousness, he gives that passage a meaning quite different from that found in its original setting. Instead of using this passage to show, as Deuteronomy does, that the commands of God can be followed naturally, and not through extraordinary means, Paul uses the passage to justify his claim that is is precisely that performance of the law that Christ's coming has rendered useless (Rom. 10:5–9).

In using this Old Testament tradition with such freedom, Paul was following previous interpreters, doing nothing different from how earlier biblical authors and compilers used older traditions. As Old and New Testament examples show, finding new meanings in old traditions, even meanings not originally intended, is a scriptural commonplace. Thus, when New Testament authors quote an Old Testament text in a form that differs from the Hebrew original, or when modern readers discern in a text a meaning it may not have carried in its original context, they are doing what the biblical authors did repeatedly in their use of tradition. It is one more example of the dynamic nature of tradition that is evident in the literature that comprises our scriptures.

In this context, the question arises as to whether modern readers of scripture wish to be oriented to the past and the old, or to the future and the new. The way in which the prophets of the Old Testament and the evangelists of the New used the traditions of the past clearly indicates that they followed the latter approach. Evidently, a rigid adherence to the forms that sacred traditions represent is the wrong way to honor the belief in a God who is living, who is God not only of the past but of the present and future as well.

This distinction is essentially the difference between "true" and "false" prophets. In Jeremiah 28, when Hananiah confronts Jeremiah with the message that God would quickly restore Judah, he was citing past examples. Jeremiah, however, was compelled to denounce Hananiah, not because he was citing traditions, but because the traditions he was citing were the wrong ones for the new time. God is doing a new thing, says Jeremiah, and sometimes rigid adherence to the wrong tradition dishonors the God who is living, who is oriented to the future and the new as well as to the past and the old.

The same use of tradition characterized the preaching of Jesus. While quoting the commands of the past, he interprets them in a new way (see Matt. 5:27–48). At times, he is also quite willing to contradict tradition (Mark 10:2–9; Luke 5:33–38), exhorting his followers to do likewise. It was precisely faithfulness to holy traditions ot the past that caused Peter to miss the point of a divine directive about what he is now permitted to eat, a command he misunderstood though it was repeated three times (Acts 10:9–17).

Clearly, scripture is a dynamic reality that welcomes new things in new times, and that is therefore not bound blindly to the past. As we have seen, that dynamism is clearly evident in the way in which traditions are used in the various books of the Bible. Traditions can be used in new ways; they can be altered and reformulated, and even contradicted. To lose the dynamic tension in the biblical witness, or to attempt to eliminate it through harmonizing, is precisely to lose the witness of scripture to a dynamic God, who never allows believers to become complacent or to canonize a holy past.

As the evidence presented by scripture indicates, inspiration is best explained as a process in which traditions are formulated and reformulated, interpreted and reinterpreted. Hence, it is in a dynamic way that inspiration is best understood. This recognition will have a profound effect on the way we understand the writings produced by such a process.

Assignment

Having read chapter 3, answer the following questions, writing the answers in your journal. [If you are in a study group, be prepared to share your views with others in the class.]

1. Read 2 Timothy 3:16–17. How might this passage be read, interpreted, and applied by Christians currently committed to the perspectives and tasks of first-half-of-life spirituality? (that is, by believers concerned with establishing identity, creating boundary markers, and seeking security). How might this passage be read, interpreted, and applied by Christians currently committed to the perspectives and tasks of second-half-of-life-spirituality? (that is, by believers who, sensing new spiritual urges and vision, are ready to risk letting go of old patterns and securities for the promise of the future).

2. Read 2 Peter 1:20–21. How might this passage be read, interpreted, and applied by Christians currently committed to the perspectives and tasks of first-half-of-life spirituality? How might this passage be read, interpreted, and applied by Christians currently committed to the perspectives and tasks of second-half-of-life-spirituality?

3. Assess the merits of viewing scripture as "inspired process." How does this perspective expand your understanding of the Bible?

4. What is the primary insight I/we gained from this chapter or session?

Chapter 4

Three Things to Know about the Old Testament

Despite the Bible's diversity, most readers approach it as a whole, emphasizing its underlying unity. There is, as we have seen, a discernible thematic flow to its overarching story, with a clear beginning, middle, and ending. Yet our perception of the Bible's unity may obscure an underlying reality, namely, that there are two Bibles between its covers: a Jewish Bible and a Christian Bible. This is not a superficial difference, as we will see. It is not merely that the Christian Bible adds a New Testament and therefore calls the Jewish scriptures "the Old Testament." Despite the similarities, the differences are significant and consequential.

8. The Jewish Bible is not the same as the Christian Old Testament.

As noted in chapter 1, the books of the Hebrew Bible are fundamentally the same as the Christian Old Testament, though the arrangement differs. This is particularly true of the Protestant Bibles that, since the Reformation, restricted their Old Testament to the same books in the Hebrew Bible, despite differences in numbering and arrangement. The discrepancy is greater in Roman Catholic and Eastern Orthodox Bibles, for both traditions recognize additional books and portions of books, found in the Septuagint (Greek translation of the Hebrew Bible) but eventually excluded by the Jewish authorities that finalized the Hebrew canon early in the second century CE.

In Jewish tradition, the Bible has three parts: the Torah (the five books of Moses), the Prophets (consisting of two divisions, the Former Prophets and the Latter Prophets), and the Writings (containing historical books, historical fictions, poetical books, and wisdom literature). The Christian Old Testament rearranges the order of these books into four different divisions. The Torah and the Former Prophets form the first and second major divisions, and added to this latter group are several books from the Writings, including the book of Ruth (added after Judges) and other books viewed as historical, including 1 and 2 Chronicles, Ezra, Nehemiah, and Esther. To them are added apocryphal/deuterocanonical books such as Tobit, Judith, and 1 and 2 (and sometimes 3 and 4) Maccabees.

This grouping is followed by a third division of poetic and wisdom writings including Job, Psalms, Proverbs, Ecclesiastes, and Song of Solomon, to which are added the apocryphal/deuterocanonical books of Wisdom of Solomon and Sirach.

The fourth division of the Old Testament is the Latter Prophets of the Hebrew Bible. Added to this list are several books from the Writings, including Daniel (considered by Christians to be one of the prophets), Lamentations (associated with the prophet Jeremiah), and such apocryphal/deuterocanonical books as Baruch and the Letter of Jeremiah.

This arrangement in the Christian canon is designed to provide a chronological storyline. First come the pentateuchal and historical books, those dealing with the past (from Genesis through Maccabees). These are followed by books thought to deal with the present, from Job to Song of Solomon (to which are added the Wisdom of Solomon and Sirach). Finally come the Latter Prophets of Jewish tradition, interpreted as dealing with the future, including the books of Lamentations and Daniel. The result is that the prophetic books come immediately before the New Testament, the events of which ancient Christians traditionally interpreted as predicting.

When, during the Reformation, Protestant reformers followed Jews in declaring that only those books written in Hebrew be considered authoritative, deleting the apocryphal writings from their Bibles, the Roman Catholic Church countered by declaring the Apocrypha canonical and authoritative for all Catholic Christians, thereby upholding the Eastern Orthodox tradition. Modern Protestant Bibles, especially study Bibles, frequently include the Apocrypha in a separate section between the Old and New Testaments.

The next major difference between the Jewish Bible and the Christian Old Testament is linguistic. The first Christians either read or heard the Old Testament read in Greek, and most North American Christians currently read their Bible in English or in other modern languages such as Spanish or French. However, other than an isolated verse in Jeremiah (10:11) and parts of Ezra and Daniel, originally written in Aramaic, the rest of the Jewish Bible is written in Hebrew, and it is this version of the Bible that modern Jews read privately and in worship. To state the obvious, there is a world of difference between Hebrew, Greek, and English, not only linguistically but culturally, socially, and religiously.

More important than the external differences of order, number, and language is the different sense of the whole that is conveyed when one reads the Hebrew Bible as complete in itself or as continuing in the Jewish oral tradition codified in the Mishnah and Talmud, rather than when one reads this literature as open toward a future fulfilled in Jesus Christ and in the Christian movement.

In this latter case, the Christian Bible presents a simple storyline that unites all the diverse episodes and genres into a sweeping epic claiming to embrace all humanity. This way of reading scripture begins "in the beginning"; discloses God's electing of a special people; recounts their disobedience, punishment, and hope; declares the story's climax in the appearance of God's divine Messiah; and ends by anticipating the coming of God's final kingdom.

When read independently of the Christian lens, the unity of the Hebrew scripture looks quite different. There is no single plot or center, but many. The various voices that speak are not united in a single hope, nor do they point to a single future, other than the hope of survival and the celebration of life. The multiple plots of the narratives move forward amid echoes of the past, repetitions and rehearsals, reminders and foreshadowings. The wisdom gathered and cultivated by professional elite and trained sages stands alongside the sensibilities of poets and peasants. Codes from the time when there were no kings stand alongside laws of monarchs and temple priests. Prophets name the injustice done to the common poor by petty officials and perceive in the march of great empires the remedial will of God. Through worship, the people celebrate the manifold occasions of their national and cultic life, giving voice to their complaints, hopes, and fears. All this variety, and more, is woven together by complex threads in the Hebrew Bible, but its rhythms are quite different from the dominant pulse of the Christian Bible.

9. The Old Testament historical material is interpretive rather than factual history.

In antiquity, only two nations developed a chronological or progressive sense of history—Greece and Israel—and Israel displayed its historical sense at least four hundred years before Herodotus, the Greek author reputed to be the "father of history." In fact, the very idea that history is a process with beginning, middle, and end is original with Israel. Not only was Israel the first to develop a sense of history, but the telling of its story comprises approximately one-third of its scripture. Nevertheless, while the Jewish Bible may be seen as a history of Israel, it is not history in the modern sense of the term.

For Israel, history never stands alone or points to itself, but rather is the medium of encounter with God. Thus, the primary purpose of the scriptures is to tell the dramatic story of God's dealings with the world and, in particular, to interpret Israel's special role in God's purpose. Apart from God's will and purpose, history would have no unity and life no meaning. Already in the J (Yahwist) tradition (dated to the reign of David and said to be the first written account of the history of Israel),[1] we find the view that history is not a chance occurrence but the execution of a divine plan. For the Yahwist, history has meaning because God is active in it, guiding the ongoing events of Israel's life. Though God created nature, God is not a nature deity but the God of history, who has chosen Israel, made a covenant with Israel, and remains active in their history.

For J (found throughout the Pentateuch as well as in isolated passages elsewhere), as for the entire Old Testament, the acceptance of history as the execution of God's will demands an act of faith. The saving and judging will of God gives to history both meaning and morality—meaning, because God's will grounds both the origin and end of the human experience in history, and morality, for history is shown to be governed by a supremely powerful and entirely just moral will. Furthermore, the fulfillment of that divine will is conditioned neither by human success nor by human failure. Human achievement does not bring about the fulfillment of history or destiny, and human sin does not prevent the accomplishment of the purpose of history. Nevertheless, despite divine sovereignty, humans remain truly free and responsible agents in history.

This overlap appears frequently throughout the biblical narrative. For example, in Genesis 25 God announces to Rebekah that the elder of

---

1. For further information on this pentateuchal literary source, see chapter 5.

her twins (Esau) will serve the younger (Jacob), but two chapters later, when the time comes to deliver the blessing to the proper son, God apparently leaves the matter to Rebekah to work out, which she does with great effectiveness. In Genesis 50, Joseph declares to the brothers who, thirteen chapters and many years earlier had sold him into slavery, that "even though you intended to do harm to me, God intended it for good" (50:20), but the story makes clear that it is largely his own wits and talent, rather than any supernatural intervention, that allow him to survive and prosper in Egypt. In the Exodus account, we learn that God claims responsibility for "hardening" Pharaoh's heart so that he refuses to allow Israel to leave (Exod. 7:3; 14:4), but Pharaoh is said by the narrator to have hardened his own heart (8:15, 32). Still other times a passive voice is used, so that Pharaoh's heart "was hardened" or "became hard" (7:14; 8:15; 9:7), thereby leaving the agency behind the hardening unclear.

This ambiguity allows the narrative to retain a sense of God's sovereign activity in history, while at the same time affirming Pharaoh's own moral failure, whose repeated promise of freedom is never fulfilled and thus represents realistically the psychology of tyranny. Logically, readers may want to know, which is it? Does God harden Pharaoh's heart, or does Pharaoh harden his own heart? The story refuses to answer one way or another, giving a both/and approach that reflects a clear trend in biblical narrative to render not only the inner lives of humans and God, but also creation and history, as complex and ultimately unresolvable.

While Israel told its story in various forms, the earliest recitals of that story were doubtless in poetic and legendary forms, handed down orally. Two of the earliest poems in the Old Testament are recitals of significant events, such as the Song of the Sea (Exod. 15:1–18), which tells how God saved the Israelites as they left Egypt, and the Song of Deborah (Judg. 5:1–31), which recalls an early victory near Megiddo. Legends, too, passed through an oral stage before they were recorded.

In Israel's understanding of history, a further question concerns the universal scope of history. What is the place of other nations in the historical process controlled by the divine will? Here, as with numerous related matters, we can trace development in the insights of Israel. For early Israelites, other people are either enemies or irrelevant. If they are enemies of Israel, they are hostile to the purpose of God in history and God removes them.

With the rise of prophecy and a deeper understanding of God's moral will, foreign nations function as instruments of God's judgment on Israel. Outside of this role, they are irrelevant, for they appear to have little or no perceptible role in the historical process. Hence, much of the preexilic literature is parochial in its treatment of other peoples.

During the exile and afterward, Israel perceives that the universal lordship of God cannot be realized unless God is recognized by all peoples. As other peoples come to know and worship God, they will share the religious gift originally conferred on Israel, and ultimately, the differences between Israel and other peoples will be eliminated. The glory that belongs to God is not manifested unless God is universally acknowledged and worshiped. The function of Israel in history then becomes that of mediating the knowledge of God to the nations.

10. Most books of the Old Testament lack individual authors.

People who read the Bible with modern eyes, that is, critically, are struck by its varied contents. Here we have prose and poetry; expansive narrative and short stories; legal codes embedded in historical reports; hymns and prayers; quoted archival documents; quasi-mythical accounts of things that happened "in the beginning" or in God's heavenly court; collections of proverbs, maxims, aphorisms, and riddles; letters to various groups; and reports of mysterious revelations interpreted by heavenly beings. This variety accounts for some of the richness that generations of readers have found within its pages, but it also causes much of the bewilderment even the most devoted readers often feel. How were so many different kinds of writings brought together into one book? This question preoccupies many modern readers and scholars alike.

When we investigate the history of the Bible, a good place to begin is with the term itself. As noted earlier, the word "Bible" is derived from a plural Greek word, *ta biblia*, meaning "the little scrolls." The term "scrolls" refers to separate rolls of leather or papyrus on which ancient literary works—sacred and secular—were recorded. The physical limits of a scroll meant that many rolls were required for the writings that came to be held sacred in Jewish communities. Sometimes a long document had to be divided into two scrolls, like the books of Samuel, Kings, and Chronicles. In the prophetic writings, sometimes the contributions of prophetic schools were combined into one scroll, such as the oracles associated with Isaiah, Jeremiah, or Ezekiel. In one case, twelve shorter prophecies were combined into one scroll, called by Jews the Scroll of the

Twelve, later to be separated by Christians into the twelve scrolls of the Minor Prophets. As early as the second century CE, Christians began using a new form of book known as a codex, much like our modern books. This made it possible to enclose all the sacred writings into one large volume.

The individual books that make up our Bible were written over a period of more than a thousand years. During that time, the people of Israel underwent many changes, even deep transformations, in their national life and culture. Their patterns of government, their cultic and legal organizations, and their relationship to neighboring peoples and to the great empires of the ancient Mesopotamian and Mediterranean regions all changed. Those changes go far to account for the variety we see in content, language, and style of the biblical books.

During the oral phase of the Israelite religion, leaders propagated its tenets in cultic, legal, and private settings. As stories and laws circulated orally, we can assume that they were changed as they were told and retold by word of mouth, year after year. Often the changes were accidental, but sometimes people telling the stories changed them to make a point, as preachers and storytellers do today.

Many people assume that people living in oral societies had better memories than most of us today, but that is not the case. As current anthropological studies show convincingly, concern for verbal accuracy is fairly recent and limited to written cultures. Oral cultures actually encouraged change adaptability in each telling of a story, depending on the audience and the situation. Furthermore, once the accounts underlying scripture were put into writing, they underwent further change. Prior to the invention of movable type in the fifteenth century CE, books had to be produced by hand, by human scribes who created copies of a text by copying words one letter at a time. This process continues in Jewish liturgical settings, synagogue copies of the Torah still copied by hand on scrolls, a practice that takes up to a year to complete.

Unlike today, when copies of books are identical, in the ancient world every copy of a book was different. Some differences were due to copying mistakes, but some changes were intentional, affecting the meaning of a passage or text. Some of the changes may also have resulted by scribes trying to make sense of the texts they were copying, changing the text to change the sense. In many cases, the altered text came to be copied rather than the original text. Not until the second century CE was there a form of the Hebrew text that was later standardized by Jewish scholars known as Masoretes (active from about 600–1000 CE), who added vowel points to the consonantal text resulting in the text used today known as the Masoretic Text (MT).

No original manuscript (autograph) of any biblical book, whether written by an author or redacted by an editor, has survived; all existing copies are the work of later scribes. The oldest extant texts of the Hebrew scriptures come from the Dead Sea Scrolls, found in Cave 4 at Qumran, and even these date to a time no earlier than 250 BCE, having been copied during the first centuries BCE and CE.

Surprisingly, prior to 100 CE there did not exist a single standard text of the various books of the Hebrew Bible, that is, a *textus receptus* regarded as possessing sole authority. Rather, as we learn by comparing the Septuagint and the ancient versions of the Hebrew scriptures preserved among the Dead Sea Scrolls, there were various recensions or texts of the same Old Testament book. For example, the texts of Jeremiah found at Qumran and in the Septuagint are significantly shorter than that found in modern Jewish Bibles, shorter by at least 12 percent. The complete scroll of Isaiah found at Qumran diverges in numerous respects from the MT, and it appears to have no kinship to the Hebrew text underlying the version of Isaiah found in the Septuagint. Furthermore, while the fifteen fragmentary texts of the book of Genesis found at Qumran show a comparatively uniform text, the copies of the rest of the Pentateuch, from Exodus to Deuteronomy, show significant variations in text.

Whenever we try to classify the books of the Bible, we notice a feature common in ancient literature: many of these books are composite. They are not the work of a single author but seem to be composed from fragmentary earlier works. Sometimes this means that they are anthologies (Psalms, Proverbs), and sometimes that they have gone through a number of editions before reaching their present form. Understanding books such as Genesis or the gospels demands the ability to trace their growth through a number of stages. At some of these stages, editors may have incorporated small units of material that originated not in writing at all but in oral tradition. These small units are classified and studied in a discipline called form criticism.

To say that we understand a book or grasp the meaning of a passage may be unproblematic with material like personal letters, newspaper reports, and most modern nonfiction, but matters are not quite so simple with the Bible. First, and most obviously, composite writings do not have an "author" in the same sense as some modern books do. We need to speak instead of the intentions of the many individuals or groups who were responsible for the various stages in the book's development: worshipers who composed and used the psalms, early preachers proclaiming the gospel by telling and retellings stories and sayings of Jesus, and so on. Where the final form of a composite biblical book is concerned, we have to speak of the intentions of the "editor" or "redactor," rather than of the "author." In the past fifty years, biblical scholars have spent much effort in trying to understand the minds of redactors and have used the term redaction criticism to describe this task.

Unlike the continuous narrative of the Christian Old Testament, the Hebrew scriptures are an anthology, a collection of writings produced and assembled in stages over more than one thousand years. As an anthology, the Hebrew Bible is a selection of texts. The ancient Israelites produced many other writings, some of which are mentioned in the Bible but have not survived, such as "The Book of the Wars of the Lord" (see Num. 21:14) or "The Book of Jashar" (Josh. 20:13; 2 Sam. 1:18). In some cases, compilers relied upon or incorporated independent source materials, such as the so-called Covenant Code (Exod. 20:33—23:33) and the Holiness Code (Lev. 17–26), and upon other traditions that reach back to ancient times.

As we know, scripture did not drop as a stone from heaven. Nor was it whispered directly into someone's ear or subconscious. It grew out of the life of a community struggling to understand itself and the God it worshipped. Once the books were written and finalized, the development of a canon took centuries to complete. For Jews, the canonical process was not completed until early in the second century CE; for Christians, not until the fourth century. Like the legal, historical, prophetic, and poetical books of the Bible, as well as the gospels and many of the letters of the New Testament, the biblical canon was formed as response to new situations that represented threats to the unity and life of the community of faith. Though the canonical process finally ended, the interpretive process continues indefinitely into the future, for that process only ends when history ends.

When all is said and done, it is apparent that the significance of the Bible is not that it is a closed canon, but rather that its composition reflects the life of two communities, that of Israel and the early church, as those communities sought to come to terms with the central reality that God was present with them in ways that outran their ability to understand or cope. In one way or another, our understanding of inspiration must acknowledge the interrelation of community and scripture, as well as the continuing process of reinterpretation imposed on scriptural tradition by the theological reflections of the communities whose life is mirrored in those writings.

Some biblical scholars today argue that the "meaning" of scripture is not the intention of the writer or compiler but the meaning that readers gain from the final form of the biblical text as it stands in the Bible as a whole. The Bible as it stands, they argue, not the fragments from which it was composed, is the Bible that Jews and Christians have received. Its "author" is the believing community that accepted this particular book or text as canonical.

Assignment

Having read chapter 4, answer the following questions, writing the answers in your journal. [If you are in a study group, be prepared to share your views with others in the class.]

1. In your estimation, what is the primary difference between reading the Old Testament with Jewish or Christian eyes? Explain your answer.

2. Evaluate the author's view that the Hebrew Bible has no single plot or center but many. Does this view square with how Christians have traditionally read the Old Testament?

3. Assess the merits of the concept that historical material in the Hebrew Bible is "theologically motivated rather that straightforward or factual history."

4. Explain the relation in the Bible between divine sovereignty and human freedom.

5. In your estimation, does composite authorship of biblical books confirm or confuse your understanding of biblical inspiration?

6. What is the primary insight I/we gained from this chapter or session?

Chapter 5

Three Things to Know about the Pentateuch

THE FIRST FIVE BOOKS of the Old Testament, traditionally called "The Five Books of Moses," are also designated as the Pentateuch, a Greek term referring to a work divided into "five scrolls." The Hebrew word for these five books is Torah, often translated as "Law" but better rendered as "Teaching." In Jewish circles, these books are viewed as divinely inspired, disclosing God's guidance and direction for everyday life, both legal and practical. As understood by later Jewish interpreters, the Torah is open-ended, for it contains principles to be applied progressively and laws adaptable to changing and unforeseen situation.

11. Moses did not write the Pentateuch.

The story of the composition of the Bible begins with the Pentateuch, five books traditionally attributed to Moses but written hundreds of years after his death. Behind the earliest written stages of the Pentateuch was a long period of oral tradition handed down by poets and storytellers. Once we have a clear idea of the compositional history of the Pentateuch, our understanding of the production of the rest of the Old Testament follows naturally.

The authorship of the Bible—particularly of the Pentateuch—remains one of the Western world's oldest puzzles. For centuries, the question of human authorship rarely arose, and when it did, it was quickly suppressed. The Bible was understood to be divinely inspired, and whether that happened through dictation or some other form of divine direction seemed irrelevant. The task of Christians was to live according to its principles, not to question its authority.

There are two basic theories regarding the authorship and composition of the Pentateuch. The traditional view is that the primary author was Moses, who incorporated both written and oral material into the Pentateuch. This view affirms the basis unity of the Pentateuch. It is maintained by many Jewish and Christian readers, particularly those who assert the divine inspiration of this material. The proponents of this view recognize that, in accordance with the practice of Near Eastern scribes, a few details have been brought up to date, including names of cities and particularly the account of Moses' death (Deut. 34). In addition, editorial comments such as Numbers 12:3 are believed to have been added later. This view of the authorship and composition of the Pentateuch is supported by later biblical material (see 1 Kgs. 2:3; 2 Kgs. 14:6; Ezra 6:18; Dan. 9:11–13), including passages from the New Testament (see Matt. 19:8; John 5:46–47; Acts 3:22; Rom. 10:5).

The second view, known as the Documentary Hypothesis, states that the Pentateuch is a compilation of at least four different sources, none of which predates 950 BCE. Each of these sources is said to preserve oral matter that may go back to the original time of the events. However, this oral material has been altered by the sources for political and theological reasons. These four sources are known as JEDP (or JEPD).

The first source, called J, was written about 950–900 BCE by an unknown author in Judah identified as the Yahwist. He (or she) was interested in personal biography and in ethical and theological reflection. E, the second source, was composed between 850–750 BCE in the northern kingdom of Israel by an unknown author identified as the Elohist. This source is more objective than J, being less interested in theological reflection. About 715 BCE an unknown editor combined J and E into what is known as the Old Epic or JE.

According to the JEDP version of the hypothesis, a third source, called D, was composed in 621 BCE by someone identified as the Deuteronomist. It was composed to undergird the Deuteronomic Reform instituted by King Josiah (see 2 Kgs. 22:1—23:25). Its purpose was to show the necessity of Jerusalem as the only legitimate place of worship. The author is believed by scholars to have been the prophet Jeremiah or his scribe Baruch. The final source, according to JEDP scholars, was P, written by an unknown author identified as the Priestly writer. P is concerned with the systematic account of the origins and institutions of the Israelite theocracy. P is said to have been written in various stages, mostly during the Babylonian Exile, beginning around the time of the prophet Ezekiel (580 BCE) and completed about the time of Ezra (400 BCE), the scribe who is said to have redacted (edited) the Pentateuch into the final version we have today. Some scholars reverse the order of D and P, arguing that P was preexilic and written before D, possibly around 700 BCE, during the period of the prophet Isaiah and the reform enacted by King Hezekiah. The debate concerning the authorship of the Pentateuch is ongoing.

Though there is widespread agreement that Exodus 25–Numbers 10 belongs to the P tradition, there is no question that this tradition incorporates older material. Furthermore, the uniqueness of the book of Deuteronomy is widely acknowledged as reflecting a source formed over the course of the eighth through the sixth centuries. The distinction between J and E remains a source of controversy, many scholars now thinking of E as representing expansions of J or seeing in E the role of a redactor (R).

The literary history of the emergence of the Documentary Hypothesis in modern times is fascinating and instructive. From time to time throughout history, isolated voices raised questions about the Mosaic authorship of the Pentateuch, but it took the rise of deistic philosophy in the eighteenth century to create the intellectual context to seriously question the possibility that Moses may not have been the author of the Pentateuch.

The critical study of the Bible[1] did not begin as an investigation into its authorship. It simply started with individuals raising questions about problems that they observed in the biblical text itself. It proceeded as a detective story spread across centuries, with investigators uncovering clues to the Bible's origin one by one. Investigators began with questions about the first five books of the Bible, attributed to Moses, even though the text nowhere says that he was the author. Nevertheless, the tradition that one person wrote these books presented problems: "People observed contradictions in the text. It would report events in a particular order, and later it would say that those same events happened in a different order. It would say that there were two of something, and elsewhere it would say that there were fourteen of that same thing. It would say that the Moabites did something, and later that it was the Midianites. It

---

1. In the realm of scholarship the word "critical" (as in biblical criticism or critical methods) need not imply disrespect or disagreement, but rather is an interpretive approach meaning "method of analysis."

would describe Moses as going to a Tabernacle in a chapter before Moses builds the Tabernacle. People also noticed that the Five Books of Moses included things that Moses could not have known or was not likely to have said. The text, after all, gave an account of Moses's death. It also said that Moses was the humblest man on earth; and normally one would not expect the humblest man on earth to point out that he is the humblest man on earth."[2]

At first, the arguments of those who questioned Mosaic authorship were rejected. Investigators still accepted the tradition that Moses wrote the five books under inspiration, but they suggested that a few lines might have been added later, such as the naming of Edomite kings in Genesis 36, a list that includes kings who lived long after Moses. In a second stage of the process, investigators suggested that Moses wrote the five books but that editors later added occasional words or phrases of their own. In the third stage of the investigation scholars concluded that Moses did not write the majority of the Pentateuch. In the seventeenth century, the British philosopher Thomas Hobbes collected numerous facts and statements from these books that were inconsistent with Mosaic authorship. For example, references to something happening "to this day" (see Deut. 34:6) or to "when the Canaanites dwelt in the land" (Gen. 13:7) indicate the presence of a later writer who is describing something that has endured over time. The Pentateuch also includes numerous anachronisms, such as the presence of Philistines in the region (Gen. 26:1–18) centuries before their actual arrival. Various geographical oddities also raised questions, such as the reference to the land east of the Jordan as "beyond" or on "the other side" of the Jordan (Gen. 50:10; Deut. 1:1), indicating the point of view of a resident of Palestine, a land Moses never entered. Moreover, the Pentateuch is not a first-person narrative by Moses, but an account written by other authors, often about Moses.

In Holland the philosopher Spinoza reviewed this information and concluded: "It is . . . clearer than the sun at noon that the Pentateuch was not written by Moses, but by someone who lived long after." His writings, like so many others that questioned the Bible's divine inspiration, were condemned by Jews, Catholics, and Protestants alike. His book was placed on the Catholic Index of Prohibited Books and attempts were made on his life.

---

2. Friedman, *Who Wrote the Bible?*, 17–18.

In 1753 Jean Astruc, professor of medicine and court physician to Louis XV, published anonymously his findings. In his study of Genesis 1 and 2, Astruc noticed that God was referred to as Elohim exclusively in Genesis 1 and as Yahweh Elohim in Genesis 2. His explanation was that Moses had used two different documents that provided two accounts of creation. Out of fear of repercussion, Astruc waited until the age of seventy before publishing his findings secretly and anonymously.

In 1780, John Eichhorn published a similar discovery, based on the presence of doublets or parallel accounts. For example, in Genesis there are two different stories of the creation of the world; two stories of Noah and the flood; two stories of the covenant between God and the patriarch Abraham; two stories of the naming of Abraham's son Isaac; two stories of Jacob making a journey to Mesopotamia; two stories of a revelation to Jacob at Bethel; two stories of changing Jacob's name to Israel; and more, and in Exodus two calls of Moses. In addition to doublets, we find different narrative styles and the use of distinctive divine names, such as Yahweh by the J writer and Elohim by the E writer.

To this day, the Documentary Hypothesis model continues to dominate the field of biblical studies. During the twentieth century every major premise of this model has been attacked piecemeal by critics, yet no systematic scholarly account of the origin and the development of the Pentateuch has been formulated to replace it. Of course, the complexity of the Torah is due not only to the existence of underlying sources, but also to the many phases through which the Pentateuch passed, beginning with a long period of purely oral transmission, followed by editorial activity throughout and by eventual revision by one or more redactors. Despite uncertainty of authorship and sources, we can be sure that the formation of the Pentateuch was a complex process that took shape over a long period of time.

12. *The compositional approach underlying the Pentateuch started with the Exodus tradition and worked backward to the Primeval tradition.*

Those who read the Pentateuch canonically, that is, as a continuous story beginning with Genesis and ending with Deuteronomy, are not reading the Bible historically, that is, as it developed chronologically, for the sources and books that comprise the Pentateuch were not written in that order. In fact, the creation story we find in Genesis 1, dated as late as 400 BCE, was composed centuries after the creation story found in Genesis 2–3, dated to the reigns of David and Solomon, about 950–900 BCE.

It is widely accepted that no Israelite narrative literature was written before the period in Israel known as the United Kingdom. Biblical scholars customarily date Israel's first national epic to the literary awakening that occurred during the reigns of David and Solomon. It is during this period that the literary genius known as the Yahwist composed a masterful prose epic using preliterary units of tradition to create Israel's first written source.

While the period from Abraham to Moses to David was one of oral tradition, this does not mean that beginning with David (1000 BCE) oral tradition was superseded by literary records or that before David there were no written records. What it means is that the Yahwist was the first to record the all-Israelite epic, a core story that up to that time had survived orally through stories, poems, songs, and other "memory units." Some units of oral tradition were non-Israelite in origin and were later taken over by the Israelites. For example, the stories of Abraham's sacrifice of Isaac (Gen. 22) and Jacob's dream at Bethel (Gen. 28) could have been Canaanite cult legends whose original cultural meaning is now lost to us. These independent units of tradition were not simply borrowed but rather were appropriated by Israel and given new meaning.

The compositional approach used by the Yahwist is fascinating. Rather than starting chronologically with creation, adding accounts of the patriarchs, the Exodus, the conquest, the tribal confederacy, and finally, the monarchy, the J writer worked backward, "viewing earlier stories through the prism of the crucial historical experiences that created the community of Israel."[3] Starting with the Mosaic tradition (the material that extends from the oppression in Egypt to the entrance into Canaan), the Yahwist linked it with the Patriarchal tradition (the pre-Mosaic material found in Genesis 12–50), and finally with the Primeval tradition (the early material in Genesis that extends from the Creation, through the Flood, to the new beginning after the Flood).

The all-Israelite epic, read chronologically through its three movements or "acts," begins universally (with fundamental human experiences), continues with Israel's ancestors, and culminates in the Mosaic

---

3. Anderson, *Understanding the Old Testament*, 145.

tradition. The Yahwist, it appears, was the first author to link the Mosaic tradition to a universal and cosmic context.

When we seek to understand the meaning of our individual life stories, we do not actually begin with birth or infancy, even though a written autobiography might start there. Rather, we view our early childhood in the light of later experiences that are impressed deeply in memory. Analogously, Israel's life story did not begin with Abraham or even with the Creation, although the Old Testament in its present form starts there. Rather, Israel's history had its true beginning in a historical experience so crucial that earlier happenings and subsequent experiences were seen in its light.

This decisive event—the great watershed of Israel's history—was a redemptive event, the Exodus from Egypt. This note is struck repeatedly in the Old Testament, particularly in the prophets and the psalms. For the preexilic prophets, the Exodus marks the beginning of the Israelite people, not the earlier migration of Abraham or even the Creation. In the eighth century BCE, Hosea traces Israel's formation, calling, and knowledge of God to the Exodus event: "out of Egypt I called my son" (Hos. 11:1), and "I have been the Lord your God ever since the land of Egypt" (Hos. 13:4). The theme still reverberates in literature composed late in the Old Testament period, such as Daniel 9:15 (see also the deuterocanonical Wisdom of Solomon 15:18—19:22, dated to the first century BCE).

The same accent is found, though not so obviously, in the Pentateuch, the section of the Hebrew Bible regarded as most authoritative by Jewish tradition. There, the account of primeval beginnings (Gen. 1–11) and the stories of the Israelite ancestors (Gen. 12–50) function as prequels to the Exodus story. Strange as it might seem, "when we begin with Genesis and read to the book of Exodus, we are reading the story backward, as it were, for the period before Moses was remembered and interpreted in the light of the Exodus event."[4] Even in the earliest period, long before Israel's history was composed as a written epic, Israelites celebrated the Exodus story in poetry and song. An excellent example is the ancient poem found in Exodus 15:1–18, the "Song of Moses." In this poem, which displays the influence of Canaanite style and mythology,[5] the poet extols "the glorious deeds" of the God of Israel, who liberated a fugitive people from Pharaoh's army and guided them into the land of

---

4. Anderson, *Understanding the Old Testament*, 11.
5. Cross, *Canaanite Myth and Hebrew Epic*, 112–44.

Canaan. Here we find Israel's primary confession later elaborated in epic narrative and poetry (see Pss. 77, 114).

13. In its written form, the Pentateuch reflects a long period of prior oral recitation.

In antiquity, few people could read or write, and traditions were often passed on through oral performance on ceremonial or informal occasions. Undoubtedly, the early period of Israel's life (before 1000 BCE) was a creative time, when the story of Israel was rehearsed and elaborated by the various tribes, each with its own experiences and traditions. Many irregularities and diversities that biblical scholars have tried to explain by literary analysis are probably vestiges of the period when the tradition was transmitted by word of mouth, in word and song. In such recitations, it is clear that the hearers did not wish to hear something new. Rather, they wished to hear repeated something that they knew very well. The speaker recreated the story new with each recitation, though limits were set to the originality of the treatment by the conventional and well-established forms of the tradition. In this way, common themes were developed and the Pentateuch as we currently have it took shape around six defining themes:

1. The story of primeval times (Genesis 1–11)
2. The story of Israel's ancestors (Genesis 12–50)
3. The liberation of Israel from Egyptian bondage (Exodus 1–18)
4. The giving of the Law at Sinai (Exodus 19:1–Numbers 10:10)
5. The wandering in the wilderness (Numbers 10:11–36:13)
6. The entrance into the Promised Land (Deuteronomy 1–34)

The Pentateuch is the result of a long and dynamic process. Excluding the first theme—which we may well credit to the Yahwist and later authors and editors—and the last theme—which is anticipated in the book of Deuteronomy—the Israelite story was shaped, expanded, and reinterpreted orally, with specific contributions from the various tribes. It was given literary form during the monarchy and then circulated in independent sources until it was shaped by editors and redactors into canonical form.

Though the Pentateuch evolved over a long period, the entire Torah became ascribed to Moses (2 Chr. 30:16; Luke 24:44), the leader to whom, Israel believed, God had spoken as to no other person (Deut. 34:10–12). In the future, great religious reforms, such as those that occurred in the time of Elijah (1 Kgs. 19) or of King Josiah (2 Kgs. 22–23), were regarded as a return to the Mosaic source of Israel's faith.

Despite its diversity, preserving not only Mosaic material but also overtones of meaning applied by subsequent generations, the Pentateuch displays a striking overall unity. The leading theme is honed at a moment of consequence, when the primeval history flows into the story of Israel's ancestors. To future generations represented by Abraham and Sarah, God makes a promise that has a threefold dimension: a vast progeny, a land, and a relationship with God that will benefit other peoples and nations (Gen. 12:1–3).

At times the promise is put to the test; at times it is not even mentioned; and at other times events seem to negate it. In Exodus, the promise is threatened by Pharaoh's attempt to destroy his own slaves. In Leviticus, attention shifts to matters pertaining to cultic life. In Numbers, the people are on the move again, though murmuring in doubt and disbelief. Finally, in Deuteronomy, Moses preaches to the people about God's faithfulness to the covenant despite their infidelity, and about the people's obligations in response to God's acts of "steadfast love." When Deuteronomy concludes, at the death of Moses, the promise is still on the way toward fulfillment. Thus, the Torah is open-ended; it concludes with the people of Israel moving toward God's unknown future.

The priestly editors enriched the Torah story by placing it within the framework of God's covenants. The first covenant is that of (re)creation, made with Noah and, through him, with all humanity, including non-human creatures and the earth itself (Gen. 9:1–17). The second covenant, made with Abraham and Sarah, guarantees to the people of Israel the promises of land, posterity, and relationship with God (Gen. 17:1–21). The third covenant, the one mediated by Moses at Sinai (Exod. 19–24), is regarded as a ratification and extension of the covenant with the ancestors/patriarchs (Exod. 2:24). In the priestly view, which came to dominate the entire Pentateuch, these "everlasting covenants" cannot be abrogated. Regardless of human weakness or failure, God's covenant relationship is grounded firmly in God's covenant loyalty.

As previously noted, the decisive event of the Pentateuch is found in the book of Exodus, which deals with the Exodus from Egypt and the giving of the Law at Mount Sinai. All Jewish tradition reaches back to these foundational narratives or "root experiences," which constitute the people's basic understanding of their own identity and the character of God. Even today, the Jewish people understand their vocation and destiny in the light of this experience. As they celebrate the Passover, they recall and make contemporary the Exodus. This festival is not just a homage to the past, but a recognition that in worship believers see themselves as participants in past experience. As Christians reenact the Resurrection at Easter, so Jews reenact deliverance from threat and oppression at Passover. As Christians celebrate new beginnings and the start of the week on Sunday, Jews celebrate the culmination of the week on the Sabbath. For both, the events of the past enter the present with renewed meaning.

The centrality of the Exodus in Israelite epic tradition is evident in a liturgical creed found in the book of Deuteronomy, a statement that received its present form after the fall of Jerusalem in 587 BCE. The passage is a confession of faith to be made when presenting the first fruits of the harvest at the sanctuary (Deut. 26:5–9; see also 6:22–23). This "historical credo" is not a private prayer but a confession of faith made in the setting of worship. As the use of personal pronouns indicates, Jewish worship is a corporate affair. In worship, individuals identify with the community and with its corporate story.

The Bible portrays Israel as God's people, not simply a collection of persons but a divine company ("a priestly kingdom and a holy nation"; Exod. 19:6; 1 Pet. 2:9). Out of families, clans, and tribes God formed a nation, with a corporate personality: When one person suffered, everyone suffered; when one person was blessed, the people enjoyed the benefits; when one person sinned, the whole nation participated in the judgment; when one person received a promise, he or she did so on behalf of the nation.

The historical credo, which dwells primarily on liberating events at the time of the Exodus, concludes with gratitude that the God who delivered the people from bondage also led them into "a land flowing with milk and honey" (Deut. 26:9). Israel's credo, like the Pentateuch, is the Hebrew scripture in miniature, for the Hebrew Bible is an exposition of the major themes enunciated in the Pentateuch, when Israel entered history as a worshiping community.

The original setting of the Pentateuch, we must not forget, is corporate worship, a practice that continues in synagogue worship to this day, According to the Jewish Talmud, the practice of reading appointed scriptures on given Sabbaths or during annual festivals dates back to the time of Moses. Some synagogues follow a pattern of Sabbath readings that covers the entirety of the Torah within the space of a year, while the three-year lectionary requires shorter reading during worship.

In worship, the Jewish people experience what Moses sensed at Mount Sinai, that God wishes to relate to humanity through a covenant community. There Moses learned that Israel was to be a "priestly kingdom" (Exod. 19:6), that is, a community separated from the world and consecrated to the service of God (see 1 Pet. 2:5, 9–10).

Assignment

Having read chapter 5, answer the following questions, writing the answers in your journal. [If you are in a study group, be prepared to share your views with others in the class.]

1. Read Genesis 22:1–18. This moving account of Abraham's testing brings to a climax the history of God's promise to Israel.
2. What does this story tell you about God's faithfulness?
3. What does this story tell you about Abraham's response to God's faithfulness?
4. In your estimation, what is God's promise to you and your family, and what is your response?

Chapter 6

Three Things to Know about the Historical Books

TRADITIONALLY, THE HEBREW BIBLE has been divided into three sections: the Law, the Prophets, and the Writings. From a logical point of view, however, this division leaves something to be desired, for placing the historical books together with the prophetic books under one heading is hard to justify. Moreover, there is not a lot of sense in placing Ruth among the Writings when its historical setting (see Ruth 1:1) makes it an obvious appendage to the book of Judges, or in including Daniel among the Writings rather than among the Prophets.

Since we are studying the Christian Old Testament, we utilize the fourfold Christian division rather than the Jewish grouping: the Pentateuch (Genesis to Deuteronomy), the Historical Books (Joshua to Esther), the Poetical and Wisdom Books (Job through Song of Solomon), and the Prophetic Books (Isaiah through Malachi). As mentioned in the preface, we disregard the apocryphal/deuterocanonical books in our study, limiting our examination to the number and order of books found in Protestant Bibles.

As we explore "historical writings," we need to recall that, like the books of the Pentateuch, the biblical authors and editors of the historical literature were less concerned with establishing documentable facts than with producing literature of high drama tinged with miracles and divine interventions. In this respect, biblical narrators often weave textures of metaphor and imaginative description into their accounts, elements that lend legendary and archetypal proportions to characters and themes.

In short, the historical books in the Hebrew scriptures resist modern categories of either history or fiction; rather, they are theological and didactic historiography. For these authors, like all other biblical writers, the primary goal of scripture is to make plain the purposes of God rather than the policies of nations and their rulers. Even the darkest pages of the record convey the sense of the continuing divine purpose on behalf of Israel, whose great glory is not any achievement of its own, but the fact that it is God's chosen people.

The historical books present different and sometimes overlapping versions of ancient Israel's past, each one shaped by the conviction that God was committed to intimate dealings with the descendants of Abraham, and each asserting that this reality of faith and religion is of continuing relevance to the author and ancient reader. This perspective, which was central to the production of these books, is still held by observant Jews and Christians, who look to these books for divine instruction.

In each historical writing, there is ample evidence of composite authorship. In some cases, this evidence resembles the data for the Documentary Hypothesis in the composition of the Pentateuch. Scholars have found signs of conflation of sources in the books of Joshua and Judges, including evidence of J, E, and P, though the framework of the narrative is Deuteronomic. In 1 and 2 Samuel, signs of composite authorship are particularly evident in 1 Samuel 8–12, where at least two accounts of the origin of the monarchy appear, one supportive (the Saul Tradition) and the other critical (the Samuel Tradition). In the earlier Saul source, Samuel is depicted as a seer and Saul is chosen by divine lot from among the tribes, whereas in the later revisionist Samuel source, Samuel is depicted as judge, and the idea of the monarchy displeases both Samuel and God.

Most scholars assume that Israel's earliest historians drew upon oral traditions as well as written sources when constructing a connected narrative of Israel's past. If ancient Israel followed the ways of other ancient Near Eastern monarchies, its scribes would also have produced records that commemorated and praised the religious and political accomplishments of various kings. Some of these sources include palace and temple records. In the books of Kings and Chronicles we find repeated citations to sources such as "Book of the Annals of the Kings of Judah/Israel" (1 Kgs. 14:29; 16:5), "Book of the Acts of Solomon" (1 Kgs. 11:41), "the record of the seer Samuel" (1 Chr. 19:29), and "The Commentary on the Book of the Kings" (2 Chr. 24:27).

Many scholars believe that the earliest example of theological and didactic historiography in the Bible is the "Court History of David" (2 Sam. 9–20 and 1 Kgs. 1–2). Here a variety of sources was assembled into a literary unity and given a consistent theological point of view. Commonly admired for its literary qualities, this version of history tells the intricate story of David and Solomon, using the twists and turns of love, envy, greed, and struggle for power to proclaim the assurance of the continued vitality of God's promise to be with Israel through the longevity of the Davidic dynasty. Later, other narratives and records of kings who ruled after David were added to this "court history," and, supplemented with materials relating to pre-monarchical times (now found in the books of Joshua, Judges, and Samuel), resulted in an expanded version of Israel's past known as the Deuteronomistic history, with the book of Deuteronomy serving as as introduction for the work's governing theological perspectives.

14. The Old Testament contains two alternative (and conflicting) narratives of the history of the Israelite people.

The narrative books of the Old Testament contain two distinct story sequences, alike in many ways but that also show surprising and important differences. The first narrative sequence, called the Deuteronomistic History, runs from Joshua to 2 Kings, and the second, the Chronicler's History, from 1 Chronicles to Esther. Both sequences cover some of the same periods of the story, but they conclude at different points in the history; the first concludes with the end of the Judean kingdom at the fall of Jerusalem in 587 BCE, and the second finishes about 400 BCE, with Jews under Persian rule.

The different ending points are not the only sign that the two histories have different outlooks on the past. The Deuteronomistic History consistently stresses elements of decline, disaster, and failure in the national history, whereas the Chronicler's History emphasizes positive aspects. The two histories thus represent alternative ways of retelling the past, and in being included within the Hebrew scriptures—without any explanation of why both exist—they invite readers of the Bible to make their own assessment of their significance. In this way readers are compelled to reexamine their own notions of what constitutes success or failure, blessing or curse, promise and fulfillment—which is to say, in examining scripture, readers are expected to reflect theologically in creative ways.

The Pentateuch ends with Moses dead and Israel camped on the east bank of the Jordan, poised to conquer the land of Canaan. A central theme of the J tradition is the promise that Israel would soon possess that land. While it is likely that J originally included an account of how the promise of the land was fulfilled, the J source ends abruptly, as do E and P, at the end of the book of Deuteronomy. The original ending of J seems to have been suppressed in the final shaping of the Bible in favor of the narrative in the book of Joshua. The narrative of the books of Joshua, Judges, Samuel, and Kings (these books make up the "Former Prophets" in the Hebrew Bible) are part of a larger work called the Deuteronomistic History because of their close connection with the book of Deuteronomy, which functions as a sort of theological and thematic preface to that historical narrative.

The basic theme of Deuteronomy, meaning the "second law," is the reaffirmation of the covenant between God and the people of Israel. Here the legal tradition of the book of Exodus is not just repeated (notice, for example, how Exodus 20 and Deuteronomy 5 are a doublet, repeating the Decalogue—the Ten Commandments—practically verbatim), but reinterpreted for the worshiping Israelite community already in possession of the Promised Land. Deuteronomy contains three addresses of Moses (1:6—4:40; 5:1—28:68; 29:1—30:20). The remaining chapters (31–34) continue the story left at the end of Numbers. A distinctive teaching of Deuteronomy is that the worship of God is to be centralized in one place (12:1–31). When Deuteronomy was written, the Jerusalem temple was already in place and was regarded as the only sanctuary at which sacrifices to God could be performed. Although Deuteronomy rests upon ancient traditions, it signifies a rediscovery and reinterpretation of Mosaic teaching in the light of later historical experience.

The Deuteronomistic "theology of history" is found in capsule form in Judges 2:11–16. As noted earlier, this cycle of four elements—disobedience, punishment, repentance, and deliverance—is repeated seven times in the book of Judges. Through this pattern, the Deuteronomistic historians emphasize the central truth that Israel's vitality and solidarity lay in united loyalty to God. The parents' faith does not necessarily become the faith of their children; each generation must renew the covenant in its own way.

The Deuteronomistic History probably underwent several editions. The latest, a product of the Babylonian Exile, views almost the entire history of Israel as characterized by apostasy. This exilic edition interprets the destruction of the capitals of the northern kingdom of Israel (Samaria) and the southern kingdom of Judah (Jerusalem), the loss of autonomy, and exile as deserved punishment from God.

Covering Israel's history for over six centuries, the Deuteronomistic History is the earliest extended historical narrative known from ancient times. Three themes are prominent in that account: (1) the exclusive worship of God (Yahweh) as a prerequisite for Israel's continued possession of the Promised Land (idolatry will result in divine punishment); (2) the centrality of the city of Jerusalem as the only legitimate place of worship; and (3) the unconditional covenant with David, whereby God establishes the dynasty founded by David.

In the Deuteronomistic History, this perspective is expressed in speeches by God and by key human characters. In the earlier parts of the narrative, God often speaks directly to individuals, such as Moses, Joshua, and Samuel. In the later books, God speaks indirectly through prophets. These prophetic speeches function as an ongoing commentary on the narrative.

The Deuteronomistic narrative may be described as one of favorable beginnings and unfavorable endings. The first of those beginnings builds on the promise in Genesis 12 to Abraham that his descendants—the Israelite people—will be vastly numerous, that they will inhabit a land of their own, be the object of divine blessing, and be a blessing to other nations. However, by the end of 2 Kings these promises are shown not to have been ultimately attained, even though there have been signals of their potential success along the way. By the end of the Deuteronomistic narrative, ten of the twelve tribes of Israel have been lost to Assyrian captivity, and the remainder are subject to Babylonian Exile, to the point where God has "expelled (Jerusalem and Judah) from his presence" (2 Kgs. 24:20).

Beginning with Saul (1 Sam. 11) and ending when the last of the rulers in David's line goes into exile (2 Kgs. 25), the monarchy is seen as problematic; it is a threat to God's rule, and finally becomes a moral, political, and religious failure. Destruction of Jerusalem and the temple, and dissolution of God's people, are divine punishments necessary to set things right. Not even the righteousness of occasionally admired kings such as Hezekiah (2 Kgs. 18–20) or Josiah (2 Kgs. 23:26) can forestall or turn it aside. The writer allows a hint of hopefulness to intrude into this bleak picture by noting at the end that Johoiachin, the last of the Davidic line, was treated kindly by his Babylonian captor (2 Kgs. 25:27–30).

Favorable beginnings are also announced by the various styles of leadership Israel experiences in the Deuteronomistic History. Every type of leader—warrior, judge, king, and prophet—though represented as God's gift to the nation, proves disastrous or at least ineffectual. Moses can lead the people to the Promised Land but not into it because of a personal failing; he can bring them divine law, but he cannot prevent the curses of Deuteronomy 28 falling upon them if they fail to be obedient. Joshua the warrior, whom no one is able to withstand in his fight for territory (Josh. 5:1) and whose function is to gain the land of Canaan as a possession for the Israelites (Josh. 1:6, 15), is at the end still exhorting the Israelites to remain loyal to God rather than "the gods of the Amorites in whose land you are living" (Josh. 24:15). In his estimation, the land still belongs to the Amorites.

The history of the judges, who are "raised up" by God (Judg. 2:16), is likewise a story of decline, from the first and unexceptional judge Othniel to Samson, who, unlike other judges, cannot bring peace to his nation, cannot control the Philistine threat, and in the end must suffer the indignity of having his era called "the days of the Philistines" (Judg. 15:20). Even Samuel fails conspicuously, appointing his unscrupulous sons as successors to his judgeship (1 Sam. 8:1–3) and resisting God's intention to institute a monarchy (1 Sam. 8:22).

The monarchy as an institution holds out great promise, but it soon proves its potential for disaster. The first king, Saul, chosen by divinely directed lot (1 Sam. 10:20–24), is rejected from being king over Israel" (1 Sam 15:26). Even David, the most esteemed king of Israel, is condemned for sinning against God in the matter of Bathsheba and Uriah (2 Sam. 12:13) and in the numbering of the people (2 Sam. 24:10). Though he is promised that his line will rule over Israel "for ever" (2 Sam. 7:13, 16), he is also threatened with a prophecy that his dynasty will never be free from feuds and attacks (2 Sam. 12:10). His son Solomon, who begins his reign by building God a temple (1 Kgs. 6–7), in the end proves not to be true to the Lord (1 Kgs. 11:4), and is threatened with the destruction of his kingdom (1 Kgs. 11:11). In consequence, Solomon's son Rehoboam loses the allegiance of all the tribes except Judah, and Jeroboam, his northern rival, commissions competing sanctuaries to the temple at Jerusalem that are condemned as idolatrous. In the northern kingdom of Israel, the kings regularly follow the example of Jeroboam, whereas in the southern kingdom of Judah, only two kings are wholeheartedly approved by God: Hezekiah, who nevertheless is the first to hear of the forthcoming exile to Babylon (2 Kgs. 20:16–19), and Josiah, who is killed in battle despite a prophecy that he would be gathered to his ancestors in peace (2 Kgs. 22:20).

The other institution of leadership in Israel is that of the prophets. They appear at various times in the course of the narrative, from Moses (Deut. 34:10), who functions both as God's mouthpiece and as an intercessor for the people, through anonymous prophets in the period of the judges, to bands of prophets in the time of Samuel (1 Sam. 10:5) and schools of prophets in the time of Elisha, to the famous individual prophets Samuel, Nathan, Elijah, and Elisha.

As a channel of communication between the divine and the human, the prophets hold greater promise than other leaders, but even they are remarkably ineffectual in influencing national history. In the large narrative given over to the activity of the prophets Elijah and Elisha (1 Kings 17–2 Kings 10), there is clearly the successful confrontation between the prophets of God and those of Baal (1 Kings 18); nevertheless, it is not the prophet Elijah but the king Jehu who most decisively defends the worship of God by "wiping out Baal from Israel" (2 Kgs. 10:28).

Despite early promise, in the Deuteronomist's mind, Israel's leadership fails in the end. This does not augur well for the Jewish people, for not even the prophets can reverse the downhill direction in which the whole of the Deuteronomistic History has been moving.

15. By comparison with the Deuteronomistic History, the Chronicler's History is far more hopeful.

The second major historical work, written about the fifth or fourth century BCE (at the time of Israel's restoration from exile), is called the "Chronicler's History." This writing encompasses 1 and 2 Chronicles and may have included the books of Ezra and Nehemiah, though this view is disputed by scholars. Working in much the same way as earlier historians, the Chronicler[1] selected and shaped materials from a variety of sources, many of which are cited as written works (1 Chr. 29:28; 2 Chr.

---

1. Scholars use the term "Chronicler" to refer to the author, or as is more likely, the authors or team of authors that produced the books of 1 and 2 Chronicles.

13:22; 26:22). Presupposing the earlier Deuteronomistic History, the author for the most part repeats, rewrites, and supplements large portions of 1 Samuel 31–2 Kings 25, while also drawing upon other portions of the Bible.

By comparison with the Deuteronomistic History, the Chronicler's History is remarkable for its omission of any narrative for the period from the Creation to the death of Saul (1 Chr. 10)—genealogies fill the narrative gap—and for its exclusion of the history of the Northern Kingdom. Clearly the first crucial event in this history is not the Exodus or the conquest of Canaan, but the reign of David and the establishment of his dynasty. In this history, David does not rule over Judah and then extend his power over the northern tribes (see 2 Sam. 5:5); he is made king over all Israel from the beginning (1 Chr. 11:1).

The importance of David in the Chronicler's History is that he is represented as the institutor of the Israelite system of worship, particularly of the temple, which is his idea and which he instructs his son Solomon to build (1 Chr. 17:22). Likewise the Levites, who perform the worship in the temple, are appointed by David (1 Chr. 23–26). Nothing is said of David's faults, and even the narrative of his exploits as a warrior seems to be included only by way of introducing the story of his bringing the ark as the focus of the worship of God to Jerusalem (1 Chr. 13).

This special concern for David and the worshiping community of Israel is already reflected in the genealogical tables of Chronicles 1–9, where Judah and his descendants, including David, come first in the genealogical history of Israel (2:3—4:23; see 5:1–2). In addition, more space is devoted to Judah and Levi (6:1–81) in these tables than to all the other sons of Israel (Jacob) combined. According to the Chronicler, it was David in Jerusalem and not Moses in the wilderness who founded the true Israel (that is, the worshipping community).

The section of the history devoted to Solomon also has as its theme Solomon as the builder of the temple (2 Chr. 1–9). Here, too, any negative aspects of the king's personality are overlooked (see 1 Kgs. 2:1—3:1). While later kings of Judah are not depicted as uniformly righteous, nevertheless, special emphasis is given to those who effect religious reforms or repair the temple. The history of the monarchy thus seems to be primarily a history of the establishment and maintenance of the worship of God; the function of kings is primarily to promote correct and lavish worship, and the function of the people is to provide the necessary funds and personnel for temple services.

In the postexilic section of the Chronicler's History in Ezra and Nehemiah, the same interest is evident. The return from exile in Babylon is authorized by the Persian king Cyrus specifically to rebuild the Jerusalem temple (Ezra 1:2), and the first action of the returned exiles is to rebuild the temple altar "on its foundation" (Ezra 3:3) and to reinstitute sacrifices there, even before the temple is rebuilt. The initial climax of these books is the completion of the temple (Ezra 6:14) and the celebration of the traditional religious festivals (Ezra 6:10–22). Nehemiah's closing words affirm the Chronicler's primary interest: the establishment of temple worship (Neh. 13:30–31), even though Nehemiah is not a professional religious individual but a Jewish official in the Persian civil service.

The book of Esther, while not technically part of the Chronicler's History, is set in Persia. Its theme, the preservation of the Jewish people from the threat of genocide, makes it a fitting conclusion to the historical literature. In its Old Testament context, it affirms that the continuance of the worship of God by the Jews is guaranteed. Thus, the Chronicler's History concludes on an optimistic note. It harmonizes well with the outlook of the narrative as a whole, that the purpose for which history exists is the worship of God. And the people of Israel, aided by the righteous kings of Judah, have, throughout this historical narrative, been carrying out that worship faithfully and joyfully.

This quite different perspective on national history from that of the Deuteronomistic History is well illustrated by the way the two histories handle the question of the meaning of the Exile. For 2 Kings, the Exile is a punishment for national iniquity, an unredeemed disaster, and the end of the entire narrative. However, for 2 Chronicles, the Exile is punishment for pollution of the temple (2 Chr. 36:14), destined to come to an end at a time predicted by the prophet Jeremiah (2 Chr. 36:21). The book concludes not with the Exile but with an announcement of the plans of Cyrus to rebuild the temple (2 Chr. 36:22–23).

Our understanding of the biblical history of Israel as essentially two competing historical narratives is not the way in which this story has been generally understood by the communities that have preserved it. This is because it has not been customary to look at these ancient sacred books as literary works that generate meaning through their overall shape, structure, and dominant tendencies, that is, through their identity as wholes. When biblical books are valued or interpreted piecemeal, much of their meaning is lost.

While the Deuteronomistic History has received greater attention by students of the Bible, the Chronicler's History has been less highly esteemed. This may be due partly to the Septuagint, which presents 1 and 2 Chronicles under the heading *Paraleipomena* ("the omitted things"), giving the impression that Chronicles is no more than a supplement to Samuel and Kings rather than a work presenting a distinctive view of the past and indeed of the purpose of creation. Ezra and Nehemiah, for their part, have been treated more as a continuation of the Deuteronomistic History, rather than as further evidence for the argument of Chronicles.

While some scholars now think that Ezra and Nehemiah are not the work of the Chronicler, there can be no doubt that these books come from the same literary and religious circle. Further evidence that these books are part of the same work is shown in the first two and a half verses of Ezra, attached to the end of 2 Chronicles (36:22–23), with the result that they further strengthen the forward-looking conclusion of the Chronicler.

The Chronicler's version of Israel's history runs from Adam through the Davidic monarchy and down to the Persian period, when Cyrus decreed that exiled Israelites might return to their homeland. The Chronicler's vision is both idealized and practical. A genealogical chain leads from Adam to the house of David (1 Chr. 1–9), and from this point David emerges as the archetypal king and religious figure. He rules in obedience to God and establishes authentic divine service, including the temple, its priesthood, singers, prayers, and offerings. Subsequent kings fall from this standard until the Exile, as divine punishment, brings closure to Israel's monarchy. In its place, there will be a newly constituted, priest-directed people, living in commonwealth with God and focused on holy space, temple, and worship. The books of Ezra and Nehemiah chronicle the rebuilding of Jerusalem and the successful creation of such a theocratic order.

In its interpretation of history and in some of its themes, the Chronicler's work has much in common with the pentateuchal source P. Chronicles has sometimes been thought to be politically motivated as a defense of the legitimacy of the Judean community against its northern neighbors, the Samaritans. Others have thought of the Chronicler's History as an implicit expression of hope for the restoration of the Davidic monarchy. It seems more probable, however, that its audience was primarily the author's own community, and its purpose was to assure the Judeans of the value of their life, even under foreign rule. As a community, they are to sustain the worship of God, which is the primary function of Israel and the primary purpose of the world's creation.

16. God's covenant with David is the basis for hope in a coming kingdom of God and for a messianic ruler.

First Samuel portrays David as a heroic figure, viewed as the legitimate successor to the divinely rejected Saul. David comes to prominence as a court musician (1 Sam. 16:17–23) and then by slaying the Philistine giant Goliath (1 Sam. 17). Anointed king by Samuel, David takes Saul's daughter Michal as his first wife in order to establish a claim upon Saul's throne. He begins his reign in the southern city of Hebron, ruling there for seven years. Desiring a greater centralization of power, he captures the old fortress of Jerusalem, a neutral site bypassed by Israelite forces during the earlier occupation of Canaan, and makes it his capital. The city, naturally fortified and ideally located on the boundary of the southern and northern tribes, comes to be known as "the city of David" (1 Sam. 5:9).

In order to capture the allegiance of all Israel, David brings to Jerusalem the ark of the covenant, shifting the religious center of Israel from the confederate sanctuary of Shiloh to the royal shrine in Jerusalem. Establishing his throne on the religious sanctions and Mosaic traditions of the tribal confederacy, David lays the groundwork for the theocratic fusing of religion and politics. With the ark stationed in the tent of meeting, David joins the two major cultic objects inherited from Mosaic times. Thus the city of David became Zion, the city of God.

His defeat of the Philistines, followed by successful wars against Moab, Ammon, Edom, Amalek, and Aram (Syria), leads to a treaty with the Phoenician king, Hiram of Tyre. David comes to be recognized as the ruler of an empire that stretches from Phoenicia (southern Lebanon) to the borders of Egypt, and from the Mediterranean Sea to the desert of Arabia. Never before or after did Israel exceed this zenith of political power.

Having established his capital, David designates Abiathar and Zadok as chief priests and guardians of the ark, appointing some of his sons as priests to work with the Levites in administering Israel's religious rituals. David also calls upon the guidance of the seer Gad, who advises him to purchase the threshing floor of Araunah on which to build an altar to God. This property, adjacent to David's palace, would become the site of

Solomon's temple. To help govern, David also selects Nathan the prophet, adding the prestige of the prophets to his cabinet.

In managing his kingdom, David builds on the foundations that had been laid by Saul, beginning with a professional army. Second Samuel contains two lists of David's appointees, in 8:16–18 and 20:23–26. In addition to prophets and priests, David centralizes authority through commanders, secretaries, and cabinet members, probably according to Egyptian standards. He appoints Joab commander over the army, Jehoshaphat as "recorder" (perhaps the equivalent of a prime minister), and Seraiah as "secretary" or scribe. The second list includes a new official, Adoram, who oversees the "forced labor," a group consisting of war captives, subjugated populations, and perhaps Israelites, in addition to responsibility for public building projects.

Another monarchic innovation is the census (2 Sam. 24), its purpose being to ascertain the number of males to be drafted into the army. The census also demonstrates a royal attempt to impose further centralization on the kingdom by assessing the population's resources for taxation and labor. The census is opposed by the Deuteronomistic historians as sinful (even David is said to have regretted this decision; see 2 Sam. 24:10), probably because it implies a lack of confidence in God, who should have been trusted to provide for Israel.

David's innovations mark the beginning of "royal theology," the view that God has made a special covenant with David, promising to establish David's throne securely though all generations (2 Sam. 7:1–17). This passage, placed immediately after the establishment of the capital in Jerusalem and the ark's transfer there, sets forth for the first time the Deuteronomistic ideology of kingship. It opens with David's desire to build a temple (a "house") for Yahweh. The prophet Nathan expresses his approval, but Yahweh has other plans, which are transmitted to David through the prophet: Yahweh does not want a temple, but rather wishes to establish a covenant with David and Israel, guaranteeing the security of Israel and the dynasty ("house") of David unconditionally and in perpetuity. According to the prophetic word, a temple will be built by David's successor (Solomon), who will be regarded as God's son, punished if he "commits iniquity," but never to lose God's "steadfast love" (*hesed*), phrases that reflect a covenant relationship.

Because royal ideology (God's covenant with David) is so pervasive in the Bible, especially in the historical books, the prophets, and the

Psalms, it is appropriate to summarize its main features. God's covenant with David:

1. Establishes a permanent dynasty (2 Sam. 7:13, 16; 23:5; see Ps. 89:4, 29, 36–37; 132:12); the covenant is said to be unconditional and everlasting (a covenant of promise, not law). David's dynasty would remain unbroken in Israel (the United Kingdom) and in Judah (the Southern Kingdom) for some four hundred years.

2. Guarantees Israel land, security, and stability (2 Sam. 7:10).

3. Centralizes worship in a temple (2 Sam. 7:13; Ps. 132:1–5).

4. Establishes the king as covenant mediator, with whom God has a special relationship (2 Sam. 7:14–15; Ps. 2:7; 89:27–33).

Periodically throughout Judah's history, particularly in times of national crises, two different but related hopes emerged from royal theology: (1) *Kingdom hope*: the hope for rule by God, so important in both the Old and New Testaments, and (2) *Messianic hope*: the hope for a Davidic ruler that would guarantee the promissory terms of the Davidic covenant. After the end of the Davidic dynasty in 587 BC, elements of the royal ideology continued to play an important role in later Jewish and Christian traditions. The earliest Christians applied the language of divine sonship to Jesus. One of the titles used for him is "Christ," a Greek term that translates the Hebrew *mashiah* ("Messiah," meaning one who was "anointed" or consecrated for an exalted office such as prophet, priest, or king). Royal theology also survives in the hope for a restored or new Jerusalem, in which the promises attached to the city would be fulfilled.

Assignment

Having read chapter 6, answer the following questions, writing the answers in your journal. [If you are in a study group, be prepared to share your views with others in the class.]

1. Evaluate the author's statement that the presence of two alternative and competing accounts of Israel's history invites readers of scripture "to reflect theologically in creative ways."

2. Read Psalm 89 and respond to the following questions: (a) what elements of Royal Theology can you find in this psalm? (b) How do

you reconcile or explain the tension between the opening thanksgiving (89:1–37) and the closing lament (89:38–51)? Many psalms, like Psalm 13, follow a threefold pattern, moving from disintegration (13:1–2), through a hopeful transition (13:3–4), to integration (13:5–6). Psalm 89 seems to reverse the pattern (but note the conclusion in 89:52). In your estimation, does this closing verse reflect faithful perseverance, realistic hope, or simply religious resignation? (c) What happens to your relationship with God when things don't go as expected? Do you praise God in bad times as well as in good times? Why or why not?

3. What is the primary insight I/we gained from this chapter or session?

Chapter 7

Three Things to Know about the Poetic and Wisdom Books

IN ADDITION TO HISTORICAL literature, legal material, and prophetic collections, the Hebrew Bible contains numerous songs, prayers, compilations of wisdom sayings, and similar compositions. These are sometimes found in the midst of narratives (as the "Song of the Red Sea," Exodus 15, is found in the midst of the Exodus narrative and as Psalm 18 is found in 2 Samuel 22), but they exist as well in independent collections such as those of the books of Psalms, Proverbs, Job, and Ecclesiastes. These books are classified as the "poetic and wisdom books of the Bible," and the reference epitomizes the view that such books stand apart from the rest of the Bible by virtue of their special literary or poetic character. Despite their similarities, these writings are quite diverse concerning their origins, literary types, life setting, and structure. Although there is some overlap between the two broad categories "Psalms" and "Wisdom" (some psalms, for example, are classified as "wisdom psalms"), it is best to deal with each category separately.

Poetic Books: Psalms

The word "psalms" (meaning "praises") refers to a collection of 150 songs of supplication, thanksgiving, and praise found in the Bible. The hymns in the book of Psalms (or "Psalter") represent a wide variety of styles and moods, ranging from thanksgiving hymns, festival psalms, national and historical psalms, wedding psalms, royal psalms, laments, penitential psalms, and wisdom psalms.

Like most biblical poetry, the psalms (and many of the proverbs) have as their primary poetic device the use of parallelism. This technique, common to Middle Eastern poetry, is a kind of thought rhyme, in which an idea is developed by the use of repetition, synonym, or contrast. In synonymous parallelism, two lines express essentially the same idea (see Ps. 3:1; 49:1); in antithetic parallelism, opposites or contrasts are used (see Ps. 37:21, 22; Prov. 15:1); and in synthetic or ascending parallelism, the ideas build cumulatively (see Ps. 1:2; Prov. 4:23)

The book of Psalms is divided into five parts, probably in imitation of the Torah, the first five books of the Bible. This is also suggested by the content of Psalm 1, a wisdom psalm that introduces the entire collection by describing reward for those who observe Torah and punishment for those who fail to do so. Other than Psalms 1 and 2, which introduce the anthology, the five collections are:

1. Book I (Pss. 3–41), characterized by the use of the word Yahweh ("Lord") for God, is thought to be relatively early.

2. Book II (Pss. 42–72), characterized by the use of the word Elohim ("God"), is a collection of "northern" psalms (from the northern kingdom of Israel during the period of the divided monarchy).

3. Book III (Pss. 73–89), characterized by instructions given for singers in the headings, was designed for use in the temple.

4. Book IV (Pss. 90–106), taken from a royal collection, was often used in the celebration of Jewish festivals in the fall of the year: Sukkot ("Booths") and Rosh Hashanah ("New Year").

5. Book V (Pss. 107–150) appears to be a second collection of Davidic royal psalms.

Each of the first four of these divisions ends with a blessing (Ps. 41:13; 72:18–19; 89:52; 106:48). The final psalm, Psalm 150, may be considered a conclusion to the fifth division as well as to the book of Psalms as a whole.

An important clue to the origin of the Psalter is found in the postscript following Book II: "The prayers of David son of Jesse are ended" (72:20). This passage indicates that at one stage in the formation of the Psalter the "Davidic" collection ended here, although after Psalm 72 eighteen more psalms are attributed to David, showing that "the prayers of David" was a temporary edition. In this first division almost all of the psalms are prefixed with the words "of David." This does not mean that they were composed by David, however, but it does point to the antiquity of the collection.

The psalms were composed by many individuals over a long period of time and collected under the patronage of David, in part because he was regarded as the ideal king with whom the people identified as they approached God in worship and as the prototype of the Messiah (God's "anointed one"; Ps. 2), who would fulfill the hopes of Israel. The Psalms are quoted in the New Testament some seventy-five times; more than fifty represent Christ as the speaker or are directly applied to him.

In addition to David, the Psalms ascribe authorship or association with "the sons of Korah," one of the principal priestly families in Jerusalem; twelve are attributed to Asaph, a musician associated with David and one of the sons of Korah; ten are attributed to King Hezekiah. Within the book of Psalms there are other collections as well, including the Songs of Ascents (Pss. 120–134), so called because pilgrims used these psalms as they went up to Jerusalem to participate in the annual festivals; some psalms deal with divine kingship (Pss. 93–99), and another group, known as "Hallel" psalms, open or close with "hallelujah" ("praise Yahweh"; see Pss. 104–106; 111–113; 135; 146–150).

Additional evidence that the book of Psalms is an anthology is the repetition found therein. Thus, Psalms 14 and 53 are identical, except for the shift of the divine name from Yahweh to Elohim; Psalm 40:13–17 is the same as Psalm 70; and Psalm 108 is a combination of Psalms 57:7–11 and 60:5–12. The book of Psalms is therefore the result of a long process of compilation and editing. Its present shape was probably formed before the end of the Persian period in the late fourth century BCE. Perhaps the final editing was done by Ezra the scribe (c. 400 BCE), the same person said to have edited the five books of Torah, putting them into their final form.

Many of the psalms are from the time of the monarchy, with their repeated references to the king and the temple. Others are from the exilic period, including Psalm 137. Many of the psalms also reflect pentateuchal traditions, such as Psalm 8, which is related to the Priestly creation account in Genesis 1, and Psalms 78, 105 and 106, with their references to the ancestral history. As an anthology, the book of Psalms contains poems from several periods in Israel's history, though most individual psalms are impossible to date precisely.

An important connection can be made between the book of Psalms and God's Torah ("teaching"), the revelation of God's will. Significantly, the first psalm emphasizes the benefits of meditating on God's Torah (see also Ps. 19:7–14). Furthermore, the book of Psalms seems to reach its climax with Psalm 119, the longest of the psalms and the most formal in its structure. This psalm consists of twenty-two stanzas, each corresponding to one letter of the Hebrew alphabet. In addition, each stanza contains eight verses, every line in the stanza beginning with the same letter of the alphabet. Psalm 119 is a celebration of love for God's gift of Torah. The chapter has been titled, "The Love of God's Law," based on the exclamation in verse 97: "Oh, how I love your law!" The reference to "love" in this psalm should not be taken as an emotional outburst of support or delight at specific commandments. The psalmist is not displaying a feeling but a commitment, a commitment to God and to Torah as God's greatest gift. In a larger sense, Psalm 119 is a prayer for wisdom.

The psalm opens by saying, "Happy are those whose way is blameless, who walk in the law of the Lord" (119:1). The wording and sentiment are similar to the opening of Psalm 1; in both cases, the focus is on the delight of pondering Torah day and night, much as does someone who enjoys chemistry, computer science, history, literature, mathematics, music, or some other academic discipline. As scholars love their subject, so people are exhorted to love and study Torah. There is a difference, however, for the psalmist is speaking of a cultivated devotion to God that results from committing oneself to study of Torah. The desired result is to be transformed by study and thereby inspired to live the life that the study of Torah requires. It is possible that at one stage of editing the Psalter ended with Psalm 119, in which case the book concluded on the same note as it began: God's revelation in the Torah.

17. *The Psalms represent Israel's conversation with God.*

Looking back from the postexilic period, Israel understood its history to be a life of coexistence with God, that is, a "partnership with God" in a historical drama. In times of nationhood and even in the most catastrophic event, the end of Israel as a nation, Israel viewed history as the dramatic narrative of God's presence in the midst of the people. Though

Israel felt called to be a partner with God in this historical drama, the accent always fell on the "mighty acts" of God. As a covenant partner, Israel did not remain silent. Not only did the Israelites recall God's actions in narrative and written traditions, but they also addressed God in personal ways. The finest examples of Israel's relationship with God are found in the book of Psalms.

Throughout the biblical period, Israel's primary bond of unity was worship of God. According to the Bible, the enslaved Israelites were liberated from Egyptian bondage so that they might worship God at Sinai (Exod. 3:12). During the period of the tribal confederacy, instituted by Joshua, the Israelites gathered at cultic centers such as Shechem and Shiloh to celebrate the great annual festivals and to renew the covenant tradition. During the time of David, Jerusalem became the cultic center of the nation, to which Solomon added the impressive temple. During the period of the divided monarchy, when the northern kingdom became independent from Judah and Jerusalem, the kings of Israel gathered at pilgrimage shrines in their own territory, especially at Bethel. When the exiles returned from Babylon, their first thought was to rebuild the Jerusalem temple. Throughout its history, Israel was a worshipping community, recalling God's actions in narrative and written traditions but also addressing God in bold, honest, and deeply personal ways. For this reason the book of Psalms represents the very heart and center of the Hebrew Bible, Israel's "conversation" with Yahweh.

About one third of the Hebrew Bible is poetry. Awareness of this feature of Israel's liturgical and literary expression is invaluable for reading and interpreting scripture. Poetry is a personal way of expressing faith, both individually and communally. Poetry appeals to our human nature, making us realize the importance of emotion and signifying that we are more than intellect. Worship, like other interpersonal communication, involves both head and heart.

The book of Psalms in its present form is the product of postexilic Judaism. Insofar as the Psalter reflects the liturgical practice of this period, one can speak of it as the Hymnbook of the Second Temple, though this material continues to be chanted in Jewish synagogues. The collected psalms were intended to be sung, generally as a kind of chant and often accompanied by instrumental music. Some psalms provide hints of the original musical setting in the titles, headings, and opening words, largely added later but still preserving ancient tradition. In addition to their use as hymns, the psalms also function as prayers, recited corporately and privately.

There are, of course, numerous psalms that are expressions of community celebration, and these doubtless served as liturgies for such occasions as the various festivals and holy days described in the Pentateuch. But there are others of a more individual character, psalms that evoke states of distress such as illness or personal intrigue, or that offer thanks for God's having "heard my cry" in times of need. Yet these psalms lack detail. The identity of the psalmist's "enemies" or the precise nature of the predicament involved is glossed over. They are alluded to starkly as "Sheol" or "the Pit," but they remain ambiguous. Apparently, this lack of specifics was intentional, a way of tailoring the individual's plea or praise to his or her circumstances, but in such a way as to permit the reuse of a particular text repeatedly by different worshipers.

Classification of the psalms by literary type, such as whether its intent is principally praise or lament, or whether a psalm is apparently intended for the individual or the community, may well lessen its impact and meaning. There is clear evidence that within the biblical period, psalmody had already developed something of an independent existence, the singing or speaking of the words of existing psalms, as well as the creation of new ones inspired by existing models, became a form of individual and group devotion outside of the temple setting. Under such new circumstances, the very words of the Psalms sometimes took on new meanings. Because the book of Psalms reflects many aspects of the religious experience of Israel, its intrinsic spiritual depth and beauty have made it from earliest times a treasury of resources for public and private devotion in both Judaism and Christianity.

18. While Israel's poetic literature is adaptable to both private devotion and corporate worship, wisdom literature focuses on the individual.

From the earliest days, humans have sought to understand the nature of reality, going beyond their first and often mistaken impressions to a more profound level of truth. They have learned to discern life's patterns and to respond to life's vicissitudes by acting wisely, doing what brought everyone happiness and success. The Bible is a record of that journey. It represents the inspired attempt to become wise at the deepest level.

Through stirring teachings, the sages of the biblical wisdom tradition offer time-honored advice about some of life's most difficult questions, including the problem of pain, the suffering of the innocent, the nature of evil, the justice of God, and dealing with death. They also address such themes as friendship, virtue and vice, marriage and spousal choice, decision making, life priorities, child rearing, illness, and death. The insights offered in the biblical tradition and the efforts of the biblical sages to integrate faith, reason, revelation, and human wisdom rival those of the renowned philosophical schools of ancient Greece.

In Israel there were probably three separate settings for wisdom teaching: the clan, the court of the king, and the school. In the clan, the father and mother were the sages. In the royal court, the kings were associated with sages who advised them (see 2 Sam. 16:23; 17:14). Later wisdom writings give evidence of a house of learning, that is, a school in which sages instructed the young. The primary purpose of the book of Proverbs is to instruct youth in the life of wisdom, principally the children of wealthy elite connected to the royal court. It is likely that Ecclesiastes also emerged from school instruction, its author a scribe or teacher who lived in Jerusalem. The reference to "those who are wise" in Daniel 12:3 points to a group of trained scholars who served as exemplars in society, praised and viewed in tandem with "those who lead many to righteousness."

Our study of biblical wisdom literature includes an examination of Proverbs, Job, and Ecclesiastes. While these books of the Bible have provided perspective, guidance, and consolation to generations of believers, they can also be of significance for unbelievers, precisely because this literature provides perspective to some of humanity's greatest concerns, including suffering, educating our young, governing wisely, avoiding temptation and vice, growing in virtue, choosing better vocations, selecting friends, and choosing marriage partners.

While the Torah and the prophets agreed in placing the nation at the center, during the period of the Restoration, which followed the Babylonian Exile, the individual gradually came to the fore. Personal happiness and success, together with individual fears and hopes, had been recognized in the Torah and by the prophets, but after the Exile, the problem of individual suffering became central to Jewish thought. Increasingly, too, the prophets, concerned with the ideal future of the nation, focused on the happiness of the individual. "It was the decline of faith in the fortunes of the nation, coupled with the growth of interest in the individual and with individual destiny, that stimulated the development of wisdom.

Wisdom was not concerned with the group, but with the individual, with the realistic present rather than with a longed-for future."[1]

In ancient Israel there were three principal intellectual and spiritual currents, found in the three sections of the Hebrew Bible: Torah (the Law), Nebiim (the Prophets), and Ketubim (the Writings). The Septuagint, the Greek version of the Hebrew scriptures, expanded the Writings to include a fourth category: Wisdom Literature, adding to that literature the books of Sirach and the Wisdom of Solomon. A tripartite division of scripture appears in Sirach: "How different the one who devotes himself to the study of the law of the Most High! He seeks out the wisdom of all the ancients and is concerned with prophecies" (38:34b–39:1). What is unusual about this division is that "wisdom" is placed second, after "law" but before "prophecy." The passage continues by extolling the activity of the scribe: "he preserves the sayings of the famous and penetrates the subtleties of parables; he seeks out the hidden meanings of proverbs and is at home with the obscurities of parables" (34:2–3).

It is clear that Hebrew wisdom was not an isolated creation in Israel. On the contrary, it was part of a vast intellectual activity that had been cultivated for centuries in the Fertile Crescent, especially in Egypt and Babylonia. Situated at the cultural crossroads of the ancient world, the Israelites were influenced from an early time by Eastern wisdom writings. These writings, which circulated far beyond the land of their origin, dated back to the Egyptian Pyramid Age (about 2600–2175 BCE) and to the Sumerian era in Mesopotamia. However, wisdom had a timeless quality, transcending time and culture. Though ancient sages reflected on problems of society as they knew them, these were human problems found in varying forms in every society. Thus the wisdom movement was fundamentally international.

According to the historian Charles A. Beard, one of the lessons of history can be summarized by the proverb, "The bee fertilizes the flower it robs."[2] This is particularly true of the Jews during the Exile and the Restoration. Although the experience seemed bitter to many at the time, the people came to realize that God was working for good. While the surrounding culture was regarded as a threat to Israel's faith, the Exile also awakened a new world-consciousness, enlarging Israel's faith to an extent never before seen, not even in the cosmopolitan age of Solomon.

---

1. Gordis, *God and Man*, 40.
2. Cited in Anderson, *Understanding the Old Testament*, 425.

The exiles realized that they must look beyond their own community to the whole civilized world, if they would behold the glory and majesty of God's purpose in history. The time was ripe for a deeper understanding of the conviction that Israel was called to be God's agent in bringing blessings to all the nations of the earth.

The view that world-shaking events may have a double and seemingly contradictory effect on people's lives characterized a small but highly literate and influential group of Palestinian Jews living in Judah under Persian rule during the fourth and fifth centuries BCE. These sages flourished during this "Golden Age of Wisdom," a peaceful era of two hundred years aided by a common lingua franca (Aramaic) across the Persian Empire, a new sense of Jewish identity, and a new internationalism. During this period the books of Job and Ecclesiastes were written and the wisdom material found in the book of Proverbs was collected and finalized.

The wisdom of the biblical sages, unlike the regulations of the priests or the oracles of the prophets, usually made no claim to being divine revelation. It was, of course, self-evident that God was the source of Hebrew wisdom, as of every creative aspect of human nature. Thus, when Isaiah described the ideal Davidic king who would govern in justice and wisdom, he envisions the spirit of the Lord resting upon him, "the spirit of wisdom and understanding, the spirit of counsel and might, the spirit of knowledge and the fear of the Lord" (Isa. 11:2). Some of wisdom's most fervent advocates went further. By endowing wisdom with a cosmic role, they sought to win for wisdom a status almost equal to that of Torah and Prophecy. In their most lavish praise of wisdom, the Hebrew sages attributed her with great antiquity, declaring her to have been established "at the first, before the beginning of the earth" (Prov. 8:23). In Job's magnificent "Hymn to Wisdom" (Job 28), wisdom is endowed with cosmic significance and is virtually personified (28:20–28).

In Palestinian Judaism, where the study and interpretation of the Torah ultimately produced the Mishnah, wisdom was equated with the Mosaic Law. In the Diaspora, outside of Palestine, where Greek ideas were more influential, wisdom received a more philosophic interpretation. In the case of Philo, the celebrated Alexandrian Jew of the first-century CE, wisdom assumed the doctrine of the Logos or the Divine Word, which became the instrument by which God creates and governs the universe. It is only a further step to conceive of the Divine Word as the intermediary between God and the world, even as a distinct "person" or "aspect" of the divine nature (cf. the Logos Hymn in John 1:1–5).

Ultimately, however, biblical wisdom's claim to authority rested on its pragmatic truth. The Hebrew sages insisted that the application of wisdom "worked," meaning that when coupled with human reason and careful observation, it brought human beings success and happiness. Its origin might be in heaven, but its justification was to be sought in society and nature: "keep sound wisdom and prudence, and they will be life for your soul and adornment for your neck. Then you will walk on your way securely and your foot will not stumble. If you sit down, you will not be afraid; when you lie down, your sleep will be sweet. Do not be afraid of sudden panic, or of the storm that strikes the wicked; for the Lord will be your confidence and will keep your foot from being caught" (Prov. 3:19–26).

The origin of Israel's wisdom movement is unknown. A vigorous Canaanite wisdom movement might have been assimilated by Israel in the pre-monarchic period, as suggested by various affinities between the book of Proverbs and the Ugaritic Ras Shamra literature. From the earliest period of Israel's oral tradition come the proverb (1 Sam. 24:13), the riddle (see Judg. 14:14), and the fable (Judg. 9:8–15), ancient types of Near Eastern wisdom. By the time of the early monarchy, sages were well-known and respected leaders in Israelite society. We are told that the counsel of Ahithophel, one of David's court advisers, was "as if one consulted the oracle [word] of God" (2 Sam. 16:23). During Absalom's rebellion a wise Israelite woman used dramatic skill as well as literary inventiveness to present an imaginary case to King David (2 Sam. 14:1–24); later, during the same crisis, another wise woman negotiated with Joab (2 Sam. 20:14–22). The remark that the woman went to the people "with her wise plan" indicates that she was a recognized leader with professional standing, perhaps like the "wisest ladies" found in the Canaanite court in the "Song of Deborah" (Judg. 5:29).

The Bible regards Solomon as the source and symbol of its wisdom. Just as the Pentateuch was ascribed to Moses and the Psalms to David, so Israelites attributed much of their wisdom literature to Solomon, including the books of Proverbs and Ecclesiastes as well as the Song of Solomon. Though their connection with Solomon is not to be taken literally—this literature was written over a period of nine hundred years—claims to Solomonic authorship reflect the established historical fact that Solomon's reign was marked by wide international contact and internal prosperity, which contributed to the flowering of culture in general and to the intensive cultivation of wisdom in particular.

In biblical times, religious texts were often attributed to a famous person from the past. Such practice, called pseudepigraphic because authorship was falsely attributed, was commonly accepted in the ancient world, when "old" was considered superior to "new." In the biblical tradition, the attributed author was usually either a famous person from the remote past (such as Enoch, Moses, David, Solomon, and Ezra) or the actual author's own teacher (after his or her death). A pseudepigraphic work, then, was composed *as if* it were written by a person from the past, while the actual author remained anonymous.

The reasons for such practice are well known. For example, if an ancient or biblical author claimed her teaching was "new" or "original," few people would pay attention. But if she wrote in the name of a recognized authority, or if she transmitted what her teacher said (who may have learned from previous authorities), then people would be interested. In addition, writing in the name of a famous personage or authoritative teacher such as Moses, Solomon, Isaiah, or Daniel stressed continuity with tradition, enabling the "actual" author to adapt or apply that tradition to new historical circumstances. Pseudepigraphy characterized the wisdom literature of antiquity, including the Jewish wisdom tradition.

The Literary Forms of Wisdom Literature

If we are correct in assuming that the wise constituted a distinct class within Israel, we may also assume that these sages used a characteristic mode of discourse. The introduction to the book of Proverbs (1:6) mentions four kinds of sapiential teaching that students must understand: the *proverb* (a basic similitude or likeness in which a given phenomenon is set alongside another as illuminating it significantly); the *parable* (a saying or narrative conveying a stinging message hidden within a clever formulation); the "*wise saying*" (a general category or collection of sapiential instruction; and the *riddle* (an enigmatic saying leading to reflection on the meaning of life and its inequities). By extension, all of the above use admonitions and warnings as powerful expressions of cultural truth.

A broader examination of the Hebrew wisdom literature reveals additional literary forms, which, taken together, constitute ten categories. The wisdom saying we call (1) *proverb* (*mashal*) is expressed in a short pithy form, characterized by the usual Hebraic feature of parallelism. While proverbs need not include a pedagogic intent, usually the saying is clearly didactic, describing a particular act or attitude as wise or foolish. Numerical sayings may be related to (2) the *riddle*, as in "what item is common to the things enumerated?" (see Prov. 6:16–19; 30:18–31). While no pure riddles have survived within biblical wisdom literature, there can be little doubt that ancient sages coined enigmas and that the solving of riddles belonged to the essential tasks of the wise. Several (3) *allegorical texts* stand out as worthy links with riddles, such as the clever description of old age in Ecclesiastes 12:1–8 and the exquisite advice about marital fidelity in Proverbs 5:15–23, in which a wife is likened to a cistern from which one drinks life-giving water. Cipher language functions on two levels at the same time and is particularly apt in allegorical contexts.

The category of (4) *hymn* was utilized by the sages to fashion their own kind of song, whether about Lady Wisdom (Proverbs 8) or about the wonders of nature and the inaccessibility of wisdom (Job 28). Perhaps the supreme rhetorical achievement of the sages was the (5) *dialogue or disputation*. Its peculiar characteristics include a mythological introduction and conclusion, the dialogue proper, and a divine resolution. The book of Job is a marvelous example (Job 4–26), for it utilizes these formal features to address the problem of undeserved suffering. The sages developed a special type of (6) *autobiographical narrative*, allowing them to communicate lessons from personal experience. Wisdom's deep roots in experience provide many lessons based on observation and reflection.

Another important literary form that the sages adapted to their own purposes is the (7) *didactic narrative*. An example of this "story-sermon" appears in Proverbs 7:6–23, where a seductress leads a young man to his ruin. The (8) *wisdom poem*, a poem containing numerous sayings or admonitions, is exemplified particularly in Proverbs 1–9 and in the speeches in Job. This device shows a tendency toward alphabetizing (Proverbs 2:1–22 has twenty-two lines corresponding to the number of letters of the Hebrew alphabet), a practice related to the acrostic pattern in which each unit begins with the next successive letter of the Hebrew alphabet (see Prov. 30:1–31 and Ps. 34). The book of Job, characterized by the disputation speech that marks the dialogue between Job and the three friends, also contains a (9) *lament* (Job 3), a dirge regarding Job's birth. Although Ecclesiastes uses various genres, the most characteristic form may be termed a (10) *soliloquy*. In passages such as 2:12–17 and 2:18–26,

Ecclesiastes proposes as points for reflection the value of wisdom and the value of toil. While the passage develops randomly, there is frequent reference to the author's personal observations and insights.[3]

The Underlying Principle for Israel's Sages

What was the goal of Israel's sages? What did they hope to achieve by coining proverbs and formulating observations about the meaning of life? One means of discovering the self-consciousness of Israel's sages as a distinct group within society is to examine the carefully worded introduction to the book of Proverbs, where we find listed a cluster of words and phrases that characterize those who master the proverbial tradition: wisdom, instruction, understanding, intelligence, righteousness, justice, equity, discretion, knowledge, prudence, learning, and skill. Taken together, they constitute individual facets of the quest for "Life," what philosophers call "the good life." The canonical sages pursued the good life in all its manifestations: health, wealth, honor, progeny, longevity, and remembrance.

A study of three books central to the Jewish wisdom literature reveals different results in describing the object of the sapiential search:[4]

(1) The book of Proverbs represents a quest for *practical knowledge*, an understanding about nature and human beings that enable people to live wisely and well. For the authors of Proverbs, finding "life" means not so much biologically but relationally, life with another. For the sage, "to live" means to live with wisdom, to banquet with her in her house.[5] According to Proverbs 9:4, living with wisdom is the opposite of living in ignorance. To live with wisdom requires "pondering," meaning that one must live with discernment. Living with the proverbs is like living in a house or a school of wisdom, where wise sayings are examined deeply. Hence the proverbial material is often couched in parables, allegories, riddles, and other enigmatic sayings, with emphasis on subtlety, paradox, and wordplay. Proverbial themes may appear simplistic or repetitive, but careful study reveals that details are important and vital to the meaning of the text.

---

3. Crenshaw, *Old Testament Wisdom*, 37–39, and Murphy, *Tree of Life*, 7–13.
4. The following segment is adapted from Crenshaw, *Old Testament Wisdom*, 62–65.
5. Clifford, *Wisdom Literature*, 64.

(2) The book of Job is not primarily a search for knowledge about how to cope with the enigmas of ordinary existence, but rather represents a quest for *God's presence*. The author, like the character of Job, acknowledges God's gracious presence in the past, and therefore cannot endure a God who is hidden in the present. Job searches the darkest depths of despair in pursuit of his God, and eventually risks death and even damnation to achieve restored communion. To Job, God is "Life," the highest good, and compared to that *summum bonum*, biological life pales.

(3) The book of Ecclesiastes represents the quest for *meaning in a silent universe*. Like Job, Qoheleth (the author of Ecclesiastes) cannot affirm biological life as the supreme good, but unlike Job, Qoheleth does not enter into dialogue with the living God. Lacking confidence in life's goodness, he searches in vain for some meaning that can enable him to endure his empty existence.

19. The Old Testament contains two distinct (and opposing) streams of wisdom literature.

In *Jesus the Sage*, Ben Witherington divides early Jewish wisdom into two major traditions: conventional wisdom (as found in Proverbs) and counter-order wisdom (as found in Ecclesiastes and Job). He maintains that through his teaching and way of life Jesus modeled the latter tradition, particularly in his parables and aphorisms of reversal (as exemplified by his care for weak and marginalized individuals).

Wisdom literature, thus, falls into two classes. The first consists of (a) practical advice to the young on how to attain a successful and good life. This *conventional approach* is illustrated in the maxims found in the book of Proverbs as well as in the longer essays of Sirach. The second consists of (b) reflective probing into the depth of human perplexity about the meaning of life, often skeptically. This *unconventional approach* is illustrated by the biblical books of Ecclesiastes and Job. Though the sages of this reflective perspective had been trained to apply observation and reasoning to the practical problems of life, they were intrigued more by fundamental issues such as the purpose of life, life after death, the basis of morality, and the problem of evil. When they weighed the religious and moral ideas of their time by these standards, they found much that they felt compelled to reject as either untrue or unproved. Hence, the speculative wisdom books are basically skeptical, at variance with the approach of the practical school. In seeking to penetrate the abiding issues of suffering and death, these rare wisdom teachers were unwilling to rely on tradition and conventional ideas. When they insisted on applying experience and reason to the ultimate questions of life, "they courted tragedy—but achieved greatness."[6] Both types of wisdom literature, however, isolated the human problem from the particulars of history, and in this respect they stand in contrast to most biblical literature.

In one sense wisdom authors are highly conservative, for they revere tradition. Yet in another sense they are highly innovative and progressive, for they also revere their own experience and value their own insights. In the biblical tradition, the understanding and insight that constitute "wisdom" ultimately come from God, but are accessible in three primary forms: wisdom taught by God, wisdom taught by nature, and wisdom that arises from reflection on human experience. In these writings, wisdom is the rare attainment of intelligence, sound judgment, ethical conduct, humility, and the distinctive piety identified in the motto of the book of Proverbs: "The fear of the Lord is the beginning of wisdom" (Prov. 9:10). Within the biblical wisdom tradition, certain themes take on increasing significance: the fear of the Lord, God's self-manifestation through personified wisdom, the problem of innocent suffering, the meaning of life, the justification of God's ways, the limits of human knowledge, and the inevitability of death. Given the range of this literature, we may conclude that Israel's sages struggled with life's fundamental questions. Their way of addressing these, and the solutions they reached, point to a remarkable group of people.

Wisdom's practical goals for temporal success appealed primarily to those groups in society that benefitted from the status quo—government officials, rich merchants, great landowners, even high-priestly families. The goal of upper-class education was the training of youth for successful careers. These needs were admirably met by the wisdom teachers who arose, primarily in Jerusalem, the capital city.

The upper-class orientation reflected in the book of Job emerges in the treatment of the book's basic theme—the problem of suffering. While wisdom writers could not ignore the inequities of the present order. at the same time, as representatives of affluent social groups, they did not find the status quo intolerable. The lower classes, oppressed by poverty and marginalized at the hands of domestic and foreign masters, were deeply

---

6. Clifford, *Wisdom Literature*, 43.

afflicted by the prosperity of the wicked and the suffering of the righteous. Holding resolutely to their faith in God, they were nevertheless unable to see divine justice operating in the world. Their solution to this problem was the espousal of the doctrine of the afterlife, a future world where the inequalities of the present order would be rectified. Thus, the idea of life after death became an integral feature of Pharisaic Judaism and of Christianity.

The teachers of wisdom, on the other hand, felt no need to adopt these views. The sages of the conventional wisdom schools continued to maintain the old view of collective retribution here and now, where the sins or virtues of the fathers determine the destinies of the children (Prov. 13:22; 14:26; 20:7). The idea of a future life is not mentioned in Proverbs, probably because the material is comparatively early. However, by the first century BCE, the doctrine of an afterlife could no longer be ignored. In fact, it is clearly affirmed by the author of the Wisdom of Solomon: "But the righteous live forever, and their reward is with the Lord; the Most High takes care of them" (Wis. 5:15). The unconventional authors of Job and Ecclesiastes are too sensitive to overlook the undeserved suffering and prosperity in the world, yet neither accepts the solution of life after death, although both are familiar with it (Eccl. 3:19–21; 9:10). The author of Job lacks the tough-mindedness of Qoheleth. He cannot pretend to be indifferent to the hope for an afterlife. He wishes he could accept it as true, but he sorrowfully comes to the conclusion that the renewal of life after death is not given to mortals (14:7–19).

The Jewish wisdom tradition profoundly influenced the New Testament community. Wisdom images and ideas appear in every layer of the New Testament, from the letter of James, an early document attributed to the brother of Jesus, to the gospels, which portray Jesus as a wisdom teacher, to the letters of Paul, where Christ is called the wisdom of God (1 Cor. 1:24). Early christological hymns, embedded in the New Testament, utilize wisdom motifs to express Christian belief in the incarnation of Jesus (John 1:1–18) and in his cosmic rule (Col. 1:15–20; Heb. 1:1–4). Among the various influences on the New Testament was the identification of wisdom (Jesus) with divine spirit (2 Cor. 3:16–18), word (John 1:1), and law (Matt. 5:17–20; 7:24–29). The study of Jewish wisdom literature as found in the Hebrew Bible provides readers of the New Testament with an entirely new and intriguing perspective on Jesus and early Christianity. Following the resurrection of Jesus, when early Christians were looking for language and concepts to express their experience and understanding of Jesus, one of the most helpful resources was the wisdom literature. Of course, other parts of the Hebrew Bible were valuable, such as the prophets, the psalms, and the historical traditions of Israel, but the authors of the New Testament and the leaders of the early Christian communities saw in the wisdom literature important resources for understanding Jesus and their new life in Christ.

The Virtue of Patient Moderation

An outsider to the world of wisdom might say that acquiring wisdom is first and foremost an act of faith, a willingness to believe despite at times considerable evidence to the contrary, that all happens according to a plan, and that the necessity for fair and righteous conduct is still the best guide in leading one's life. However, biblical wisdom texts present another answer, that evidence of the workings of this pattern does present itself, but only if one is sufficiently discerning and takes the "long view." As the author of Ecclesiastes observes, "Better is the end of a thing than its beginning; the patient in spirit are better than the proud in spirit" (7:8). For only with patience can one refrain from snap judgments and escape the tyranny of the moment. In fact, the English word "patience" corresponds well to Israelite wisdom, for it suggests not only an ability to wait things out, but also an ability to accept discomfort and suffering (the English word "patient" refers to one suffering from a disease and under a doctor's care). So, too, the sage is one who has patience and knows that, however much at any given moment the world seems to be in imbalance and common folks are forced to suffer in a manner that appears unjust, sooner or later the underlying order will appear, either because things are set aright or because a previously unknown explanation will become apparent.

As we note in the story of Joseph, who is swept up by events beyond his control and yet displays many of the characteristics of a sage, he rides out the storm and patiently greets each new turn, ultimately assuming his place as ruler over Egypt. When, at last, he reveals his identity to his brothers, he urges them to consider their actions as part of a divine plan: "Even though you intended to do harm to me, God intended it for good" (Gen. 50:20).

This virtue of patience is evident in the biblical wisdom literature. The book of Proverbs regularly contrasts the "fool" or the "wicked" with the "sage" or the "righteous," and it is the latter who win out in the end (see Prov. 10:17–18). Indeed, in Proverbs the attitude of patient moderation is the hallmark of the righteous sage. In Job, the notions of "patience" and "suffering" are intertwined, and Job is portrayed as challenging conventional wisdom, putting all advice to the test. This is an author disturbed by suffering and evil (perhaps in response to the suffering of innocent Jews during the Babylonian Exile), although he is willing, in the end, to give God the last word.

Qoheleth also questions conventional wisdom, although in a somewhat different fashion from Job. He knows the version of the world espoused by sages but sets out to put everything to the test, finding the best in life thwarted by "folly" (the word in Ecclesiastes means self-indulgence and hedonism). Although the answer is quick in coming (2:13), the book's search is far from over; indeed, the book implies that learning the truth of wisdom is a lifelong task. While claiming that all is "vanity" (the Hebrew word *hebel* is not so much "vanity," but something ungraspable and therefore futile), this judgment is nevertheless a summons to move forward. As the author continues, he concludes with an allegorical poem on old age (12:1–7). Looking from the vantage point of old age and death, he exhorts his readers to keep the conversation with God alive at an early age, while they are still able: "Remember your creator in the days of your youth, before the days of trouble come" (12:1).

Assignment

Having read chapter 7, answer the following questions, writing the answers in your journal. [If you are in a study group, be prepared to share your views with others in the class.]

1. Read Psalm 1. How many forms of poetic parallelism can you find in this wisdom psalm?
2. Read Psalm 119. This psalm speaks of God's justice and God's mercy. How do you understand these concepts? How are they reflected in how you relate to God, others, and yourself?
3. Explain how "patience" works, and why it is considered a virtue.
4. What is the primary insight I/we gained from this chapter or session?

Chapter 8

Three Things to Know about the Prophetic Books

TOGETHER WITH THE HISTORICAL books (known in the Hebrew Bible as the "Former Prophets"), fifteen prophetic books form the central section of the Hebrew scriptures. Following the Torah, these writings join the Pentateuch to form the earliest sacred canon of Judaism, constituting "the law and the prophets," a phrase familiar from the New Testament.

The canonical inclusion of historical writings within the category of prophecy can be detected as early as the fourth century BCE, when the author of Chronicles listed prophets and seers among his sources, thereby attributing inspired origin to his writings. In 1 Chronicles 25:1, the author expanded the meaning of the term "prophecy" to include the composition and rendition of liturgical music. In the first century CE the Jewish historian Josephus explained the inclusion of the historical books within the category of prophecy by attributing to this literature prophetic authorship.[1] In addition, the writers of apocalypses also thought of themselves, and were thought of by others, as fulfilling a prophetic role (2 Esd. 15:1; Rev. 1:3).

When considering the meaning of the term "prophecy," it is important to bear in mind that those whom we think of as biblical prophets formed only a small and in some respects an unconventional minority among Israelite prophets, the rest having cultic or royal institutional roles. Furthermore, when the "true" biblical prophets speak of contemporary

---

1. *Against Apion*, 1:37–41.

prophecy, they regularly condemn it as false or inauthentic (see Jer. 23 and Ezek. 13).

The Christian Old Testament distinguishes between major and minor prophets, adding Daniel to Isaiah, Jeremiah, and Ezekiel while expanding the Scroll of the Twelve into twelve individual prophets (Hosea, Joel, Amos, Obadiah, Jonah, Micah, Nahum, Habakkuk, Zephaniah, Haggai, Zechariah, and Malachi). Though Daniel is included among the prophetic books in Christian Bible, in the Hebrew scripture Daniel is placed with the Writings, the third and closing body of literature in the Jewish canon. In the Septuagint, however, the order is different, the prophetic books coming at the end, after the poetic and wisdom literature. Technically, the book of Daniel more appropriately belongs to a form of prophetic literature known as apocalyptic.[2]

The "classical period" of Old Testament prophecy extends from the middle of the eighth to the middle of the sixth centuries BCE. It includes Amos, Micah, Nahum, Habakkuk, Isaiah, Zephaniah, Jeremiah, and Ezekiel, and ends with the prophecy of Second Isaiah (Isa. 40–55) and Obadiah, both exilic prophets. The postexilic prophets, including Third Isaiah (Isa. 56–66), Haggai and Zechariah (520 BCE), Malachi (c. 450), Joel (c. 400), and Jonah (c. 350), belong to the declining period of prophetic activity.

The Hebrew Bible arranges the prophetic writings chronologically. The three major prophets are grouped together for practical reasons, and the twelve minor prophets also appear to have been arranged in what was thought to be their chronological order (Haggai, Zechariah, and Malachi were always known to be postexilic, but modern scholarship has altered the dates of other books). As we now know, the prophetic writings originated over a period of six hundred years, beginning with Amos (c. 750) and Hosea (c. 745) and ending with Daniel (c. 165).

20. The prophetic movement is the most astonishing phenomenon in the history of Israel, though not because of its predictive power.

Popularly viewed, the role of the prophet is to predict future events. Modern scholarship downplays this understanding of the role of prophets. Biblical scholars now understand the prophetic role as having involved

---

2. Further discussion of this topic appears at the end of this chapter, in the segment "From Prophecy to Apocalyptic."

three distinct yet related tasks, each with a different temporal focus: (a) they were predictors of the future (*foretelling*); (b) they were reformers who kept alive the Mosaic past through continuous appeal to the theocratic ideals expressed in the covenants (*retelling*); and (c) they were social critics who spoke out boldly and without compromise against current disobedience and disbelief within the social, religious, and political establishment (*forthtelling*). Of the three tasks, the most significant was forthtelling and the least significant was foretelling. Biblical prophets rarely, if ever, made open predictions about the distant future, and when they did so, the predictions were linked to their role as social critics, which focused on the consequences for unrepentance. The prophet's futuristic role was associated primarily with the certainty of the coming of the Lord, a coming to make things right through judgment and reward.

Most cultures in antiquity had diviners, that is, individuals trained or skilled in interpreting dreams and signs in nature, or mediums able to communicate with the dead. Some had magical powers and the ability to heal and even to restore the dead to life. In most of these capacities, they functioned as intermediaries and channels of communication between the natural and supernatural realms. Such individuals were widely attested in the ancient Mediterranean and Near Eastern regions long before their appearance in Israel, primarily in Egypt, Mesopotamia, Syria, Canaan, Asia Minor, and Greece.

Like other forms of interpretation of the supernatural, prophecy was widespread in the ancient world. As a religious phenomenon, it flourished in Israel long before the days of Elijah and Elisha or the emergence of writing prophets such as Amos and Hosea in Israel or Isaiah in Judah. Thus, the Bible refers to the "four hundred and fifty prophets of Baal and the four hundred prophets of Asherah" during the reign of the northern king Ahab, brought to Israel by Jezebel from her native Phoenicia (1 Kgs. 18:18).

In Israel, traces of prophetic activity appear as early as Mosaic times (see Num. 11:26–30), but not until the eleventh century BCE does prophecy emerge in the life of Israel as a recognized institution. At that time, two distinct types of prophet appear: the ecstatic group of prophets, such as those who met Saul before his coronation (1 Sam. 10:5–13; see also 19:18–24), and the lone seer type, represented by Balaam, the Syrian diviner hired to curse Israel (see Num. 22), and later by Samuel (1 Sam. 9:5—10:8). Some two hundred years later, prophetic communities appeared in Israel under the leadership of Elijah and Elisha.

Other well-known charismatic prophets in the monarchic period include Nathan and Gad, who served in David's court, Ahijah, who advised Jeroboam, and Micaiah, who prophesied in the time of Ahab.

After the eighth century, prophecy flourished for the most part in times of national crisis. Amos and Hosea in Israel and Isaiah and Micah in Judah warned the people that Assyria was God's tool of judgment, and that her armies would destroy Israel if she did not repent of her evil ways. Israel refused to heed the warning, and the Assyrians took the northern kingdom of Israel into captivity in 722. Although the kingdom of Judah was spared, she was left a weak vassal state.

The climax of Old Testament prophecy was reached in the period just before and after the fall of Jerusalem to the Babylonians in 587. Once again prophets arose, this time to warn the people of Judah of impending doom unless they repented. Jeremiah, Zephaniah, and Habakkuk bravely tried to avert the tragedy with their powerful preaching and consistent witness, but to no avail. After the fall of Jerusalem, Ezekiel comforted the exiles in Babylonia with his message of a restored nation in Palestine, worshiping in a new and glorious temple. New elements appearing in his prophecy led ultimately to apocalypticism on the one hand and to the emergence of institutional Judaism on the other. He was followed shortly thereafter by Second Isaiah, the greatest poet-theologian among the prophets, who inspired his people with images of the good news of imminent release from the Babylonian captivity.

With the fall of Babylon to Cyrus of Persia in 539 came freedom for exiles to return to their ancestral homeland. The small group of Jews that returned to Palestine soon fell on hard times. Crop failures, widespread poverty, hostility of neighbors such as Edomites and Samaritans, and spiritual indifference reduced the morale of the people to a dangerous low point. Even the rebuilding of the temple, which was the only rallying point for the people, was temporarily abandoned. At this critical time (520 BCE) Haggai and Zechariah arose to revive the hopes of the people and to urge them to finish the temple. The people responded by completing the project in 515.

The prophetic office now fell from repute (see Zech. 13:2–6), and, with the exception of Malachi, Joel, and Jonah, disappeared until its restoration in the ministries of John the Baptist and Jesus of Nazareth. Prophecy became a recognized phenomenon in early Christianity, as we see exemplified in the book of Acts (11:27–30; 13:1; 21:9; see also 1 Cor. 12:28–29).

The Role of the Prophet

Given the diversity of their lives and activities, various terms are used to describe Israelite prophets. The English word "prophet" comes from the Greek and literally means "spokesperson." The most frequently used term in the Hebrew Bible is the word *nabhi*; while its etymology is not certain, its origin is from a word meaning "to call." Thus, a *nabhi* is "one who speaks a word on behalf of another," implying, in the religious sense, someone called by God to deliver divinely sent messages. The primary content of these messages was the interpretation of phenomena and current events from a divine perspective. In this respect, the biblical prophet received a status similar to that later assigned to "angels," also viewed as divine messengers.

In the Bible, the first human to fit the prophetic office was Moses. Interestingly, in Exodus 7:1, Moses is designated as "God" to Pharaoh, and Aaron is to be Moses's *nabhi* (that is, Moses is to tell his brother Aaron what to say, and Aaron is to speak on behalf of Moses to Pharaoh). In Deuteronomy 18:9–22, we find an attempt to normalize the concept of prophecy. Here, in a polemical context opposed to the Canaanite practice of divination, we find a distinction between true and false prophecy (18:21–22).

During the history of Israel, the prophetic office evolved through three stages: ecstatic prophecy (this type was exhibited in guilds of prophets; 1 Sam. 10:5–6, 10; 19:23–24); royal or court prophecy (2 Sam. 7:2); and classical or literary prophecy. In the second stage, there was always the danger that the prophetic office might deteriorate into a "professional trade" (a condition that easily befalls priest and kings and other holders of theocratic offices in Israel), whereby representatives of God would become "yes-men," serving the status quo or their own aggrandizement rather than being "troublers of Israel" (see 1 Kgs. 18:17). Thus, instead of being voices "crying in the wilderness," many became voices "singing in the city," uttering predictable words instead of bold and honest messages "from the Lord." This compromise led to the emergence of the classical prophets, viewed as the true, faithful prophets through whom God spoke and to whom God gave the divine Spirit.

How did prophets receive messages from God, we wonder. Such communication must be possible, but at the same time God's essential otherness must also be preserved. A common way of dealing with this paradox is through metaphor. The two most common metaphors in the prophetic literature are those of speech and vision. Hence, to take such forms of communication literally can distort their meaning.

In secular contexts, we often find the role of the prophet marginalized, the figure itself often reduced to a state of cognitive dissociation, and the perspective that emerges is of an odd figure relating almost exclusively to societal insecurity and gullibility. However, as anthropological scholars such as Nora Chadwick and Kenelm Burridge demonstrate, it is not appropriate to think of prophets as schizophrenic or paranoid, or as mystics suffering from mental disorder. Rather, as evidence shows, in social settings such as primal societies, shamans or prophets are persons of formidable intellect who serve valuable roles as preservers of tradition and, when needed, as agents of social change.

As the ancient Greek philosopher Plato noted, the ideal form of prophetic activity lies not in marginal individuals but rather in those ruled by understanding and objective judgment, namely, in the conception of the philosopher. In this vein, the apostle Paul speaks highly of prophecy in 1 Corinthians 14, praising it above all spiritual gifts (14:2-5, 39-40). For Paul, prophecy is beneficial in church because the prophet speaks to others intelligibly (14:9), with the mind (14:19), and in such a way that the message is grasped by the hearer, who is both edified (14:4) and convicted (14:26-26) by the inspired message. It is worth noting that in Rabbinic Judaism, wise men (that is, learned scribes and rabbis) were seen as the legitimate successors of the Hebrew prophets. According to Philo, the first century Hellenistic Jew, those who are righteous are bearers of the prophetic spirit, and every wise person has the prophetic gift.[3]

This relationship between wisdom, righteousness, and the prophet can be seen in the New Testament as well. In Matthew 23:31-36, Jesus is quoted as saying that "prophets and wise men and scribes" would be sent as righteous messengers to confirm the unrighteousness of members of his own generation. In the parallel passage found in Luke 11:49, further insight may be gained: "Therefore also the Wisdom of God said, 'I will send them prophets and apostles . . .'" Here we are reminded of the statement in Ephesians 2:20, where apostles and prophets are said to be the foundation upon which the church is built. Throughout this epistle, prophets are found in positions of prominence in the church (see Eph. 3:5; 4:11). In Matthew 10:41, a deliberate parallel seems to be drawn between the prophet and the righteous person.

---

3. *Quis Rerum Divinarum Heres*, 259.

The sociologist Max Weber operates out a broad framework when he includes "founders of religion" and "renewers of religion" in his study of the prophetic type. Attributing the genesis of prophecy, especially in the Near East, to the growth of great world empires, he connects the prophet with great social ferment, demonstrating that economic and political conditions play a prominent role in the production of prophets and seers. Weber associates the success of the great prophets of the world's religions with their ability to provide their followers, both through their lives and by their teachings, with a unified view of the world, derived from a consciously integrated and meaningful attitude toward life.[4] In this respect, the prophet's role is to orient the conduct of humanity to this systematic and coherent meaning that the prophet finds to underlie human life and that of the natural realm.

In his study of millenarian movements, Burridge realizes that the prophet is not a person to be taken lightly. Rather, the prophetic figure is extraordinary, due to strong personal qualities such as keen intellect and specialized training, the ability to speak authoritatively and to command power, the ability to impose certainty on a situation characterized by uncertainty, the ability to articulate new assumptions or symbolize new realities, and the awareness of moral dilemma.[5] The true prophet, then, is characterized by a sense of mission and personal call, acting, in traditional societies, as the midwife of change, and serving as the conscience of a religion or a people. In this lies the greatness of the prophetic type.

In the biblical literature, while most of the named prophets are men, it is clear that women are also prophets. During the period of the monarchy, the best example is Huldah (2 Kgs. 22:14). Other named women prophets are Miriam (Exod. 15:20), Deborah (Judg. 4:4), and Noadiah (Neh. 6:14). Also identified as a prophet is the unnamed wife of Isaiah (Isa. 8:3). In his vision of the "day of the Lord," the prophet Joel speaks of God pouring out his Spirit on the entire population, so that "your sons and your daughters shall prophesy" (Joel 2:28–29). In Joel's vision of restoration, the gift of prophecy will be universal, as the first Christians quickly affirmed (Acts 2:2:16–18).

---

4. Weber, *Sociology of Religion*, 59.
5. Burridge, *New Heaven, New Earth*, 153–64.

21. *Some of the material in the prophetic books derives from interpretive schools inspired by the named prophet.*

The prophets are generative personalities, having the capacity to shape perception of public reality in a rich variety of images and metaphors. Because they were imaginative and sometimes irreverent in their utterance, the speech of the prophets was daring and unpredictable, confronting even modern-day readers with their bold message. The prophets voiced a restlessness about social reality that reflects the restless rule of God, opening society to God's new possibilities.

Despite their highly individualized vocations, Israel's prophets did not operate alone or in a social vacuum. They were deeply engaged in the social, economic, and political issues of their day. They failed to see the world as others saw it, and they dared to proclaim what others did not dare to utter. Despite their remarkable extraordinariness, they did not act alone. Around these awesome figures there were loyal friends, allies, and disciples who remembered and cherished their words and who regarded their message as having enduring authority. This residue of remembered words and actions became the core of the prophetic books. In sum, most prophetic books reached their present form as the result of a cumulative process of editing, adapting, and expanding. This redactional history continued until the individual books and the collection as a whole achieved such an authoritative status that no further adaptation or commentary was deemed permissible.

The prophets left words, but they also left a vision of reality that continued to inform and empower others after them. These others continued the rhetorical, interpretive tradition of their mentors and teachers, so that in the wake of the prophetic person, the prophetic tradition continued with new prophetic speech that was faithful to and congruent with the originating personality. Thus, because of the prophetic personality, the prophetic tradition that derived from that personality continued to be powerful and passionate, claiming the authority of the original person. Consequently, the words in a collection, even those from a derivative tradition, became ascribed to the original prophet. This is particularly evident in the book of Isaiah (see 8:16, which speaks of a tradition perpetuated by Isaiah's disciples and followers). Only chapters 1–39 can be assigned to the prophet Isaiah, who proclaimed his message to Judah in Jerusalem from 742 until 701, and even these chapters contain later material.

Chapters 40–55, commonly called Second Isaiah, originated as much as a century and a half after the original prophet, dating to about 545–540, to the period immediately before the end of the Babylonian Exile. The anonymous author exults in joyful anticipation of exiled Judah's restoration to Palestine. A noteworthy feature of his prophecy is the figure of the Servant of the Lord, heralded in four "Servant Songs" (42:1–4; 49:1–6; 50:4–11; and 52:13—53:12) and identified by interpreters variously as a reference to the exiled Jews, a righteous remnant, a prophetic individual, and by Christians as the Messiah. Chapters 56–66, commonly called Third Isaiah, date to the postexilic period, about 530–510 BCE.

What applies to Isaiah relates to a lesser degree to other prophetic books as well. The reason is clear. Much of the prophetic literature originated in oral form, particularly in the preexilic period, and only certain prophets created written works. Scholars believe that books such as Ezekiel, the latter portions of Isaiah, the narrative material in Jeremiah, and most of the postexilic prophetic books are exceptions, not having passed through an oral stage but having originally been created in written form.

The process by which the prophets' oral sayings were collected and preserved in writing is not fully understood. Scholars usually assume that disciples or supporters remembered and collected the oracles and eventually wrote them down or paid scribes to record them. In 605, for example, Jeremiah dictated from memory sayings delivered by him over a period of more than two decades. When this collection was read to King Jehoiakim by Jehudi his secretary, Jehoiakim tore it up and threw it on the fire, after which Jeremiah produced a second and amplified edition, now part of the biblical book (Jer. 36). The book also contains long biographical passages (Jer. 26–45), authored likely by Baruch, Jeremiah's faithful scribe. The book as a whole, including its continuous narrative sections, was later edited and expanded by a Deuteronomistic redactor during the exilic period. Not surprisingly, Jeremiah 52 is identical with the conclusion of the Deuteronomistic History (2 Kings 24:18—25:30).

Clearly, the prophets did not intend to create scripture, nor did people at the time of the recording phase think they were preserving scripture, for the idea of scripture, certainly as applicable to contemporary figures, was foreign to all participants. Rather, scripture results through the ongoing theological reflection of the religious community. On the one hand, the process of making a holy text (that is, canonization) consists in recognizing that the literature has ongoing authority. The community finds the literature to be enduringly true, in that words uttered in one context are found to be compelling and powerful in subsequent contexts. On the other hand, the process of shaping a prophetic book is not done around a literary topic or a historical event but around theological themes and convictions. Characteristically, the prophetic books are thematized around the notion of God's purpose, judgment, and enduring promise. Thus, the prophet urges the listening community to come to terms with God's will, which cannot be overridden or nullified.

There would have been at least two reasons for wanting to record a prophet's words. First, the written record could be used to test the accuracy of what a person had predicted. Second, at least in some cases, prophecies that had been fulfilled might have been thought to be still applicable to new situations, so that written records could benefit future communities experiencing circumstances similar to those of the original audience.

With the advent of oracle collections and written prophetic narratives, a new phase began in the development of the prophetic writings. As long as oral prophecies were still being delivered, the collecting and shaping of prophetic materials presumably remained in the hands of the prophets and their supporters. However, once the transition to written prophecy began to take place, a new influence in the growth of the prophetic literature began to emerge. Over time, the production of lengthy written texts required specialized skills, and, as a result, about the time of the Exile trained scribes began to play an increasingly important role in the shaping of prophetic texts.

The degree to which the scribes influenced the contents as well as the shape of prophetic texts is uncertain. It is possible that some prophets such as Ezekiel were scribes themselves and therefore capable of shaping their own prophetic writings. Others, such as Jeremiah, may have hired scribes and then dictated the contents of their prophetic writings. However, it is also likely that in many cases the scribes who produced or copied oracle collections also felt free to edit their contents. Eventually, some of the smaller prophetic collections, known today as the Minor Prophets, were organized loosely into a unit, perhaps in stages, with smaller collections eventually giving rise to larger ones.

22. Central to understanding the Old Testament prophets is their relationship to the covenant.

Despite the fact that some prophets were also priests (this certainly holds true for Jeremiah and Ezekiel), scholars once emphasized the contrast between the prophetic and the priestly offices, at least in the preexilic period. Though Israel carefully distinguished the functions of priest and prophet, nevertheless, these functions coincided in part. Jeremiah 18:18 speaks of the "law" of the priest, the "counsel" of the wise man, and the "word" of the prophet. While these three offices conveyed their teachings in different ways, they doubtless contributed to a common objective. When the prophets condemned the priesthood, as they often did, it was not for what the priests were teaching but rather for what they failed to teach; they had rejected knowledge and had ignored the law of God (Hos. 4:6). In the same spirit, they condemned "false" prophets, not to exclude the idea of prophecy, but rather to reject its perversion. At best, the priesthood did the same work that prophecy did, namely, it transmitted the revealed moral will of the God of Israel. The priesthood did so by maintaining the tradition of religious law preserved in the sanctuaries; prophecy accomplished the task by communicating the living word.

During the Intertestamental Period, the disappearance of prophecy led to an expanded role for the priest and the sage. In the two centuries prior to the emergence of Christianity, wisdom writers consciously carried on the tradition inherited from prophecy (see Sir. 24:31; Wis. 7:27), without, however, claiming to possess the prophetic spirit. In the end, Jews considered themselves to be "people of the Law," and it was only with the cessation of sacrifices precipitated by the destruction of the temple in 70 CE that the role of the priest ended, to be replaced by the new sage, the rabbi.

The concept of the covenant is central not only in the Pentateuch but also throughout all scripture. As in a marriage or a business contract, a covenant describes a binding relationship between two parties (nations, individuals, or a person and God), based on commitment. The Old Testament speaks of covenants established by God with Noah (Gen. 6), Abraham (Gen. 15 and 17), Moses (Exod. 20 and Deut. 5), David (2 Sam. 7 and Ps. 89), and Israel (Jer. 31:31–34 and Ez. 36:22–38). In reality, these are differing views of the covenant between God and Israel.

In antiquity, secular covenants could be divided into two main types: (a) *parity treaties* governed relationships between equal parties, and (b) *suzerainty treaties* governed relationships between unequal parties. In the second type of covenant, the superior was known as the suzerain and the inferior as the vassal. In the Bible, God is the suzerain and humans are the vassal. Suzerainty covenants involve specific obligations, with sanctions (blessings or curses) to follow, depending upon the carrying out of the obligations. Often a solemn oath gives force to the covenant.

Two forms of the suzerain-vassal treaty are found in the Old Testament, depending on whether the text emphasizes God as being bound to Israel unconditionally or Israel being bound to God conditionally: (1) In a *promise covenant*, God swears an oath of unconditional loyalty to Israel. In this case God assumes the responsibility and obligations set down in the agreement. A prime example is Genesis 15, where God promises to give posterity and land to Abraham. In this account Abraham prepares the ritual of the covenant, dividing sacrificial animals into two pieces with the intention of walking through them to seal the treaty. A deep sleep, however, overcomes Abraham, and God alone passes between the parts, thereby assuming full responsibility for the covenant and its promises.

(2) In a *law covenant*, both parties swear to uphold the terms of the treaty. God establishes the laws (stipulations) by which Israel is to live. Because both God and Israel are required to fulfill certain covenantal demands, both stand under what is known as the "sanction," which describes the results of obedience or disobedience to the stipulations. In conditional covenants with Israel, such as the Mosaic covenant at Sinai, God enacts the sanctions, which can be either positive (a reward or blessing) or negative (a punishment or curse).

Of special importance in understanding the prophets is the "covenant lawsuit," a concept related to the ancient Hittite suzerainty treaties. There we find a provision related to covenant disloyalty. In cases where a vassal failed to fulfill the stipulations of a sworn treaty, the suzerain would institute a lawsuit, a procedure carried out through messengers and consisting of two distinct stages. The first stage consisted of *warnings*, delivered by the messenger, reminding the vassal of the suzerain's benefits and of the stipulations agreed upon. In addition, the vassal would be reminded of the curses or sanctions of the covenant. Using interrogation, the messenger would require an explanation of the vassal's offenses against the suzerain, charging the vassal with a change in behavior and warning of the vanity of appealing to alien help as a means of escaping the consequences. Finally, the messenger would issue an ultimatum: "if you continue, the curses will go into effect." If the messenger of the suzerain was rejected, the legal process moved into the second distinct stage: *declaration of war* as an execution of the sanctions of the treaty.

Like messengers of the Hittite suzerain, the mission of the Old Testament prophets was to serve as Yahweh's messengers to enforce the covenant mediated to Israel through Moses. Amos, the first of the classical writing prophets, was a vigorous upholder of the Mosaic tradition. The keynote of Amos's prophecy is struck in Amos 3:1–8, a passage that begins by recalling the crucial event of Israel's history: the Exodus from Egypt. Through God's action in this event, Israel had become a "family" bound together by religious loyalty. Through this event God had entered into a covenant relationship with Israel: "You only have I known of all the families of the earth; therefore I will punish you for all your iniquities" (Amos 3:2).

This passage, marked by solemnity, raises immediate questions: In what sense is it true that Yahweh has known only Israel, and why the "therefore"? What is the logical connection between God's knowledge of Israel and her fate? The passage makes little sense unless we know that we have here a usage of "know" borrowed from international relations. Hittite and other ancient Near Eastern texts reveal that "to know" in this technical legal sense means to recognize treaty stipulations as binding. In this context the term could be translated "recognize" or "be loyal to" a suzerain.[6] This clarification makes Amos's terminology understandable. Yahweh had recognized only Israel as legitimate servants, "therefore," since this sort of covenant involves obligations that were not fulfilled, "I will punish you for all your iniquities."

Other prophets speak in the same way. Jeremiah uses "know" in this way when describing a future repentance of the people: "I will give them a heart to know that I am the Lord; and they shall be my people and I will be their God, for they shall return to me with their whole heart" (Jer. 24:7). That this kind of knowledge is closely related to the people's conduct is evident from another passage in Jeremiah, where the prophet indicts the reigning monarch for thinking that being king is a matter of privilege rather than of justice: "Are you a king because you compete in cedar? Did not your father eat and drink and do justice and righteousness? . . . He judged the cause of the poor and needy . . . Is not this to know me?" (Jer. 22:15–16).

---

6. Hillers, *Covenant*, 121–22.

Hosea, best known for his extended use of the marriage metaphor to describe the relationship between Yahweh and Israel, makes the same connection. "Hear the word of the Lord, O people of Israel; for the Lord has an indictment [lawsuit] against the inhabitants of the land. There is no faithfulness or loyalty, and no knowledge of God in the land. Swearing, lying, and murder, and stealing and adultery break out; bloodshed follows bloodshed. Therefore the land mourns . . ." (Hosea 4:1–3a). In addition to using the technical Hebrew term meaning "covenant lawsuit" (*rîb*), Hosea provides a list of specific words very much like the Ten Commandments.

Along with Hosea 4, various additional texts in the prophetic literature contain references to the covenant lawsuit literary form, including Isaiah 1 and Jeremiah 2, but the classic passage is Micah 6:1–8, often cited as the sum and substance of Old Testament ethics. Like the book's opening oracle, this passage employs the imagery of a controversy in a law court. Notice the dramatic structure of the lawsuit pattern:[7]

a. *Summons* (Mic. 6:1–2): the trial opens with a summons by the prophet, who acts as God's prosecuting attorney. As we find in Hittite and other ancient international treaty patterns, the mountains serve as witnesses, before which Israel must present its case.

b. *The Plaintiff's Charge* (Mic. 6:3–5): Here God, through the prophetic attorney, interrogates the people, appealing to Israel's historical traditions rather than to specific laws recorded in a treaty. The appeal is based on events that displayed *hesed* or covenant love toward the people, beginning with the Exodus from Egypt and culminating in the occupation of the Promised Land. The prophet is appalled at the incongruity between God's benevolent deeds and Israel's disloyalty.

c. *The Defendant's Plea* (Mic. 6:6–7): Finally Israel speaks, but finds no case to plead save to confess betrayal of the covenant. Empty religious ritual does not satisfy the covenant demands, but seemingly adds to the offense.

d. *The Indictment* (Mic. 6:8): The passage reaches a climax as the prophet proclaims the essence of the covenant stipulations: "to do justice (*mishpat*), to love kindness (*hesed*), and to walk humbly with God." This simple statement expresses the prophetic demand for justice, righteousness, and steadfast love. Is this not to know God?

---

7. Anderson, *Understanding the Old Testament*, 311–12.

The prophets predict that in the end there will only be a remnant who will be faithful, hence only a portion of the people will experience covenant blessing. The prophets are often considered to have been messengers of doom, because they proclaimed a message of judgment. The truth is that before there can be good news, there must be truthtelling. The story of the Old Testament is the record of Israel's failure to live by covenant principles. Because God's people broke their covenant with God, they were eventually conquered by an invading nation, Babylon, and taken into exile. However, all hope is not lost. In the latter years of Israel's history the prophet Jeremiah promised that God would do something new in the future, once again restoring the people to proper relationship with God and one another.

From Prophecy to Apocalyptic

During the Intertestamental Period, when the culture and religion of the Jews were seriously threatened by the rise of Hellenism, a new phase of prophetic activity, known as apocalypticism, emerged. Some of its literary and theological characteristics are already perceptible in Ezekiel, Third Isaiah, and Zechariah 1–8. Joel and Zechariah 9–14, in addition to Isaiah 24–27, are later examples of this category. However, the classic representation of this type of literature in the Old Testament canon is Daniel, written during the Maccabean crisis of 168–165 BCE.

While the distant future was not central to the prophets, it was not overlooked, for eschatology was basic to the prophetic message. Israel's prophets consistently looked beyond the present, in which God's purpose seemed to be temporarily opposed by Israel's rebellion, to a time when God would triumph over the forces of evil. Prophetic predictions of the triumph of God's purpose were expressed in phrases like "the Day of the Lord," "the Age to Come," and "the Kingdom of God." In their vision the consummation of history was to be a time of reckoning, when all rebellious powers would be judged and destroyed. It was also to be the beginning of a New Creation in which nature and human nature would be transformed. No longer would there be war, and even wild animals would be tame (Isa. 65:17–25). The pictures of the messianic age remind us of the idyllic peace and harmony of the Garden of Eden prior to the expulsion. The prophets proclaimed that the Day was imminent, as near as the next moment of history.

The theme of apocalyptic literature, which flourished in the postexilic period, was, like that of prophecy, the nearness of the time when God would assert sovereignty over history and nature. It is characteristic of apocalyptic, however, that specific historical events receded into the background, and the contest between God and rebellious forces assumed a cosmic scale. Apocalyptic writers were dualistic in their view of history. They perceived two dominions (kingdoms) struggling for dominance. The kingdom of God stands opposed to the well-organized kingdom of Evil that is under the leadership of Satan. This is not a metaphysical dualism, rooted in ultimate reality or in the depths of divinity, for God's original creation was good. Rather, this is a postcreation dualism rooted in creaturely rebellion against God—rebellion that is evident not only in human sin but also in cosmic revolt by celestial beings. The conflict between the forces of God and the forces of evil was eventually expressed in terms of the myth of Satan, a heavenly being who revolted against God and set up a rival kingdom into which human beings are enticed. These two dominions may also be described as two "ages" or "worlds," that is, times of history. The present "age," in the apocalyptic view, is under the dominion of evil, and it will be succeeded by the "new age," when evil is overcome and all things are made new.

The End will be heralded by unusual "signs" and cataclysms in nature. On the Day of Judgment God (or God's messianic agent) will destroy all powers of evil and will create a new heaven and a new earth. As we see in the book of Daniel, the purpose of apocalyptic writers was to encourage the faithful to remain steadfast in a perilous hour when allegiance to God was temporarily eclipsed by foreign tyranny or the victory of evil The use of fantastic imagery in books like Ezekiel and Daniel clearly indicates that the language was intended to be imaginative. The heart of the apocalyptic message was the certainty that God's purpose could not be frustrated—a certainty that found expression in the nearness of the End. This is the only way that a new age of peace and justice can come: God must destroy the whole evil system.

The movement from classical prophecy to apocalyptic can be traced within the book of Isaiah, from its inception in the message of the eighth-century prophet Isaiah of Jerusalem (chapters 1–39), to the message of the so-called Second Isaiah during the Exile (chapters 40–55), to the message of the so-called Third Isaiah, dated to the postexilic period and found at the conclusion of the book (chapters 56–66). To appreciate the theological significance of this shift, we turn to the message of Second

Isaiah, which represents the transition from prophecy (First Isaiah) to apocalyptic (Third Isaiah).

Like a pastoral theologian, Second Isaiah offers comfort to a dislocated, suffering people whose faith in God has been strained to the breaking point: "Comfort my people, says your God. Speak tenderly to Jerusalem, and cry to her that she has served her term, that her penalty is paid, that she has received from the Lord's hand double for all her sins" (Isa. 40:1–2). The substance of the "good news" that is to be carried from heaven to earth is that the time of the coming of God's dominion is near. While Second Isaiah does not refer directly to the Mosaic covenant, the people are told that though they have suffered the penalty for their sins, they are assured that God's covenant promises made of old are still valid: "the word of our God will stand forever" (Isa. 40:8). Like the former exodus from Egyptian bondage, God is about to do a "new thing," which will be so wonderful that the former things pale in significance: "I am about to do a new thing, now it springs forth, do you not perceive it?" (Isa. 43:16–19). The heart of Second Isaiah's message is the proclamation that the new creation is happening in the present as God conquers the chaos of the Babylonian Exile and makes a path through the sea for his redeemed to pass over and return with singing to Jerusalem (Isa. 51:10). The prophet has taken creation completely out of the realm of mythology. For him creation is a historical event in the now. Here is a faith that turns not to the archaic past, longing for the good old days, "but stands on tiptoe, facing the new age that God is about to introduce."[8]

Second Isaiah turns to the Davidic covenant, announcing the rebuilding of the temple through the agency of a foreign ruler, Cyrus of Persia, here called God's anointed (Messiah) because he will accomplish God's purpose (Isa. 44:28—45:7). The Davidic covenant is reaffirmed by shifting the promises of this "everlasting covenant" from the Davidic dynasty to the new community (Isa. 55:3). The poet continues by stating that this community will be instrumental in including other nations in the saving purpose of God, as promised in the Abrahamic covenant (Isa. 55:5; see Gen. 12:3; 22:18).

The final section of the book of Isaiah, Third Isaiah, is sometimes designated proto-apocalyptic or the "dawn of apocalyptic," since it is not apocalyptic in the full-blown sense. In the final edition of the book of Isaiah, materials of more definite apocalyptic character were added,

---

8. Anderson, *Contours of Old Testament Theology*, 294.

including "the little apocalypse" of Isaiah 24–27 and chapters 34 and 35. In these passages we notice a shift in emphasis from the history of the people Israel to the cosmic dimension, which includes heaven and earth and the whole course of human history from Creation to Consummation. Nations like Assyria and Babylon are no longer agents of God chastening the people Israel, but are symbols of sinister powers at work in history, threatening God's divine plan for Israel and the nations. God's victory over these forces of evil represents a new creation in which God vindicates Zion, the city of God, and ends the suffering of the poor and helpless of the earth (see Isa. 65:17–19).

Whereas classic prophecy explained suffering as retribution for the people's failure or sin, apocalyptic writers found this explanation of evil to be inadequate. It was not enough to call for repentance or to blame the people for their irresponsibility. Apocalypticists perceived that Israel and all peoples were caught in the grip of monstrous forces that challenged the sovereignty of God. Evil, in their view, is located not in the human heart but in oppressive empires and other structures of power. Accordingly, apocalyptic writers revived the ancient myth of the battle of the Divine Warrior against the powers of chaos and the decisive victory that demonstrated God's power as King. This ancient myth influenced the pattern of the Song of the Sea (Exod. 15:1–18), a poetic response to the Exodus. At one point Second Isaiah invoked the myth to portray Yahweh's power to create a people and give them a future. In this poetic view, the victory over the army of the Pharaoh is symbolized by the monster of chaos, Rahab (Isa. 51:9–10), and the author implores Yahweh to achieve a similar victory in the future.

In apocalyptic imagination the Divine Warrior's victory is not restricted to Israel's history but belongs to a universal drama, in which the kingdom of God opposes the powers of evil that afflict people. These visionaries portray a New Jerusalem, a new age, indeed, a new creation. In this perspective, the coming of God's kingdom on earth will be the time of God's triumph—not only over human sin but also over all the powers of evil that have corrupted human history. In the Isaiah Apocalypse (Isa. 24–27), the writer portrays the final triumph of the Divine Warrior over the monster of evil known as Tiamat in Babylonian tradition and as the sea serpent Leviathan (Rahab) in Canaanite mythology (Isa. 27:1).

Thus in apocalyptic literature the entire historical drama, from Creation to Consummation, is viewed as a cosmic conflict between the divine and the demonic, Creation and Chaos, the kingdom of God and the kingdom of Satan. According to this view, the outcome of the conflict will be God's victorious annihilation of the powers that threaten creation, including death, which apocalyptic writers regarded as an enemy hostile to God. Seen in this perspective, the role of the Messiah would be not just to liberate humanity from the bondage of sin but to battle triumphantly against the powers of evil.

A line can easily be drawn from this apocalyptic passage to the portrayal of the consummation found in the book of Revelation. In this Christian apocalypse, at the time of the final triumph of God, the powers of evil—symbolized by "the great dragon . . . that ancient serpent, who is called the Devil and Satan" (Rev. 12:9)—will be overcome. Moreover, "the sea"—the locus of the powers of chaos—will be no more (Rev. 21:1).

Assignment

Having read chapter 8, answer the following questions, writing the answers in your journal. [If you are in a study group, be prepared to share your views with others in the class.]

1. Assess the three tasks of the prophet. In your estimation, which task best describes the biblical role of a prophet? Explain your answer.

2. Read the four Servant Songs in Isaiah (42:1–4; 49:1–6; 50:4–11; and 52:13–53:12). The identity of Isaiah's "Servant" is much debated by scholars. In your estimation, which identity (the exiled Jews, a righteous remnant, a prophetic or righteous individual, or the Messiah) best suits your understanding of this figure? (Keep in mind the possibility that the author may have more than one figure or identity in mind).

3. Read Jeremiah 31:31–34. Which aspects describe the restored community of Israel, and which elements best describe the Christian community's self-understanding as the new Israel of God? (See Gal. 6:16).

4. What is the primary insight I/we gained from this chapter or session?

Chapter 9

Three Things to Know about the New Testament

SINCE THE DAWN OF Christianity, "Old Testament" has been the standard label for the scriptures that the early Christian community inherited from ancient Israel. The term "testament," meaning "covenant," indicates that the Christian movement began in the heart of Judaism, that the Christian proclamation was based on the Jewish scriptures, and that the two communities of faith belong to the Abrahamic tradition, sharing a common Bible and therefore a common story.

"Covenant" is the word that the Bible uses in referring to the relationship that God established with humanity. In a sublime passage written some six hundred years before Jesus, the prophet Jeremiah predicted that the covenant God instituted through Moses on Mount Sinai would give place in the future to a more inward and personal one (Jer. 31:31–34). In the Christian era, it became natural for the followers of Jesus to refer to him as the mediator of that new covenant (Heb. 9:15–20). Hence, early Christians insisted that the Bible they read did not belong exclusively to the Jewish community; it belonged also to them. They could say, as did Paul: "For whatever was written in former days was written for our instruction, so that by steadfastness and by the encouragement of the scriptures we might have hope" (Rom. 15:4). Nevertheless, what was happening in their time seemed so radical and comprehensive as to constitute a "new covenant" (2 Cor. 3:6), a new beginning for Judaism and the world.

For Christians, the relationship between the Old and New Testaments is one of continuity and discontinuity. Like two partners joined in marriage, neither testament is a substitute for the other, nor are they independent of one another. Rather there is relative independence, whereby they complement one another. For Christians, the gulf between the testaments is bridged by Jesus Christ, whose person and work "establishes a deep discontinuity with Israel's scripture and, at the same time, a deep continuity in the purpose of God."[1] The discontinuity is expressed in the gospel of Matthew: "You have heard that it was said to those of ancient times, . . . but I say unto you" (Matt. 5:21–22, 27–28); the continuity is expressed in the same gospel: "Do not think that I have come to abolish the Law or the Prophets. I have come not to abolish, but to fulfill" (Matt. 5:17). In short, both testaments are theologically necessary if the church is to hear in the human words of the Bible the word of God.

The mystery of the relation between the testaments seems consonant with Paul's discussion in Romans 11 about the relation between the Jewish and Christian communities. In the face of Israel's rejection of Jesus as the Messiah, Paul grapples with the "mystery" of God's election that includes both Jews and Gentiles in "the Israel of God" (Gal. 6:16), declaring that "all Israel will be saved" (Rom. 11:26). God is thereby faithful to the promises made to the ancestors of Israel and extends the meaning and power of those promises to all who have faith.

The Jewish and Christian communities, bound together in God's creative purpose, have a common Bible and a shared history as the people of God while differing over the climax of the story, whether the pilgrimage of God's people leads to the Talmud and a continued life of messianic hope, or whether that pilgrimage leads through the Old Testament to Jesus the Christ, who came not to destroy but to fulfill the Law and the Prophets.[2]

One of the implications of this view of the relationship between the testaments is that it allows the Old Testament to speak with its own voice, even if that means interpreting passages differently than New Testament authors do. Of course, it is proper for Christians to regard the Hebrew scriptures as a whole in a christological perspective, but this does not mean forcing particular texts to bear witness to Jesus Christ or to carry a Christian meaning if they do not. If the Old Testament can be understood

---

1. Anderson, *Contours of Old Testament Theology*, 12.
2. Anderson, *Understanding the Old Testament*, 597.

as promise and the New Testament as fulfillment, as Christians maintain through their canonical approach to the Bible, this should not lead to the loss in the Old Testament of its unique Hebraic character.

The Canonical Process

The New Testament comprises the twenty-seven books that constitute the second of the two portions into which the Bible is naturally divided. Within the New Testament we may broadly distinguish four main types of composition: gospels, letters, theological history, and apocalypses. The New Testament consists of four gospels about Jesus' life, teachings, death, and resurrection; one book of Acts, which describes the activities of Jesus' disciples during the first thirty years following his death; twenty-one epistles written to Christian churches and communities; and an apocalypse, a revelation or disclosure that describes God's will for the future. These books have exercised an enormous influence over the religious lives of Christians for two thousand years and have made a significant impact on the history of Western civilization.

The language in which the books of the New Testament was written was the *koine* or common Greek of the time. This form of Greek was known and used widely across the Roman empire when Christianity emerged. Different grades of Greek are found in the New Testament documents. The most highly literary forms are found in Hebrews and the two books attributed to Luke. Those that are closest to colloquial Greek are the gospel of Mark and the book of Revelation. Occasionally in the gospels and the first half of Acts, we find preserved in Greek certain turns of expression that reflect an underlying Aramaic idiom, the mother tongue of Jesus and his disciples.

Unlike the books of the Old Testament, which originated during a period extending over many centuries, the books of the New Testament were written within a period of some seventy-five years, from about 50 to 125 CE. Because Jesus left no literary remains, information regarding his words and works was circulated orally by his immediate followers (the apostles and their disciples). As the tradition developed, the communities that comprised early Christianity became quite diverse. This was also due to their wide geographical distribution. In Palestine the church was predominantly Jewish. Antioch, the third largest city of the Roman empire, contained both Jews and Gentiles. Alexandria in Egypt was known for its mystical and allegorical interpretation of religion. Philippi was a Roman colony, Corinth a cosmopolitan port, and Ephesus a rich Greek city fanatically devoted to the Roman empire. Colossae, far inland in Asia Minor, had a peculiar spiritual life of its own in which Jewish and Hellenistic elements were mingled. Rome, the empire's capital, while initially open to every type of influence that existed in the early church, eventually became a mainstay of proto-orthodoxy.

Individual personalities also influenced every phase of Christianity's development. Paul, a Pharisaic Jew prior to his conversion, was eloquent in Greek and had an original and creative mind. While in his letters he emphasized human inability in the process of salvation, the author of James taught a simple religion of obedience to the moral law. The author of Luke–Acts, often thought to have been Paul's companion, was sympathetic both to Paul and to the Jewish-Christian mission. Matthew's sensibility, with its concern for community life and the new law of Christ, was entirely different from that of the author of John's gospel, who emphasized the spiritual life of individual Christians. A church that read and valued Revelation, with its proclamation of the imminent end of the age, would have had an outlook different from one that read Luke and John, which expected an indefinitely long continuation of church life and the preaching of the gospel.

The Bible of the earliest Christians was the Old Testament. Of equal authority to this writing were the remembered words of Jesus. Parallel with the oral circulation of Jesus' teaching were apostolic interpretations of his person and significance for the life of the church. It is natural that when gospels and apostolic letters were written, incorporating various kinds of authoritative materials, they would be treasured, circulated, and read in services of worship. At first a local church would have only a few apostolic letters and perhaps one or two gospels. During the course of the second century many churches acknowledged a canon that included the four gospels, the Acts, thirteen letters of Paul, 1 Peter, and 1 John. Seven books still lacked general recognition: Hebrews, James, 2 Peter, 2 and 3 John, Jude, and Revelation. On the other hand, certain writings, such as the letter of Barnabas or the Shepherd of Hermas, were accepted as scripture by several ecclesiastical writers, though rejected by the majority. During the third century there was a sifting of the disputed books; some came to be acknowledged as canonical and others were rejected as apocryphal.

The twenty-seven books of the New Testament were not the only ones written by the early Christians, but they were the ones that Christians of later times opted to include in their sacred canon. The process of forming the New Testament canon took over three hundred years to complete, being finalized in the late fourth century. By then Christian unity was symbolized by the councils of bishops, beginning with Nicaea in 325 CE. However, there were still bishops and congregations seen as heterodox, resulting from centuries of disputes and schisms in the church. While the earliest surviving list to include the twenty-seven books now known as the New Testament is from the year 367, appearing in an Easter letter written by Athanasius, bishop of Alexandria, the Council of Laodicea meeting that same year still rejected the book of Revelation. Meanwhile, Egyptian Christians had a larger New Testament and Syrian Christians a smaller one.

An important criterion of selection for canonicity was apostolic origin; the book in question had to have derived from the initial community of Jesus and his disciples. To us there may seem little reason to choose Jude and 2 Peter instead of 1 Clement, but the former bore apostolic names. An apostolic name also helped the Fourth Gospel to be included. However, the criterion of apostolicity was also augmented by the criteria of orthodoxy and catholicity. To be considered canonical, documents had to demonstrate theological and devotional power, established by widespread acceptance and usage by a broad range of communities, particularly those considered authoritative or apostolic. Such criteria led to the rejection of gospels, acts, letters, and apocalypses bearing the names of Peter, Andrew, James, and Thomas. On the basis of three criteria, then, the twenty-seven books of the New Testament were accepted at the councils of Hippo (393) and Carthage (397), thereby bringing the canonical process to a close.

23. Despite its status as the single most important book in the history of Western civilization, the New Testament is widely misunderstood.

There are a number of ways people approach the New Testament. Most people do so for religious reasons, approaching it from the perspective of faithful believers. Many people revere the Bible as the Word of God and want to know what it can teach them about what to believe and how to live. However, there are other equally valid ways of approaching the New Testament. In addition to religious reasons, there are literary reasons. The New Testament contains great literary gems, such as Matthew's Sermon on the Mount (Matt. 5–7), the gospel of John's portrayal of Jesus and his teachings, the apostle Paul's Hymn to Love (1 Cor. 13), and the symbolic imagery of the book of Revelation.

Nevertheless, however we approach the New Testament, we must read and interpret it historically, that is, in its own historical context. The books of the New Testament emerged out of the life of the Christian community, particularly out of the hopes and fears of early Christians in a Greco-Roman world. To understand the New Testament, we must acknowledge and appreciate not only the context of individual passages, but the broader Greco-Roman context as well. Those who don't understand the New Testament in its historical context necessarily take it out of context, thereby changing its meaning. Furthermore, to understand the New Testament from a historical perspective also means readers must initially suspend their own belief or disbelief about its message and meaning, something nearly impossible to do, at least without guidance.

The vast influence of the New Testament on Western civilization in general and particularly on American Christians may be a good reason why it should be studied. No one can doubt that sincere believers have frequently done much good in society, often through enormous personal sacrifice. The New Testament teaches to "love our neighbor as ourselves" and "to do unto others as we would have them do unto us," but the New Testament has also been read and interpreted to negative effects as well, for example, in helping to justify war, murder, and torture during the Crusades and Inquisitions, or more recently, to justify slavery, white supremacy, misogyny, and homophobia.

One important aspect of the context of the New Testament is the religious and political environment of the Greco-Roman world. When scholars used the term Greco-Roman, they are referring to the political, social, and cultural conditions prevalent in the Mediterranean world from roughly the time of Alexander the Great in the fourth century BCE to the time of the Roman Emperor Constantine in the fourth century CE, that is, a period of some 650 years. Alexander (356–323 BCE) was the great military genius who conquered most of the Mediterranean and lands east, including Persia and India. As he conquered, he spread Greek religion and culture, so that by the time of the New Testament, most of the educated elite throughout the Mediterranean world spoke Greek, in addition to their native language. The Roman empire arose in the context of the Hellenistic world and took full advantage of its unity—promoting the use of Greek language, accepting aspects of Greek culture, and even taking over features of Greek religion—to the point that the Greek and Roman gods came to be thought of as the same, only with different names.

Romans eventually conquered most of the Hellenistic world, ruling Palestine, Syria, North Africa, Asia Minor, Greece, and much of Europe during the emergence of Christianity, and establishing the Pax Romana (the "Roman peace"), a period of peace and stability that lasted for about two hundred years. The Roman world enjoyed a common language, coinage, and legal system, and had a good road system and other benefits that helped the spread of Christianity.

To maintain peace, prosperity, and stability, Rome ruled with an iron fist. In addition, it required tribute from conquered peoples. Roman provinces were ruled by governors, chosen from the Roman aristocracy with two major responsibilities: to raise tax revenues and to keep the peace. To achieve these objectives, they were granted near absolute authority. It was assumed that the governor, on location, would know how best to handle any situation, using whatever means necessary to maintain public order and maximize revenue collection. Using any means necessary meant having the power of life and death. Christians were occasionally persecuted and prosecuted, not because their religion violated Roman law, but because they were perceived as public nuisances. Authorities took care of problems on an ad hoc basis. This is what we see in the crucifixion of Jesus. From a Roman administrative point of view, Pontius Pilate was completely justified in condemning Jesus to death, not only as a political threat, but mostly as a public nuisance who might stir up trouble and create riots.

From both the letters of Paul and the book of Acts, we see that Christian missionary activity sometimes led to public disturbances, often with Jews over differences in belief and practice, but at times with Gentiles as well. Christians occasionally abandoned their own families to join the new communities. These splits in the family were often painful to those who were left behind (see Matt. 10:34–37). Because Christians were known to be a closed community, they often came under suspicion as a secret society. In particular, widely believed slanders were leveled against them. The problem was exacerbated by the fact that Christians refused to participate in the public ceremonies honoring the state and local gods, which was an affront to the prevailing paganism.

Scholars usually refer to the religions of the New Testament world as "pagan," meaning that they were polytheistic, inclusive, and tolerant. One way to understand the forms of paganism scattered throughout the Roman world is to contrast them with what we think of as religion today. Nowadays, most people think monotheistically; it makes sense for us to think that there is only one God. For most ancient people, however, such thinking was nonsensical. They were polytheistic, believing in many gods. There was, of course, a hierarchy of deities, from the great gods known from ancient mythology to numerous local deities who protected and cared for cities, towns, and villages, down to family gods and even demigods—humans believed to be partly human and partly divine.

While it is common today to view religion as a matter of proper belief, this is not how most ancient people thought. Odd as it might seem to us, it didn't much matter to the ancients what you believed about the gods. What mattered was that you worship them, which involved cultic pagan acts. Public sacrifices were viewed as essential, and any calamities that might occur in life were the result of the gods' anger at not being properly acknowledged. Because Christians didn't make these acknowledgements, they found themselves liable whenever disasters hit a town or city.

While most people today believe only one religion can be "true" or valid, most ancient peoples disagreed. Because there were many gods, there was no reason to think that one was better than any other or that only one was to be worshiped and praised. All deities were gods, so all deserved to be worshiped. For this reason, the religions of the Greco-Roman world were tolerant of one another. You could worship as many gods as you chose, and following one religion did not prevent you from following any other as well. However, everyone was expected to worship the state gods. These gods had made the Roman empire great, and thus, they deserved to be worshiped. Not to do so was to oppose the state they had created and helped to maintain, which was a political offense. These gods were often worshiped at major state festivals, which were eagerly awaited and enjoyed with family and friends. Christians, of course, refused to participate in these forms of pagan worship, which ultimately led to their persecution.

It took several centuries before the Roman administration felt threated in any serious way, however, and it wasn't until the middle of the third century that serious and systematic persecutions began, ending only in the fourth century when Emperor Constantine converted to Christianity.

24. The central theme of the New Testament is Jesus of Nazareth, a wandering preacher of the first century who changed the course of history.

Whether Christian or not, all who live in the Western world have been influenced by the teachings and life of this individual. Early disciples envisioned Jesus as the climactic historical figure, the Messiah who brought the long-awaited messianic kingdom of God, a rule that by ending evil and suffering would usher in an age of bliss. Later followers viewed Jesus' role as pivotal, representing the midpoint of history. This view is maintained by the famous nineteenth-century scholar Ernst Renan, who wrote: "All history is incomprehensible without Christ"; by Napoleon, who confessed toward the end of his life: "This man, Jesus, vanished for eighteen hundred years, still holds the character of men as in a vise"; and by H. G. Wells, who once declared: "I am an historian. I am not a believer. But I must confess, as an historian, that this penniless preacher from Galilee is irresistibly the center of history."

The message of the New Testament is reducible to two claims: (1) that Jesus' appearance and career came at the climax of a series of historical events of which the Old Testament is witness, and (2) that God was in Christ, confronting humanity with reconciling power and transforming truth. The paradoxical emphasis upon both Jesus' humanity and deity is evident not just in his message but in his life, his actions, and his person.

The New Testament is best understood as the early Church's response to the historical Jesus (who he was, and what he said and did), envisioned as five widening circles of response leading from "the Jesus of history" to "the Christ of faith," that is, from the experience of Jesus *by his disciples* to the confession of him *by the church*. Most of these periods lasted approximately twenty years, with occasional overlap.

1. The period of *the earliest disciples* (27–30 CE): this includes their involvement with Jesus in ministry and their return to fishing and other occupations following his crucifixion.

2. *The oral period* (30–50): the years between the date of the Crucifixion and the first letter written by Paul are years of silence, from which no writings have survived. During this period, characterized by preaching and proselytizing activity on behalf of the early followers of Christ, the "Jesus material" (sayings of Jesus and stories about Jesus) circulated as single and detached units. Some scholars argue for the existence of proto-gospels and for the possibility that the passion narrative reached a fixed form at an early period, but these assumptions cannot be corroborated with literary evidence.

3. The period of *the Pauline epistles* (49–64): this phase includes Paul's missionary travels and the authentic letters of Paul, Christianity's earliest written documents.

4. The period of *the gospels* (65–95): this material, while going back to actual events in the life of Jesus, represents an expanding tradition of faith. To the gospels should be added the book of Acts, written by the same author as the gospel of Luke. Acts can be viewed as a sequel to the gospels in that it describes the spread of early Christianity through the work of the apostles.

5. *The church* conscious of itself as society (80–100): this period overlaps significantly with that of the gospels; literarily it features the writing of the latest books of the New Testament, including disputed letters of Paul such as the Pastorals, the General Epistles, and the book of Revelation.

To summarize, the message concerning Christ in the New Testament involves a process of development from the free period (the historical situation of Jesus) to the binding period (the historical situation of the Church), from faith *in* Jesus to *the* faith. The New Testament writings, therefore, represent a total response to the person of Christ, from experience to confession, from fact, through faith, to truth. When, at the close of the biblical period, the author of the epistle of Jude speaks of "the faith that was once for all entrusted to the saints" (verse 3), this is biblically atypical. In the Bible faith is generally a relationship between human beings and God. Jude's view, referring to "the faith" with a definite article, reflects the situation of the church at the end of the apostolic age, when it became necessary to have a "rule of faith," a consistent system of teaching for the purpose of maintaining the identity of the community and defending its doctrines against novel teaching.

25. The whole of the New Testament is theology: every book, chapter, and verse was written to explain and promote faith in Jesus Christ.

The New Testament was written by believers for the edification of other believers, or for those who are not yet believers, that they might be brought to faith. Each gospel, for example, has its own point of view and special reading public, and these communities guided the selection, arrangement, and synthesis of the many units handed down concerning the life, deeds, sayings, death, and resurrection of Jesus. Despite their differences, all four gospels show the same basic intention: they are addressed to readers in order to minister to their faith. In fact, two of the gospels contain expressions of their author's intentions. The prologue to Luke's gospel states that it was written so that Theophilus would "know the truth concerning the things about which you have been instructed" (Luke 1:4). A similar expression of intention stands near the end of the Fourth Gospel: These things "are written so that you may come to believe that Jesus is the Messiah, the Son of God, and that through believing you may have life in his name" (John 20:31).

The gospels, then, are not biographies of Jesus in any traditional sense. Their intent is not to memorialize the deeds and words of a revered but deceased master. Rather, they explain the universal significance of the life and death of someone whom they proclaim to be still alive and knowable. In a word, they are evangelizing—and consequently, for good reasons, the authors of the gospels came to be known in the church as the four evangelists. What can be said of the gospels holds true for the rest of the books of the New Testament as well.

Assignment

Having read chapter 9, answer the following questions, writing the answers in your journal. [If you are in a study group, be prepared to share your views with others in the class.]

1. On what grounds were some books included but others excluded from the New Testament? In your estimation, how would modern-day understandings of the New Testament differ if some of these decisions were now called into question?

2. Explain why "context" is so important for meaning. Think of some examples from your own experience in which a misunderstanding occurred because someone took a word or action out of context.

3. Imagine you are a pagan in the Roman empire, and you are trying to convince your Christian neighbor to give up worship of the Christian God and to become a follower of the Roman gods. Make your argument.

4. Summarize the most important ways that religion in the Greco-Roman world was so different from what most people today think of as "religion." Can you think of examples when "common sense" in one context can become "nonsense" in another?

5. What is the primary insight I/we gained from this chapter or session?

Chapter 10

Three Things to Know about the Gospels

THE NEW TESTAMENT INCLUDES four canonical gospels, known as Matthew, Mark, Luke, and John. Each is a narrative of the life and teachings of Jesus of Nazareth, proclaiming him to be the Christ, which means the Messiah, the one anointed by God to fulfill the promises made to Israel. What began as a largely oral tradition, handed down in no particular order, gradually became a set of texts. The first three gospels, similar in structure and content, are known collectively as the Synoptics, whereas John, the last to be written and distinct in structure and point of view, is known as the Fourth Gospel.

The gospels do not appear in the New Testament in the order in which they were written historically. Having been written some a generation or more after the death of Jesus, they represent not so much a composite history of Jesus' words and deeds as the church's expanding understanding of Jesus. While they certainly contain accurate information, they should not be viewed as factual. Their intent was not primarily to provide factual knowledge but to enhance faith.

The first gospel was Mark (written about 65–70 CE), followed by Matthew (written in the early 80s), then by Luke (written in the mid- to late 80s), and finally by John (written in the early to mid-90s). The first three gospels are not separate witnesses, since Matthew and Luke copied large portions of Mark into their works. John may have been familiar with some or all of these, but his version is clearly independent.

The English word "gospel" means "good news." Each of the four gospel writers—or "evangelists," as they are known—sets out a basic perspective about the "good news." The gospel genre, as it appears in the New

Testament, is a distinctively Christian literary form. We have, of course, examples of biographical writing from this period, but comparison indicates that the gospels are not biographies. They tell us practically nothing of the youth and upbringing of Jesus, his education, or the influences that molded his attitude and outlook. Even the material they do record is only a selection (see John 20:30; 21:25). This does not mean that the early church had no biographical interest in the life of Jesus, as we see from the apocryphal infancy gospels; it means only that the biographical interest was not primary. Here again we must consider the purpose of the author, which in John's case is expressly stated: "But these are written so that you may come to believe that Jesus is the Messiah, the Son of God, and that through believing you may have life in his name" (John 20:31).

The gospels, then, do not give a neutral account of what happened; rather, they tell of the work of God in the career of Jesus, and they present their story as an offer of salvation for all who will believe. In short, the gospels represent a genre all of their own because they present the tradition of Jesus from the viewpoint of faith in him as redeemer. Hence, it was the intention of the four evangelists that their gospels be understood not only as narrative, but at the same time and especially as proclamation.

26. The earliest traditions about Jesus' life and teaching circulated orally and were modified in the process of transmission.

It was at one time customary to distinguish between John and the synoptic gospels, the Fourth Gospel being viewed as presenting a theological interpretation whereas the others, especially Mark, as supplying straightforward history. This is now known to be erroneous; even Mark is theologically oriented. All four are the product of the life and mission of the early church and present one community's perspective or tradition of the events it portrays, namely, the tradition of early apostolic preaching modified and adapted in the light of Christian experience.

At some point it is possible to recognize the motives that prompted the preservation of an element in the tradition, the interest that made it important for the life of the early church, such as the topics of prayer and fasting, Sabbath observance, tribute to Caesar, and the temple tax. The Old Testament quotations probably belong to a later but still early stage at which the church was striving to attain a more complete understanding of its place and function or of its understanding of Jesus in the light of the

Jewish scriptures. Even in Mark some sections seem to be grouped under a common theme, suggesting that they may have been brought together for liturgical or catechetical purposes. Each evangelist has selected from the material available, Matthew and Luke building on the work of Mark but at the same time modifying it to suit their own purposes. Scrutiny of these modifications, and examination of the gospels reveals to us something of the outlook and the theology of the authors.

The gospel story, most scholars now agree, was put together over a period of several decades and in several stages; the time between Jesus' death and the gospel accounts of his life was 35 to 65 years. During that time, Christianity spread to major urban areas throughout the empire. People converted to this new religion when they heard about the spectacular words and deeds of Jesus. However, given the rapid growth of the religion, the people spreading most of these stories were necessarily people who were neither eyewitnesses nor had known someone who was. Obviously, the stories about Jesus changed over time, given the fact that they were being told in different languages in different regions. As a result, the traditions about Jesus were modified in the process of transmission. As we see clearly through a comparison of the various gospel stories concerning Jesus' birth and death, discrepancies in the tradition indicate that the stories were being altered to suit the occasions for which they were told.

Concerning the birth of Jesus, neither the first canonical gospel written, Mark, nor the last, John, provide a birth or infancy narrative. Only Matthew and Luke have stories about Jesus' birth and early life. Yet these accounts are at odds with one another on a number of points. Luke alone indicates that Joseph and Mary went to Bethlehem to register for a census; only he mentions the shepherds. Matthew alone mentions the wise men, the wrath of King Herod, and that Joseph and Mary escaped by fleeing to Egypt, where they stayed until Herod died, only to relocate in Nazareth to avoid the wrath of Herod's son, who was now ruling. If Joseph and Mary fled to Egypt, as in Matthew, how is it that they returned to Nazareth just thirty days after Jesus was born, as in Luke?

The accounts of Jesus' trial and crucifixion in our earliest and latest gospels (Mark and John) are also difficult to reconcile. In Mark's account, Jesus, Pilate, the Jewish leaders, and the crowds are all in one place. The trial is very short, and Jesus only speaks a couple of words. In John's account, the Jewish leaders refuse to enter Pilate's residence. As a result, Pilate moves back and forth between Jesus, who is inside, and his accusers, who are outside. Jesus, rather than being silent for most of the proceeding, delivers several speeches to his judge.

There is also a discrepancy over when the event took place. Both Mark and John indicate that Jesus died during the Feast of the Passover. According to Mark, Jesus is arrested *after* he participates in the Passover meal. The following morning he appears before Pilate, who orders him executed. He is crucified at 9:00 a.m. (Mark 15:25). According to John, Jesus has a last meal with his disciples, but there is no indication that it is a Passover meal. After supper, Jesus goes out to pray, is betrayed by Judas, is arrested, and spends the night in jail. He is crucified at 12:00 noon on the Day *before* Passover (the Day of Preparation for Passover). In other words, in John's gospel, Jesus was executed before the Passover meal began. As we notice with this and other accounts of Jesus, the earliest version is generally to be preferred, and later gospels make alterations to suit expanded understandings of Jesus' identity and mission.

John is the only gospel that explicitly identifies Jesus as "the Lamb of God that takes away the sins of the world" (John 1:29, 36). Thus, John's gospel differs from the synoptic gospels by stating that Jesus dies on the afternoon of the day before the Passover, at precisely the time when the lambs are being sacrificed by the priest in the temple, in preparation for the Passover meal. In this case, John appears to change a historical fact to make a theological point.

The process of gospel transmission underwent at least three stages. (1) During the time of oral transmission, the teachings of Jesus and individual stories about him were communicated among his followers by word of mouth. Of these stories, the most lengthy and important would have been the "Passion Narratives" (accounts covering the week or so leading up to his death, and the subsequent accounts of his resurrection). It was also during this time that some of the materials were retold in Greek, the common language outside of Palestine, instead of the Aramaic that Jesus and his first followers spoke. (2) Subsequently, written collections were assembled, consisting of selections of these teachings and stories. Included among such accounts would have been a complete passion narrative, along with a collection of short sayings and parables. (3) Finally, the four evangelists collected these materials, both oral and written, and combined them into the gospels that we have today.

The literary relationship among the first three gospels is also of interest. Many of the sayings, parables, and incidents appear in more than one gospel, often in similar or virtually identical words. Among various explanations for this, the most widely held view holds (a) that Matthew and Luke depended on Mark for the general outline and many of the incidents of Jesus' ministry; (b) that there also existed a separate list of sayings of Jesus, which scholars call "Q" (for the German *Quelle*, "source"), used only by Matthew and Luke; and (c) that each synoptic writer had additional materials (for instance, the story of the wise men in Matthew 2, or the parable of the Good Samaritan in Luke 10, said to come from sources called "M" and "L" respectively). Scholars generally agreed that John derives largely from a different tradition, since most of the material in his gospel differs from those in the Synoptics.

Each of the four gospel writers had his own point of view and special reading public, and these would have guided the selection, arrangement, and perspective of the many units handed down concerning the life, deeds, sayings, death, and resurrection of Jesus.

27. *The gospels were written anonymously.*

Biblical scholars remain uncertain about the authorship of the gospels. These writings did not originally come with titles and authors appended. Whether individuals named Matthew, Mark, Luke, or John actually penned these documents matters less than the fact that four different early Christian communities saw fit to tell the story of Jesus from four distinct perspectives. Whether the gospels represent eyewitness accounts or were redacted by second or third generation believers, these documents are not primarily historical narratives of the life of Jesus. They are essentially testimonies of faith, written to bolster the faith of those who believed that Jesus was the Messiah and to win converts to a community that believed Jesus to be the Lord and Savior of the world.

None of the letters or books in the New Testament were written for the purpose of inclusion in the New Testament, the idea of which had yet to be conceived when they were written. Rather, they were composed for specific communities and their immediate needs, much as the New Testament itself was created for the needs of emerging Christian communities in the Mediterranean world. The New Testament is a selection from a much larger body of texts, many of which were written anonymously or pseudonymously by Christians during the latter half of the first century CE. Most of the titles and authorial attributions given to these books emerged in the last half of the second century. This includes the gospels as well. Even the title "Gospel According to" originated at the end of the second century, and was applied to noncanonical texts as well as the four canonical gospels.

There are, in fact, good reasons for doubting that the traditional ascriptions are accurate. On the one hand, these books were written by highly educated and literate Greek-speaking Christians, whereas Jesus and his immediate disciples (the apostles) spoke Aramaic. According to the New Testament accounts, Jesus' disciples were mostly lower class, uneducated peasants (see Acts 4:13). Furthermore, the gospels are written in the third person, making no direct references to the authors' own involvement with Jesus. The books were ascribed to apostles long after their lives as a way to secure their authority as scripture. Such traditional ascriptions are late and therefore questionable. Who, then, were the authors? We cannot know for certain, except that they lived several decades after Jesus and that they were relatively highly educated Greek-speaking Christians.

28. A critical examination of the gospels reveals that Jesus was an apocalyptic Jew.

Biblical scholars famously distinguish between the "Jesus of history" and the "Christ of faith." While the New Testament writers had a great deal to say about the latter, what about the former? Who was Jesus of Nazareth? Biblical scholars have devised three major criteria for examining the gospels as historical sources for the life and teachings of Jesus.

The first criterion used is called *independent attestation*. This criterion maintains that traditions that are attested independently by more than one source are more likely to be reliable than those found in only one source. The logic behind this criterion is that if two sources independently attest to a saying or deed of Jesus, then neither of them could have made it up. It is important to stress that the sources must be independent. The evidence they present is stronger than having only one witness. A saying found in both Matthew and Luke, however, is not independently attested, because both Matthew and Luke could have gotten it from Q (such as the Lord's Prayer or the Beatitudes). However, a saying found in both Mark and John, or in Luke and the noncanonical gospel of Thomas, would be independently attested, because John did not use Mark, and Thomas did not use Luke. It is important to emphasize that independently attested traditions are not automatically authentic, only that they are more likely to be authentic.

Examples of this criterion include stories of Jesus associating with John the Baptist, which are found in Mark, Q, and John. Also included under this criterion are parables of Jesus in which he likens the kingdom of God to seeds sowed by a sower, attested in Mark, Q, and the gospel of Thomas. Of course, this criterion cannot disprove a single reference or one that is not multiply attested, but can only be used to indicate which traditions are more likely to be historically accurate. Simply because the Lord's Prayer comes only from Q does not mean Jesus did not actually teach it to his disciples. Similarly, just because the parable of the Good Samaritan appears only in Luke does not mean that Jesus could not have said it.

The second criterion is called *dissimilarity*. This criterion suggests that traditions that appear to work against the vested interests of the Christians who were telling them are more likely to be historically accurate than those that Christians may have invented to suit their own purposes. The logic behind this criterion is that we know that Christians were altering, and sometimes even creating, stories about Jesus. They did so to make their own points about him. Thus, if a story does not advance the vested interests of the Christians telling it, then it is not a story they would have made up. Such stories, then, survive in the tradition precisely because they really happened.

Examples of this criterion include the tradition that he came from Nazareth, since Nazareth was an insignificant place, or Galilee, which had no connection with the coming Messiah (see John 1:46; also 7:41). If Christians were to "make up" a place for Jesus to be born, it would probably be Bethlehem (the home of King David), or Jerusalem (the city of God). Other examples of this criterion include the tradition of Jesus as a carpenter (an occupation of low social status at the time), or that he was baptized by John (since this might suggest that he was a disciple and therefore spiritually inferior to John). Jesus' followers would not have created the story that he was betrayed by one of his own followers, or that he died by crucifixion, since no Jew expected the Messiah to be crucified as a criminal.

Like the criterion of independent attestation, this criterion can only be used to argue in favor of a tradition, not against it. It is problematic when it is used to argue that something didn't happen, such as when Jesus predicted that he would die in Jerusalem, since this is something he might have anticipated. However, Jesus' prediction that he would rise in three days does not meet this criterion, since that was exactly what his later followers said had happened. The best-case scenario, of course, is when a traditions passes both criteria. For a tradition to be credible, however, is also needs to pass a third criterion.

The final criterion is *contextual credibility*. It argues that no tradition about Jesus can be accepted as reliable if it cannot plausibly be situated in a first-century Jewish Palestinian context. The logic of this criterion is self-evident: what Jesus said and did must make sense in a particular historical and cultural context. Unlike the other criteria, this one is used to argue against certain traditions as historically implausible. For example, the gospel of Thomas contains sayings that make perfect sense in the context of second-century Gnosticism, but sound completely unlike what a first-century Jew in Palestine would have said. These things likely do not go back to Jesus. Another example is the discussion between Jesus and Nicodemus in John 3:3, in the saying about "being born from above," which Nicodemus understands to mean "being born again." That misunderstanding only makes sense in Greek, not in Aramaic, the language Jesus would have used. This criterion is particularly useful for understanding how Jesus understood himself and his role.

As we have seen, to understand Jesus we must situate him in his own historical context. Jesus was a first-century Palestinian Jew, and as such lived in a period of foreign subjugation by Rome. One consequence of foreign subjugation of Palestine included the formation of Jewish sects, which exercised some power and offered religious options for Jews living at the time. The Essenes lived at the margins of society, maintaining their own purity through separation from institutional Judaism. Through unique lifestyle and fervent study of scripture, they lived in anticipation of the imminent apocalypse in which God would judge the world, thereby ending Roman rule and purifying Judaism. The Zealots emphasized Jewish autonomy and their divinely appointed duty to reestablish Israel as a sovereign state, by force if necessary.

Despite the somewhat favored treatment of Jews by Rome, Roman rule was nonetheless felt by many Palestinian Jews as an unbearable burden. Jews responded to Roman rule in a variety of ways, from silent protest to armed rebellion. During the first century CE, various Jewish prophets arose to speak against Rome as God's enemies and were often killed as troublemakers. One form of resistance ideology, apocalypticism, became prominent in the period. As we saw earlier, this ideology claimed that the forces of evil that were currently in charge of this world and responsible for its suffering would be overthrown by God in a mighty act of judgment. This imminent event was thought to be the prelude to the appearance of God's kingdom in a utopian age on earth. John the Baptist was an apocalyptic prophet of this sort, and we have compelling reasons for thinking that Jesus held such apocalyptic views.

The only way to know what Jesus actually taught is through the sources that survive from antiquity, namely, the four gospels. However, these books must be examined critically using the various historical criteria we have discussed. To reconstruct the historical Jesus, it is not enough simply to quote verses from the Bible; every verse of the gospels must be examined carefully, not just to see what it says and to determine what it means, but more importantly, to establish whether it actually goes back to Jesus.

The view that Jesus was an apocalypticist was first popularized by Albert Schweitzer in his 1906 classic text, *Quest of the Historical Jesus*. In this book Schweitzer showed how previous critical scholars had portrayed Jesus incorrectly, because they failed to recognize that he was an apocalypticist. When we examine our gospel sources critically, we find that Schweitzer was right. To understand Jesus correctly, it is important to follow a primary rule used by historians, namely, that we should prefer sources that are closest to the time of the events they narrate and that are not tendentious. In the case of Jesus, a clear perspective emerges when we examine the earliest sources at our disposal: Mark, Q, M, and L; all portray Jesus apocalyptically. Interestingly, later sources, such as John and the gospel of Thomas, do not.

In the earliest accounts of Jesus' teachings we find numerous apocalyptic predictions: a kingdom of God will soon appear on earth, in which God will rule. The forces of evil will be overthrown, and only those who repent and follow Jesus' teachings will enter the kingdom. Judgment on all others will be brought by the Son of Man, a cosmic figure who may arrive from heaven at any moment. Jesus is said to have proclaimed this message in all of our earliest surviving sources.

This is clearly the case in Mark 1:15 and 13:14–27, the latter passage ending with Jesus' proclamation: "Truly I tell you, this generation will not pass away until all these things have taken place" (Mark 13:30). The same message is found in Luke 17:24, 26–27 and Matthew 24:27, 37–39 (this is Q material), Matthew 13:40–43 (M), and Luke 21:34–36 (L). Some of these apocalyptic traditions are toned down in later traditions.

For instance, contrast Mark 9:1 with Luke 9:27 and then with Luke 17:21 (found only in Luke). In this later gospel, Jesus no longer says that his disciples will see the kingdom come in power, but only that the kingdom will arrive in the ministry of Jesus. In Luke 17:21, Luke has Jesus state that the kingdom is "in your midst." This clearly differs from Mark's earlier "coming with power."

The author of Luke's gospel does not seem to think that the coming of a real kingdom would occur in the lifetime of Jesus' companions. Evidently, because he was writing after they had died, and he knew that the end had not come, he deals with the "delay of the end" by making changes in Jesus' predictions. Later sources eliminate the apocalyptic material altogether. Thus, in the gospel of John, the kingdom is not described as imminent but as already present to those who believe in Jesus (3:3, 36). Here, in passages written near the end of the first century, the older apocalyptic idea that a day of judgment is coming and that the dead will be resurrected at the end of the historical age is replaced by a newer view, that in Jesus a person can already experience eternal life (11:23–26). This "de-apocalypticizing" of Jesus' message continues into the second century, as we see in the gospel of Thomas, which contains a clear attack on anyone who believes in a future kingdom on earth (sayings 3, 18, 118).

From this evidence a clear picture emerges. It appears that, when the expected end did not arrive, later Christians changed Jesus' message accordingly. However, when we examine the earliest sources, it is clear that Jesus was an apocalypticist. This certainly fits in with the specific criteria of contextual credibility, dissimilarity, and independent attestation. First-century Palestine had many apocalyptic Jews, some of whom left writings (such as the Essenes, who wrote the Dead Sea Scrolls). Other apocalyptic Jews were activists, including John the Baptist and prophets such as Theudas (see Acts 5:36–37) and "the Egyptian," mentioned by Josephus.

Some of the gospel references clearly pass the criterion of dissimilarity, such as Mark 8:38, in which Jesus talks about a cosmic judge of the earth (the Son of Man), without any suggestion that the reference is Jesus, even though early Christians did make this association, equating Jesus with the coming heavenly judge. That, however, is not what Jesus taught. In some cases he clearly did speak about himself using the term "son of man" (that is, son of a human), as a reference to his humanity, but when speaking about the future coming of the heavenly Son of Man, Jesus does not appear to have been speaking about himself.

Another passage that passes the criterion of dissimilarity is the parable of the sheep and goats in Matthew 25, which indicates that at the apocalyptic judgment, the Son of Man will judge the nations based on how they live. Since this does not coincide with the view of Jesus' later followers, who believed that salvation comes only on the basis of faith in Jesus and his resurrection, not on the basis of good works, the passage was likely not created by Christians but goes back to Jesus.

The tradition about Jesus as an apocalypticist also passes the criterion of independent attestation, since Jesus is portrayed thus in Mark, Q, M, and L but not in later sources, such as John or the second century gospel of Thomas. Each of those early sources are independent of one another and all portray Jesus apocalyptically.

In addition to meeting these criteria, one final piece of evidence seems convincing. Not only did Jesus begin his ministry apocalyptically, through association with the apocalyptic prophet John the Baptist, but his ministry concluded with apocalyptic Christian communities, such as those established by the apostle Paul, who believed he was living at the end of the age (see 1 Thess. 4:13—5:10). If Jesus began his ministry as an apocalypticist, and if the first Christian communities were apocalyptic, then it seems most likely that the middle—Jesus' life and teaching—was also apocalyptic.

Jesus, as we have seen, proclaimed that God's kingdom was coming to earth imminently (Mark 1:15). These words in Mark, the first words Jesus is recorded to have said in that gospel, provide a summary of Jesus' teaching. This would be a real kingdom with real rulers, a kingdom that would welcome some people but exclude others. Before the kingdom arrived, a scene of judgment would take place, in which the Son of Man, a cosmic figure from heaven, would appear to destroy God's enemies. This coming judgment would involve a massive reversal of fortunes; those who had prospered in this world through siding with evil would be displaced, but those who had suffered would be exalted. The judgment would come not only to individuals, but also to institutions and governments. In particular, the Jewish temple in Jerusalem, the heart of all institutional Jewish worship, would be destroyed.

Throughout his authentic teachings, when Jesus refers to the coming kingdom, he seems to mean an actual earthly kingdom, with actual rulers. Consider Jesus' teachings found in Q, perhaps our earliest source: "Truly I tell you, at the renewal of all things, when the Son of Man is seated on the throne of his glory, you who have followed me will also sit on twelve thrones, judging the twelve tribes of Israel" (Matt. 19:28; cf. Luke 22:30). While the arrival of the kingdom was "good news" for Jesus' followers, it was not good news for everyone. In a mighty act of judgment, evil rulers would be toppled and punished, and the oppressed would be raised up (Luke 13:23–29; cf. Matt. 8:11–12). This coming judgment would involve a serious reversal of fortune, one that makes sense in an apocalyptic context (Mark 10:31; Luke 13:30).

Likewise, Jesus' ethical teachings make best sense in an apocalyptic context. These teachings, however, have come down to us today as perfect examples of how people ought to live normally. Nevertheless, it is important for us to understand that the meaning of Jesus' ethical teachings might have been quite different in their original context from their meaning in ours. In our context, Jesus' teachings assist us in knowing how to get along with one another, so that we can contribute to a healthier and more wholesome society, allowing us to experience peace and wellbeing for the long haul. But for Jesus there was not going to be a long haul. The Son of Man would soon come in judgment, and people needed to prepare for entrance into his kingdom by showing that they sided with God rather than with the forces of evil that were opposed to him. Jesus' ethical teachings were ethics of the kingdom—they both reflected what life would be like in the kingdom and qualified one for entrance once it arrived.

In the kingdom, there would be no hatred; thus, people should love one another now. In the kingdom, there would be no oppression; thus, people should work for justice now. In the kingdom, there would be no war; thus, people should work for peace now. In the kingdom, there would be no sexism; thus, people should work for equality now. Only those who lived in ways that are appropriate to the kingdom would be allowed entrance when it arrived.

According to Jesus' teachings in the Sermon on the Mount, his followers should regard entrance into the kingdom as their most prized possession, and even be willing to give up all their possessions for the sake of the kingdom (Matt. 6:25–33). Later on, he indicates in his parable of the Pearl of Great Price, that the kingdom is like a merchant in search of fine pearls who finds a perfect pearl and then goes out and sells all that he has to buy it. The pearl is the kingdom, and it demands our ultimate allegiance; that's how valuable it is. For Jesus, nothing made sense apart from the kingdom of God that was on the verge of breaking into history. If its coming found one unprepared, all would be lost.

If Jesus' ethical teachings make best sense in an apocalyptic context, we need to rethink their meaning. Jesus, it appears, did not deliver timeless truths to guide individuals in leading long and productive lives. His teachings were meant to show people how to live in order to enter the kingdom that would soon appear. When we examine teachings such as "love your neighbor as yourself," and "love your enemies and pray for those who persecute you," he is teaching ethics of the coming kingdom. How else can we understand Jesus' teaching to the young ruler, that he should give up everything—all possessions and everything that binds one to this world (Mark 10:17–31)—except in this context? This emphasis on giving up everything for the kingdom means that Jesus was not a major proponent of what we now call "family values" (see Luke 14:26; 12:51–53). As with other hard sayings of Jesus, these should not be explained away so that they no longer mean what they say. Instead, they should be placed in an apocalyptic context.

Understood apocalyptically, Jesus' command to love one's neighbor and God above all else points to the coming kingdom, when God will provide such things as food and clothing (Matt. 6:25–33). To those who trust God, all things are possible, for that is how God will care for us in his kingdom that is soon to come. Jesus, then, did not see himself as inventing a new system of ethics, so much as explaining the Law of Moses in view of his own apocalyptic context.

While later sources have Jesus proclaiming the kingdom as a present reality, this is not what Jesus actually taught. For him, the kingdom was imminent, but it had not yet arrived. Understanding Jesus' message of the coming judgment of the Son of Man, including the destruction of the temple in Jerusalem, helps explain Jesus' actions in the temple prior to his crucifixion. Viewed apocalyptically, they become a symbolic expression of his teaching, a prophetic gesture or enacted parable of the coming of God's imminent judgment on the earth, beginning with institutional Judaism. In cleansing the temple, Jesus was demonstrating on a small scale what would soon occur in a large way.

Jesus was betrayed by one of his own followers, Judas Iscariot. What is not clear, though, is what it was that Judas betrayed, or why he acted as he did. Some believe that he betrayed Jesus for financial gain; others argue that Judas grew disillusioned when he realized that Jesus had no intention of becoming a political Messiah; yet still others have reasoned that Judas wanted to force Jesus' hand, thinking that if Jesus were arrested, he would call out for support and start an uprising that would overthrow the Romans. While each of these explanations has merit, the clearest explanation is that Judas may have divulged insider information that the authorities could use to bring Jesus up on charges. Jesus, it appears, taught his disciples things in private that he did not state publicly.

We have several hints as to what Jesus taught about himself that Judas might have divulged to the authorities. Almost certainly, the charge leveled against Jesus by the Roman governor Pontius Pilate was that he considered himself to be the King of the Jews (Mark 15:2; John 19:33; 19:19). However, Jesus never called himself this in any of the gospels. Why would he be executed for a claim he never made? Jesus did teach that after the Son of Man executed judgment on the earth, the kingdom would arrive. Kingdoms, by their nature, have kings. Who would be the king? Ultimately, of course, it would be God. However, Jesus probably did not think that God would physically sit on the throne in Jerusalem. Who, then, would?

The earliest traditions indicate that Jesus thought he would be enthroned. For one thing, only those who accepted his message would be accepted into the kingdom. Jesus also told his disciples that they would be seated on twelve thrones to rule the twelve tribes of Israel. Who would be over them? It was Jesus who had called them to be the Twelve. Moreover, his disciples asked him for permission to sit at his right hand and his left in the coming kingdom (Mark 10:37). Of course, the current textual context, modified by later authors and redactors, changes the original meaning of Jesus' teaching. Rightly understood, his disciples would have viewed him as ruler in the kingdom, just as he was their "ruler" now.

Judas, then, betrayed this private teaching of Jesus to the Jewish authorities, and that explains why they could level the charges against Jesus that he called himself the Messiah, the King of the Jews. Of course, he meant it in the apocalyptic sense, but they meant it in a this-worldly sense. Once the local Jewish authorities learned this insider information, they had all the grounds they needed to make a quick arrest to get Jesus out of the public eye, and thus avoid any recriminations from their Roman overlords over disturbances caused by Jesus and his followers.

The Life, Death, and Resurrection of Christ as Eschatological Events

When we place the resurrection of Jesus into an apocalyptic context, it makes complete sense that it represented the new reality that was expected in the coming age. Jewish apocalypticists did not expect to be taken to heaven in the new age. Rather, that new age would be a golden age on earth. Associated with this expectation was the belief that when the time had been fulfilled for the current evil age, there would be a general resurrection of the dead (see Matt. 27:51–53). Followers of Jesus who believed in the resurrection of Jesus would draw an obvious conclusion, namely, that the new age had already begun (see 2 Cor. 5:17). In 1 Corinthians, Paul makes this connection, finding in the resurrection of Jesus clear proof of the anticipated general resurrection of the dead (1 Cor. 15:12–24). In Paul's mind, Jesus was the "first fruits" of the Resurrection, that is, the beginning of God's final winnowing or harvesting process. This meant, for Paul and other early Christian apocalypticists, that God's end-time judging and rewarding was to occur shortly. Jesus had been exalted to heaven, but would soon return as the heavenly Son of Man to judge the earth.

During his lifetime, Jesus had spoken of the coming Son of Man as a divine emissary, not to be equated with himself. Now, however, his followers began thinking of him, not as a prophetic forerunner of the final apocalypse, but as the actual coming judge referred to in Daniel 7:13–14. Whereas Jesus had taught his disciples that he would have a place of prominence in the coming kingdom, after the Resurrection his followers assumed that the kingdom had already begun, and that Jesus was already its ruler. In fact, Jesus was now ruler of all things in heaven and earth. No longer merely King of the Jews, they now understood him to be Lord of all.

The New Testament is saturated with the belief that something new happened in the history of humanity, in and through the life and death of Jesus Christ, and above all through his resurrection from the dead. Like their Old Testament counterparts, the followers of Jesus were shaped by an event so profound that it continues to be celebrated as decisive for Christians around the world. The early Christians found in Easter a correlation with the Exodus—a path from darkness to light, despair to hope, inability to possibility, bondage to freedom—and with the Creation, for the Resurrection constituted a new beginning for humanity.

In order to make sense of the New Testament, we need to begin with Easter, for Easter is central to Christianity. Whatever occurred on that first Easter, it had incredible power. Before the Easter experience, Jesus' followers forsook him and fled. After the Easter experience they were willing to die for their conviction that whatever their understanding of God, it had to include Jesus of Nazareth. This shift in God consciousness revolutionized the theology of Jesus' followers so dramatically that the world has never been the same. In addition, the Easter event led Jewish Christians to create Sunday, a new holy day, different from yet fulfilling the notion of the Jewish Sabbath.

While the line between the eschatology of Jesus and that of the church cannot be clearly drawn, it seems likely that Jesus thought in the framework of Jewish apocalyptic. However, this changed over time, and it led early Christians to view the appearance of Jesus as an eschatological event. It became their conviction that in Jesus the *eschaton* (the final and decisive event) had already entered history, giving assurance of the near approach of the Day of Judgment and "the time of universal restoration" (Acts 3:20–21). The cross, no longer viewed as a naked act of Roman cruelty, instead became God's sentence of judgment upon human sin and the powers of darkness, making possible through the Resurrection a "new creation" for those who were in Christ (2 Cor. 5:17).

While later Christians focused on the vision of a second coming of Christ, it is important to recognize that in the early Christian message the center of gravity lay not in the anticipation of Christ's return but in the proclamation that Christ's "first coming" was itself an eschatological event. The New Testament placed the emphasis on the victory that had already been won in the cross and resurrection, shunning any attempt to pry into the mystery of the future, which lies in the sole authority of God (Acts 1:7; Matt. 24:26). Oscar Cullmann expressed this matter aptly using an analogy from World War II. Speaking of the invasion at Normandy, known as the Decisive Day (D-day), he noted that the decisive battle in a war may occur at a relatively early stage of the war, and yet the war continues. While the war continues until Victory Day (V-day), the tide turns on D-day, guaranteeing the outcome. Because of Christ's resurrection, early Christians were assured that the goal of history had been achieved proleptically by Christ's victory over death. The End would merely vindicate the faith of the present.

Assignment

Having read chapter 10, answer the following questions, writing the answers in your journal. [If you are in a study group, be prepared to share your views with others in the class.]

1. Why do you suppose the gospels provide so little information about the period of Jesus' life before his baptism by John? Why do we have almost nothing of his life as a teenager or a young man?

2. If the gospels were written anonymously, why do you suppose later Christians attributed them to Matthew, Mark, Luke, and John?

3. Imagine an early debate between a non-Jewish Christian and a non-Christian Jew over whether Jesus was the Messiah. What would be the strongest arguments on both sides?

4. Explain the problems in the gospels that make each of the three historical criteria (independent attestation, dissimilarity, and contextual credibility) necessary. Given the nature of the sources, assess the logic that requires each of these criteria.

5. Read some of the more familiar teachings of Jesus, such as the Beatitudes in Matthew 5:3–12, the Lord's Prayer in Matthew 6:9–13, and the parable of the sheep and the goats in Matthew 25:31–46, and reflect on what they would mean in an apocalyptic context.

6. What evidence strikes you as most convincing that Jesus was an apocalyptic prophet? How does this view differ from what you have previously understood about Jesus? Does understanding Jesus as an apocalypticist have any bearing on the relevance of Christianity in the modern world?

7. Using the three historical criteria (see question 4 above), what conclusions can we draw as to the reliability of accounts such as the birth, trial, crucifixion, and resurrection of Jesus? Conversely, how valid are these criteria regarding a theological understanding of such accounts?

8. If you could meet Jesus and ask him three questions, what would they be? What question would you ask first? Why?

9. What is the primary insight I/we gained from this chapter or session?

Chapter 11

Three Things to Know about the Book of Acts

WHEREAS THE GOSPELS NARRATE the life of Jesus, the book of Acts narrates the life of the Christian church after his death, a period of some thirty-five years beginning with Jesus' ascension and ending with the voyage of Paul to Rome, where he remains under house arrest awaiting his trial. The book was written by Luke, the author of the third gospel, as the second part of a two-volume work that traced the history of the Christian movement from the months before Jesus' birth to the spread of the Christian gospel through Asia Minor and Greece to Rome.

When the gospels circulated independently, it was possible to appreciate the individuality, uniqueness, and perspective of each, but once they were combined, their unity became focal and their differences were de-emphasized. Another consequence of placing the four books under the heading of "gospel" is that it obscured the fact that Luke's gospel was but the first volume in a consecutive narrative. Whatever the reasons may have been for the ordering of the first four books of the New Testament, it is apparent that the position of John between Luke and Acts interrupts the literary continuity of the volumes that were composed to be read sequentially. Luke did not write a "gospel" and an "Acts"—he wrote a consecutive narrative in two parts.

Both the gospel of Luke and the Acts of the Apostles were written anonymously, though according to early tradition the author was Luke, a physician and companion of the apostle Paul (Col. 4:14; 2 Tim. 4:11; Phlm. 24). From the way in which Luke is mentioned in Colossians

4:11–14, it appears that Luke was of Gentile birth. If so, he is the only known Gentile whose writings are included in the Bible. Support for the tradition that Luke was a traveling companion of Paul comes from four passages in Acts, where the author uses the pronoun "we," switching abruptly from the third person to the first person plural (16:10–17; 20:5–15; 21:1–18; 27:1—28:16). While these references undoubtedly create a dramatic sense of being with Paul, they do not require direct partnership with Paul or even participation in his travels. Nevertheless, the sporadic nature of the "we" feature in Acts suggests that the author was relying on some type of diary, either his own or that of a minor figure who traveled occasionally with Paul.

In discussing our author's association with Paul, we should note that persuasive arguments have been adduced against associating Luke with Paul. Perhaps the greatest argument against such relationship is the claim that Luke shows little or no knowledge of Paul's epistles, little understanding of his distinctive theology, and only slight appreciation for Pauline concerns such as justification by faith and freedom from the law.

Scholars who cannot reconcile the picture of Paul in Acts with the picture revealed in Paul's own letters have proposed that the author somehow got the diary of a true companion of Paul and introduced segments of it at appropriate moments to enhance the narrative with realism and thus with greater credibility. However, the "we" sections are written in a style indistinguishable from that of the rest of the book. If we suppose that the author was using as one of his sources a diary written by another individual, we must add that he rewrote it so thoroughly as to eliminate all traces of its original style and yet so carelessly that he did not always remember to make the change from first to third person. The simpler solution is that the author was using his own diary, allowing the first person to stand in order to indicate places where he had been an eyewitness. Close analysis of the grammar, syntax, and vocabulary found in the "we" passages in comparison to those factors in the rest of Acts shows that they are consistent with the style and vocabulary in the rest of Acts. The most reasonable explanation is that Luke was present for a limited time with Paul during the second missionary journey and more extensively during the third.

While we cannot be sure about the identity of the author, one thing is clear; no matter who wrote Acts, Paul is the hero of this narrative, in Luke's eyes the man most responsible for the spread of Christianity throughout the Roman world. Despite its title, "The Acts of the Apostles,"

Acts does not tell the story of all the apostles. Only some are mentioned, and the book has most to say about Peter (the focal figure of chapters 1–12) and Paul (the focal figure of 13–28), together with selected incidents from the lives of such early Christian leaders as Philip, John, James the brother of Jesus, and Stephen.

29. The book of Acts arranges its narrative around two selective themes.

Focusing on the spread of the new religion to lands around the northeastern Mediterranean world, Luke prepared a remarkably well ordered account. Instead of providing merely a chronicle of events and a list of converts, Luke arranged his material around growth and expansion, namely, the spread of Christianity from Jerusalem to Rome. Like any historical narrative, Acts is selective in what it includes, so we would be mistaken to imagine that this book gives "the history of the early church." Its focus is oriented around the missional agenda set forth by Jesus in 1:8: "you will be my witnesses in Jerusalem, in all Judea and Samaria, and to the ends of the earth."

Christian expansion, as narrated in the book of Acts, resulted in a twofold shift: geographically, the center of the church gravitated from Jerusalem to Rome; ethnically, the church's identity shifted from Jewish Christians to predominantly Gentile Christians. According to Acts, the church expanded because it fulfilled faithfully its two tasks in society: to evangelize, that is, to serve as Christ's witnesses "to the ends of the earth" (Acts 1:8; see also Matthew's Great Commission in 28:19–20), and to live by the ethics of love and mercy that Jesus had taught.

In an orderly way, Luke traces the story of the Christian movement from Jerusalem to Rome. Within these two termini, and spanning a period of about a third of a century, Luke arranges his material in what has been described as six "panels," each concluding with a comment that summarizes the success attained. In this respect, the structure of Acts may be outlined as follows:

1. Preface (1:1–14)
2. First Panel: Early episodes in the Jerusalem church (1:15—6:7)
3. Second Panel: Extension of the church through Palestine (6:8—9:31)
4. Third Panel: Extension of the church to Antioch (9:32—12:24)

5. Fourth Panel: Extension of the church to Asia Minor (12:25—16:5)
6. Fifth Panel: Extension of the church to Europe (16:6—19:20)
7. Sixth Panel: Extension of the church to Rome (19:21—28:31)

The ending of Acts—dated to the early 60s, with Paul awaiting trial and the future of the Christian movement far from certain—raises an interesting question. Why does Acts stop at that point? Did Luke intend to write a trilogy, leaving a third and concluding volume unwritten, or did he feel his conclusion in Acts fulfilled his literary and historical purpose? If Luke did intend to write a third volume, did he accomplish his intention by penning material pseudepigraphically (in this case, under Paul's name)? In the past, occasional support emerged for Lukan authorship of the book of Hebrews, traditionally attributed to Paul but now to an anonymous writer. If not Hebrews, could Luke's concluding material constitute the pastoral epistles (1 and 2 Timothy and Titus)? The Pastorals, once attributed to Paul but now to an unknown disciple of Paul, more likely were penned by someone like Luke, a sympathetic commentator on the Pauline heritage who attempted to strengthen local church organization by weaving information about Titus and Timothy into a compatible though fictional account.

Furthermore, certain features of the Pastorals (style, terminology, the nature of the false teaching, the view of women in the church, church structure and leadership, theology, christology, and Pauline biographical information) point to authorship other than Paul, and to a date later than Paul's undisputed letters.

As many have noted, in atmosphere and vocabulary the Pastorals appear close to Luke–Acts, to the point that some have thought that the same person wrote them.[1] Historical parallels, such as the reference to Paul's sufferings at Antioch, Iconium, and Lystra, echo the journey of Paul recounted in Acts 13:14—14:20 and in 2 Timothy 3:11. The same can be said of Paul's farewell address found in 2 Timothy 3:10—4:8 and Acts 20:18-35. A further connecting tie appears between Acts, which ends with Paul imprisoned in Rome, and the Pastorals, which declare Luke as Paul's sole companion at the end: "Only Luke is with me" (2 Tim. 4:11). Because the style and vocabulary of the Pastorals differ notably from Paul's known usage, and because the atmosphere and context point

---

1. Supportive data appear in Brown, *Introduction*, 666. See J. D. Quinn in Talbert, *Perspectives on Luke–Acts*, 62-75.

to the late first or early second century, we need another candidate for authorship, and it cannot be Titus or Timothy, occasional co-authors with Paul, since they are the presumed recipients of this correspondence.

To account for the incongruities between these epistles and Paul's undisputed letters, scholars have introduced the "fragment theory," postulating that the Pastorals may have been compiled from fragments of genuine Pauline letters. Such a view, while explaining seemingly vivid biographical elements such as those found in 2 Timothy 4:9–21, introduces further difficulties, such as why such fragments survived independently, merely as scraps of personal information with no theological or pastoral context. Furthermore, if the Pastorals are the creation of a pseudepigrapher, why did this person choose as his pattern letters addressed to individuals rather than the more common pattern of letters addressed to communities? While the "fragment" thesis has had relatively little following, a better explanation is the hypothesis that Paul told a colleague what themes he wished covered and handed over to that individual the actual work of composing the three letters (for occasions in undisputed letters when Paul utilized secretarial service, see Romans 16:22, 1 Corinthians 16:21, and Galatians 6:11–18). If a colleague composed the Pastorals under such editorial circumstances, could it have been Luke?[2]

Ultimately, however, when we think of Luke's identity, what is important is not his background or upbringing so much as his conversion to Jesus Christ. Whether Luke was a Gentile Christian, as most believe, or a Jewish Christian, as some contend, is secondary to the unanimous agreement among scholars that the author of the third gospel and the Acts of the Apostles was a Christian. This insight is significant because it is as a Christian that Luke approaches the Jesus tradition, which he used to create the gospel and the early Christian story that underlies the book of Acts.

30. The book of Acts contains biased historical accounts recorded not simply for their own sake but also for their theological significance.

The book of Acts clearly paints a history of Christianity with a literary palette, using a theological brush to speak of the emergence of Christianity,

---

2. Knight, *Pastorals*, thinks Paul may have used Luke as secretary in writing the Pastorals. John Drane agrees, suggesting that Luke may have written them after Paul's death, using rough drafts of genuinely Pauline material as a starting point, *Introducing the New Testament*, 365. In view of parallels in style, vocabulary, and thought, some scholars believe Luke may also have written Colossians, Witherington, *Acts*, 170, n. 25.

the role of Christian life and ministry, and God's purpose for history. To understand the author's perspective, there are numerous literary parallels between Luke's gospel and Acts.

Even the casual reader notices the parallels between his two volumes:

Gospel of Luke	**Acts of the Apostles**
Preface	Preface
Birth of Jesus	Birth of the church
The Spirit descends on Jesus	The Spirit descends on the apostles
Mission and ministry of Jesus	Mission and ministry of the church
Journey of Jesus to Jerusalem	Journey of Paul to Jerusalem and Rome
Trial of Jesus	Trial of Paul

These parallels show that Luke was no mere chronicler of events, but that he compiled a two-part history with a clear purpose, part of which was to show that the hand of God was behind the mission of the church as much as it was behind the mission of Jesus. Thus, for example, at the beginning of Jesus' ministry in Luke, he is baptized and receives the Holy Spirit; when new believers are baptized in the book of Acts, they also received the Spirit. The Spirit empowers Jesus to do miracles and to preach in Luke; so, also, the Spirit empowers the apostles to do miracles and to preach in Acts. In Luke, Jesus heals, the sick, casts out demons, and raises the dead; in Acts the apostles heal the sick, cast out demons, and raise the dead. The Jewish authorities in Jerusalem confront Jesus in Luke; the same authorities confront the apostles in Acts. Jesus is imprisoned, condemned, and executed in Luke; some of his followers are imprisoned, condemned, and executed in Acts. In Luke, because Jesus is rejected by Jews, Jesus' message goes to the Gentiles; in Acts, because Jesus' apostles are rejected by Jews, they go to the Gentiles.

As is now clear, Luke writes with a distinct theological agenda. In his understanding, the proclamation of the gospel is made possible by the power of God, through the Holy Spirit. The early Christian evangelists and missionaries were not acting on their own, but were empowerd from on high. For this reason, their proclamation could not be stopped or even hindered (Acts 5:33–39). Luke's major theme is clear: to hinder the spread of Christianity is to hinder the work of God. This proclamation came first to the Jewish people, who accepted in large numbers (three thousand on the Day of Pentecost in Acts 2:41; five thousand in Acts 4:4; see also 5:14; 21:20). The rejection of God's salvation by the Jews led to its acceptance by the Gentiles. Moreover, this spread of the church was according to the plan of God (see Acts 1:8). Ultimately, it is God behind the scene, directing every event, which led to the ultimate triumph of Christianity. These are theological views, not historical data. Hence, historians who want to know what actually happened during the early years of Christianity must approach the text critically, much as they do with the gospels to uncover the words and teachings of the historical Jesus.

Scholars repeatedly point to the abilities of Luke as theologian and narrator, but leave open the disputed question of his role as historian. In the past, scholars and general readers viewed Luke's gospel and the book of Acts as a history of Christian origins, considering Luke's work a vast storehouse of information for reconstructing what happened in the lives of Jesus and his earliest followers. Modern times, however, have introduced a refinement of critical methodologies for conducting historical research, and Luke the historian has fallen on hard times. However, since he starts his two-volume work by talking about composing an accurate account based on rigorous questioning of original eyewitness (Luke 1:1–3), by any standard the question of history is appropriate.

Even a cursory comparison of Luke's gospel with other gospel accounts reveals how creative these authors were with their tradition. Yet, no matter how much liberty Luke may have taken with regard to traditions about Jesus, we wonder how much he knew about early Christianity, and how accurately he portrayed the Jerusalem church and the spread of Christianity. On these topics, estimates range widely. Leaving the details to specialized study, it is obvious that the accounts in Acts, like those in Luke's gospel, are highly selective chronologically and geographically. While the events recorded in Acts cover a time span of some thirty-five years, the incidents narrated in that span of time are few. For example, by concentrating on the Jerusalem Christians and the transition to Antioch, Acts does not tell us when and how the followers of Jesus spread to Damascus (9:2). The author reports Paul's travels to the west, but nothing about the spread of Christianity to eastern Syria or North Africa, or even about the initial evangelizing of Rome itself. Thus even if everything Luke reports were judged historically accurate, his account is sketchy at best.

There is no doubt that Luke romanticizes the early Christian picture at Jerusalem in terms of the rapidity and numbers of conversions, the saintliness of life, the generosity in giving up possessions, and the single-mindedness of believers. Does Luke display bias? No doubt! Notable examples from the book of Acts include (1) Luke's stress on harmony and unity among Christian leaders, and (2) his emphasis on the continuity between Israel and the church. While Acts reports some elements of dissidence and disagreement in the church, when we contrast Acts with what we learn from Paul's letters about these controversies, it is clear that Acts is overly optimistic. The early Christian movement, in Luke's view, was a harmonious movement initiated by Christ and led by the Holy Spirit. In addition, Luke views the church as an expansion of Judaism, not as a new creation having broken decisively with Judaism. Acts necessarily smooths over a rough course of events.

As for provable errors, the most obvious are in Palestinian history. Whether Gamaliel advocated tolerance toward the early followers of Jesus, his speech is undoubtedly a Lukan creation (Acts 5:34–39). Furthermore, Luke 2:2, combined with 1:5, is inaccurate about the date of the census of Quirinius, and there is a similar inaccuracy in Acts 5:37 about the revolt of Judas the Galilean directed against the census.[3] However, such minor inaccuracies do not mean that we can dismiss the general historicity of Acts' portrayal of early Christianity, any more than inaccuracies in Josephus and the discrepancies between his *Antiquities* and *War* entitle us to dismiss his general historicity.

Another obstacle modern readers face is the cavalier way in which Luke's narrative reports a predilection for the supernatural, recounting tales of fantastic miracles and adventures of good and evil spirits, of exorcisms and healings by Jesus and his followers. The antisupernaturalistic bias of modernity aside, Luke's uncritical use of oral and written sources calls into question his competence as historian. In addition, there are discrepancies between his account of the Jerusalem Council in Acts 15 and the account given in Galatians 2:1–10 by Paul, who actually attended the conference. Furthermore, Luke's knowledge of Palestinian geography seems inadequate at times, leading one prominent scholar to remark, "Jesus' route cannot be reconstructed on any map and, in any case, Luke did not possess one."[4]

In *Luke: Historian and Theologian*, conservative scholar I. H. Marshall notes that modern skeptics may be overly hasty in their assessment of Luke's abilities. The apparent discrepancies concerning the Jerusalem Council, for example, can be resolved if the account in Galatians is read

---

3. There are anachronisms in Gamaliel's speech, such as the chronology between Theudas's revolt and "after him Judas the Galilean." If this Sanhedrin session took place around 36 CE, Theudas's revolt had not yet taken place and Judas's revolt had taken place thirty years before.

4. Conzelmann, *Theology of St. Luke*, 63, n. 6.

as referring to a different, earlier meeting (see Acts 11:30). Similarly, many of the so-called geographical inaccuracies stem from a failure to recognize that Luke uses terms differently than we do today. For example, it is possible that he is not always consistent in his use of the term "Judea." Sometimes he uses the term in a narrow sense, as a reference to a particular region, while at other times he also seems to have a broader sense in mind, referring to all of Palestine. Luke is a theologian, Marshall agrees, but he is also a historian.

Luke's interest, admittedly, is not simply in recording history for its own sake, but in interpreting its significance for human salvation. In addition, Luke seems to believe that the truth is available primarily as narrative, regularly hidden from direct explanation or easy accessibility. We can expect surprises in religious history because meaning is ambiguous. More than one interpretation can be offered for events in the life of Jesus or in the early church, for no single explanation can do justice to the truth of Christ, his birth, life, death, and resurrection, or to the church's birth, life, and mission. The account in Luke–Acts is strange, inscrutable, and altogether beyond the bounds of the imagination. No flat, prosaic explanation can do justice to the truth of Jesus' life and message, or to the truth of the church's origin, meaning, and message.[5] These mysteries can only be conveyed through metaphor, story, and by inspired imagination, commitment, trust, and faithful witness.

Given that Luke was not an eyewitness of what he narrates and that he is highly selective, the author of Acts gets fairly good grades for historical accuracy. Long ago, the British scholars J. B. Lightfoot and W. M. Ramsay pointed to the extraordinary accuracy of Acts' knowledge of the widely differing titles of municipal and imperial officials in the various towns visited (see 13:12; 17:6; 18:12; 19:31, 35). Overall, the book is also accurate about the boundaries and alignments of districts and provinces in the middle of the first century. As New Testament scholar Raymond Brown demonstrates, much of what Acts tells us correlates well with what we can determine from Paul's letters.[6]

In evaluating Luke, it is doubtful whether writing history was his intent. Luke wrote to proclaim, to persuade, and to interpret, not to preserve records for posterity. It is also worth remembering that this author never called his gospel a gospel, and never calls his Acts a history. He

---

5. Willimon, *Acts*, 29.
6. Brown, *Introduction to the New Testament*, 424.

thought of both as "narrative" ("orderly account"; see Luke 1:3). In Acts, as in Luke, the narrative he recounts is primarily intended to give believers assurance (Luke 1:4), to strengthen them spiritually and intellectually with theological insight. Therefore, whatever history these books preserve is put to the service of theology and pastoral exhortation. Luke is primarily a theologian, not a historian. As theologian, his concern appears primarily practical and pastoral, not speculative or theoretical.

In antiquity, there were two ways to write history, a Greek (and more modern) way of thinking, which focused on what actually happened, and a Hebraic (and more ancient) way of thinking, more concerned with what events meant. To the Hebrews, history was "the mighty acts of God," and God was Lord of history, whose character and purpose could be known only through divine acts: "I am the Lord your God, who brought you out of the land of Egypt" (Exod. 20:2). Historical events were seen against a background of faith, and history and theology tended to become inseparably intertwined. Unlike modern historiography, concerned more with "what" and "when" questions, Luke's historiography focused on "why" and "who."

As a historian and theologian, Luke often mixed history and theology. This is not to suggest that he mixed fact and fantasy. It is to affirm, rather, that the history of a people, a nation, and a religious community cannot be understood apart from a consideration of the transcendental forces embedded in that history. As we discover in Acts, there are instances where some of Luke's details appear embellished, questionable, or even wrong. Furthermore, much of biblical language is marked by hyperbole. Such overstatement, mixed with irony and wit, is the hallmark of memorable writers and speakers. Like Jesus, Luke was a gifted storyteller.

When evaluating Luke as historian, the reader should remember that Luke was writing history in the same manner as other historians of antiquity. Ultimately, his method of writing history does not allow any easy answer to the modern historian's question, What actually happened? Luke certainly believed he was dealing with real events, but, like great historians, he was more concerned with finding patterns and meaning in human experience. As we have seen, all historiography is interpretation, and the best historians raise questions about the meaning of history and the future of humanity, questions for which, as historians, they can provide no ultimate answers. The answers belong to the realm of theology, and it is into this realm of metahistory that Luke and the other New Testament writers lead us. Whether we like it or not, when it comes to scripture, we must be content to live with a measure of uncertainty as to where fact ends and interpretation begins.

In recent years, the topic that has sparked the greatest interest in Lukan scholarship has been the evangelist's views on political and social issues. In part, this may be due to the rise of liberation theology, the development of feminist hermeneutics, and the increased appreciation for the work of scholars in the third world. In another sense, however, the tendency to understand Luke through his political views is not new, for it has long been recognized that his gospel displays an extraordinary awareness of the world in which it was written. In his gospel, Luke's historical notes (1:5; 2:1–2; 3:1–2) indicate that he intends to tie the significance of the events he reports to their social context. The book of Acts features numerous accounts that prove he is aware of the benefits and hazards that political connections can pose to the church. It is no surprise that as early as the nineteenth century, political motivations were considered important for an understanding of Luke's project. This approach was advanced in the mid-1950s by influential British scholars Henry Cadbury and Hans Conzelmann,[7] who wrote persuasively that Luke's writings had an apologetic intent, namely, to make clear that despite Jesus' crucifixion at the hands of Roman authorities, the founder of the early Christian movement and his followers posed no political threat to Roman rule.

Despite its influence, Conzelmann's thesis has been challenged and even rejected by numerous scholars, particularly by Richard Cassidy, who in his book *Jesus, Politics, and Society* argues that Luke's gospel was never intended as a political apologetic or as an attempt to make peace with the existing social order. For one thing, the words and deeds of Jesus reported by Luke are of such revolutionary consequence that no one who reads them would ever be convinced that he was politically harmless. As Cassidy notes, Jesus advocated a new society, one based on service and humility rather than on traditional power structures (Luke 22:24–27). He opposed injustice, spoke out against oppression, advocated nonviolence, affirmed new roles for women, condemned the rich, and praised those who give away their possessions. Luke presents Jesus as one who refuses to defer to authorities. He calls Herod a "fox" (13:31–33) and speaks of Pilate's atrocities (13:1–3). He defies the Jewish Sanhedrin (22:67–70) and repudiates Gentile rulers (22:24–27). In the final analysis, Cassidy concludes, Pilate and Herod were wrong in pronouncing Jesus innocent.

---

7. Conzelmann, *Theology of St. Luke*; Cadbury, *Making of Luke–Acts*, 299–316.

According to Luke, Jesus ultimately posed more of a threat to the existing social order than they could ever have imagined.

In conclusion, Luke should be evaluated not as a modern historian but as a historian of his time. In this respect, he includes items in his works that are typical of the writings of the historians of his period. Both Luke and Acts begin with formal literary prologues (Luke 1:1–4; Acts 1:1–5) that can be compared with the prefaces of classical historical and literary writers such as Herodotus, Hippocrates, Josephus, Polybius, and Thucydides. Moreover, Luke repeatedly provides chronological information that declares his intention to set the events he narrates in the context of Greco-Roman and Palestinian history. This manner of writing makes Luke a good historian, representative of his age.

Viewed by the standards of the first century, Luke was not so much taking liberties with the events he sought to narrate as he was following the conventions of history writing of his day. Luke's writings show that he was a cultured, relatively sophisticated citizen of his world. He is aware of cultural patterns from a variety of geographical regions. He also shows familiarity with political, military, and social structures and institutions. Because he assumes a sophisticated audience with his finely nuanced narrative, Luke was no mere provincial, but rather a cosmopolitan believer who styled his narrative through appreciation for subtlety.

Because he writes to inform as well as reassure his audience of God's plan in Jesus Christ, readers reaching the end of Luke's "second account" will both know the events of the origins of Jesus and the church and realize that the salvific activity of Jesus is an ongoing reality.

31. Despite focusing on Paul's life and ministry, the reliability of Acts regarding details of that story is greatly questioned by scholars.

On account of discrepancies with Paul's accounts in his own letters, there is significant scholarly disagreement about the degree to which the portrait of Paul in Acts is consistently reliable. While there is some overlap between Acts and the letters of Paul, Acts is not always consistent with the letters, making it difficult to assess the historical accuracy of Acts when there is no overlap. Furthermore, scholarly study of Acts leads us to believe that the book was most likely written near the end of the first century, some twenty-five to thirty years after Paul's death.

Because many individuals reared in Christianity are taught to take the stories about Paul in Acts literally, it might be helpful here to identify some questionable details from Luke's account.[8] The following items are representative of the broader discussion.

1. Paul's *upbringing*. While both Acts and Paul's letters mention Paul's pedigree as a zealous Jew (Rom. 11:1; 2 Cor. 11:22; Gal. 1:14; Phil. 3:5–6; see Acts 22:3; 23:6; 26:5), only Acts provides important information about Tarsus as Paul's birthplace (21:39; 22:3), and only Acts describes Paul's educational status by having him brought up in Jerusalem at the feet of Gamaliel (22:3). The latter claim needs to be examined more closely, however, for the evidence suggests that Paul received his higher education at Damascus rather than Jerusalem. If Gamaliel were his teacher in Jerusalem, Paul seems not to have followed his advice on how to handle dissident Christian Jews. Gamaliel proposed to "keep away from these men and let them alone" (Acts 5:38), whereas Paul persecuted them.

2. Paul's *political (socioeconomic) status*. Whereas Luke insists that Paul was a Roman citizen (Acts 22:25–29; 23:27), Paul himself never mentions that status and seems even to negate it. "Three times," he claims, "I was beaten with rods" (2 Cor. 11:25)—a Roman punishment forbidden to be used on Roman citizens. If Paul was a citizen, he never used that privilege for his own advantage.

3. Paul's *conversion*. Both Acts and Paul's letters emphasize Paul's conversion, but whereas Luke says Paul only *heard* Christ (in Luke's narration of this event, there is an inconsistency as to whether the bystanders heard the voice but saw nothing, 9:7, or saw a bright light but heard nothing, 22:9), Paul insists he *saw* Christ (1 Cor. 9:1; 15:8–9; see Acts 9:4; 22:6; 26:14). The difference is significant, not only for Paul, but for our understanding of Paul's call and ministry. It is his sight of Jesus that puts him on a par with the Twelve, an eyewitness—and hence an apostle—of the risen Christ. Another discrepancy appear after Paul's conversion: did he go directly to Jerusalem to meet with the apostles (Acts 9:26), or did he intentionally stay away for three years (Gal. 1:18)?

---

8. This material is adapted from Borg and Crossan, *First Paul*. For a fuller discussion of the topic, consult pages 59–92 of their work. My intent in this segment is simply to present issues, not debate or resolve them. In the past, literal readings of the biblical text suppressed creativity and led to dogmatic thinking. Exposing students of the Bible to critical readings of the text produces independent thinking and encourages less arrogant pursuit of truth.

4. Paul's *apostleship*. According to Paul, he was an apostle called and sent directly by God—just as the Twelve (generally a term for the original disciples of Jesus)—but according to Luke, Paul had no such status or authority. Whereas Paul claimed to have been sent by personal revelation made directly by God or Christ (Rom. 1:1; 1 Cor. 1:1; 2 Cor. 1:1; Gal. 1:1), Luke's account seems to counter such claims. Although Luke does call Paul an apostle on occasion, in his estimation Paul was only an apostle sent by the community at Antioch (see Acts 13:3) and was therefore subordinate to the apostles at Jerusalem. Overall, when Luke refers to "the apostles" in Acts, he means "the twelve apostles" named in 1:13 and 26. They are a closed group Jesus called at the start of his public ministry, and into that group Paul could never enter. Paul's claim in 1 Corinthians 15:9, where he calls himself "the least of the apostles," seems to suggest that he considered himself one of the original eyewitnesses of the resurrected Lord, hence one of the Twelve, in the sense of Acts 1:21–26.

5. Paul *missionary strategy*. In Acts we read that Paul's missionary strategy focuses on going into synagogues to convert Jews. That, of course, had been his method during the first missionary journey, led by Paul's colleague Barnabas. Paul tells us nothing directly about this mission, although Luke records it in detail in Acts 13–14. It began at Antioch, with Paul clearly subordinate to Barnabas (see 13:2). At the end of this mission there was a major apostolic agreement in Jerusalem (the Jerusalem Council of 49 CE; see Acts 15:1–35 and Gal. 2:1–10) and a major apostolic disagreement in Antioch (see Gal. 2:11–14), but Luke only speaks of agreement at both Jerusalem and Antioch in Acts 15.

At many points of comparison, one can find discrepancies between the accounts of Acts and Paul's own writings. It would be a mistake, though, to discount Acts for this reason. Like the gospels, Acts is written to explain the significance of what happened in early Christianity, not to provide a biographical picture or a data-driven report. Furthermore, when we examine individual events, whether in Acts or in Paul's letters, we need to be aware that in both cases, we find internal inconsistencies due to context. When we examine the matter of Paul's citizenship, for example, we notice that there are only two places in Acts where Paul's Roman citizenship is an issue, in Acts 16:37–39 and 22:25–29, and in both cases Paul uses his citizenship for the purpose of influencing the improper conduct of fellow Roman citizens. Paul does not mention his Roman citizenship while within earshot of a Jewish crowd, even when he is addressing the tribune, because such a reference would probably have impeded his cause with the Jewish audience. In other words, in general Luke makes very little of Paul's Roman citizenship, and only in limited settings. When Paul in Acts is addressing either a Jewish or pagan audience, or a Christian audience in a non-Roman nonlegal setting, he never mentions the matter. For Paul, Roman identity was low in order of importance, ahead of which came his identity as a Christian and as a Pharisaic Jew. Since there are no situations in Paul's letters where he either addresses or answers Roman charges against himself, there is no need to boast or speak about such citizenship. The reason there is no direct evidence about Paul's citizenship in his letters is that all are addressed to those who are already Christians. There is nothing in his letters that casts doubt on the evidence of Acts on this matter.

Once again, a literal reading of scripture, whether of historical narrative or in epistolary settings, is unhelpful and can actually lead to unnecessary conflict and skepticism. Awareness of intent is as important as understanding genre. Both are essential to context. As the saying goes, a text without context is mere pretext for proof-text. In other words, failure to understand context leads to faulty and often to coercive theology.

Assignment

Having read chapter 11, answer the following questions, writing the answers in your journal. [If you are in a study group, be prepared to share your views with others in the class.]

1. What role does the Holy Spirit play in the book of Acts? In the church today? In your life?
2. In your estimation, was Luke a traveling companion of Paul? If not, how do you understand the "we" passages in Acts?
3. Evaluate the reliability of Acts for a historical reconstruction of early Christianity.
4. Read Acts 15:1–35. Make a list of the principles you find about conflict resolution. How can you apply these principles to conflicts in your life?
5. After reading this chapter, what did you learn about interpreting scripture contextually?
6. What is the primary insight I/we gained from this chapter or session?

Chapter 12

Three Things to Know about the Epistles of Paul

APART FROM JESUS, PAUL was the most important figure in the history of early Christianity. One of the heroic figures in the life of the early church, he emerged from being an arch-persecutor of Christians into an unrelenting missionary of the gospel. The impact of Paul upon the church was both widespread and permanent. His influence was fourfold:

- the first great theologian of the church;
- the first full-time missionary to the Gentiles;
- the founder of numerous congregations in Asia Minor, Greece, and Macedonia;
- the author (actual or alleged) of a group of letters that now comprise one-fourth of the bulk of the New Testament.

Paul is sometimes called the second founder of Christianity. As the first great theologian of the church, he was both a practical theologian—in that he addressed specific needs arising in the church—and a task theologian. To him belonged the unique task of developing or disclosing a theology for the Gentile church, indicating how Gentiles would be brought into full participation in the fellowship of Christ, what Paul would refer to as "the body of Christ" (Rom. 12:5; 1 Cor. 12:13, 27; Col. 1:18; cf. Eph. 4:4) and "the Israel of God" (Gal. 6:16; cf. Rom. 11:25–26).

The first full-time missionary to the Gentiles, Paul helped bridge the gap as the church became less Jewish and more Gentile in its makeup.

Jesus had performed a revolution in religion, recognizing in Judaism a rich spiritual treasure, resulting in a distinct system of worship, a religious way of life, and a high ethical outlook. Yet that treasure was not available to everyone, for Judaism was an ethnic and deeply exclusive faith. Jesus believed himself to be not simply a teacher of truth but the Messiah, through whom God's eternal purpose for Israel and the nations would be fulfilled. This meant that Jesus undertook the task of liberating the spiritual treasure of Israel's faith for humanity. However, his ministry was almost exclusively to Jews, and his faithfulness to God led him to the cross. The work of Christ became entrusted to his followers, who would be empowered by the Holy Spirit to continue the mission Jesus had begun. It is in Paul and his work that we see the task being accomplished. Paul took the work of Christ and set it free from possession by any one ethnic group, sect, or clique. In so doing, Paul remains the classic exponent of the idea of freedom in Christ and of the universality of God's plan for all humanity (see Rom. 3:29–30; Gal. 3:14; 5:1; cf. Eph. 3:6).

Paul also founded new congregations during his missionary travels, providing exhortation, encouragement, and support through letters and personal visits. He helped heal doctrinal and moral difficulties in his churches, providing a form of moral instruction known as *paraenesis* (see, for example, 1 Thess. 4:1–12), such as one might expect to see in the philosophical letters of his day. His letters to the church of Corinth deal with numerous practical issues they were facing, helping later Christians more fully understand the nature of the Christian life.

In his letters Paul followed the common style of the day, beginning with introductory greetings, followed by the main body of the letter, and ending with concluding remarks, including a word of farewell, a feature that Paul regularly expanded with an expression of blessing and prayer for his readers. The middle section often consisted of two parts: doctrinal teaching (sometimes in response to questions raised by his audience), followed by practical teaching or advice concerning the Christian lifestyle.

While not all of his letters remain, by the end of the first century they became preserved through a collection that marks the church's initial Christian canon (see 2 Pet. 3:15–16). As part of scripture they became the most famous and influential set of letters ever written, impacting every major Christian thinker and practically every major revival. Central in the conversion of Augustine and Luther, they held a critical place in their life and teachings. During the Reformation, Calvin patterned his famous *Institutes of the Christian Religion* on Paul's letter to the Romans.

Who, then, was this man we call the apostle Paul? What was his heritage, and how did he become both a Christian and an apostle of Christ? While his Roman name was Paul, from his letters we know that his Jewish name was Saul, and that he was born and reared at Tarsus, an important city in the Roman province of Cilicia, in southeastern Asia Minor (present day Turkey). Though Paul was brought up in the strict observance of the Hebrew faith and traditions, his father having been a Pharisee, he was born a Roman citizen. This privilege, possessed by only a few in the provinces of the empire, proved to be of great importance later in his Christian work and more than once saved his life.

Despite the tradition that he went to Jerusalem at an early age, Paul seems to have been raised outside of Palestine and evidently did not know Jesus. He spoke and wrote Greek and seems not to be acquainted with the Semitic languages current in Palestine. Committed to the traditions of Pharisaism, he was steeped in and deeply attached to the Law of Moses as given by God (Gal. 1:13–14; Phil 3:4–6). When he was first exposed to the early Christian movement as an adult, he found it blasphemous and dangerous (Gal. 1:13). He may have held the traditional view that the Messiah was to be a figure of grandeur and power and found that the belief that Jesus was the Messiah ludicrous. How could a crucified criminal, one who was, therefore, cursed by God (Deut. 27:26; see Gal. 3:13), be the Messiah? That claim seemed to Paul to be utterly blasphemous. He may also have found offensive the Christian claim that salvation came to Gentiles apart from Jewish law. His training eventually brought him into bitter conflict with the followers of Jesus Christ.

Paul first appears in Christian history in association with the persecutors of the Christian church (Acts 7:58). Later, looking back on the advantages in which at one time he had taken pride, he described his lineage thus: "circumcised on the eighth day, a member of the people of Israel, of the tribe of Benjamin, a Hebrew born of Hebrews, as to the law, a Pharisee, as to zeal, a persecutor of the church, as to righteousness under the law, blameless" (Phil. 3:6). That's quite a pedigree!

With astonishing suddenness, the persecutor of the church became the apostle of Jesus Christ. He was in mid-course as a zealot for the law, bent on exterminating the plague that threatened the life of Israel, when, in his own words, "Christ Jesus made me his own" (Phil. 3:12). What caused this transformation? Apparently he had a visionary experience of Jesus that changed his life (Gal. 1:15–16). His own repeated explanation is that he saw the crucified Christ now exalted as the risen Lord: "Have

I not seen Jesus our Lord?" he asks when his apostolic credentials are questioned (1 Cor. 9:1), referring to that same occasion later in the same letter where, after listing earlier appearances of Christ in resurrection, he adds, "Last of all, as to one untimely born, he appeared also to me" (1 Cor. 15:8). When, in 2 Corinthians 4:6, he says that "God . . . has shone in our hearts to give the light of the knowledge of the glory of God in the face of Jesus Christ," his language implies a reminiscence of his conversion on the way to Damascus, when about midday "a light from heaven flashed around him" and he fell to the ground, hearing a voice say: "Saul, Saul, why do you persecute me?" When Paul asked who was speaking he heard the reply: "I am Jesus, whom you are persecuting" (Acts 9:3–5).

No single event, apart from the Christ-event itself, has proved so determinant for the course of Christian history as the conversion and commissioning of Paul. It is so for the author of Acts, who provides three accounts of the conversion (Acts 9:1–22; 22:6–16; 26:12–18). "With no conscious preparation, Paul found himself instantaneously compelled to acknowledge that Jesus of Nazareth, the crucified one, was alive after his passion, vindicated and exalted by God, and was now conscripting him into his service."[1]

Paul's conversion represents a radical shift in his thinking about Jesus and the church. On the Damascus road Paul learned two things about Jesus: that he was not dead, but alive, and that Jesus was not cursed, but blessed by God. Hence the cross, rather than discrediting Jesus as an imposter, is truly God's provision for humanity and the fulfillment of the promise that through Abraham all nations and peoples would be blessed (Gal. 3:6–9). Jesus was indeed the expected Messiah, but also the "Son of God." This discovery became the subject of his first Christian preaching in Damascus (Acts 9:20). As a Christian, he still believed in only one God, but he became convinced that God could only be fully known through Jesus (2 Cor. 4:6). On the Damascus road he also learned that Christians are not heretics, but God's people. He discovered that in persecuting Christians he had been persecuting Christ (Acts 9:5). That correlation would lead him to one of his most profound insights, that the church was neither a building nor a sect but the "body of Christ" (1 Cor. 12:27). Theologically, the church was a microcosm of the transformation that God's new order would bring for the whole world. To be in the church was to have a foretaste of life in God's kingdom. Socially, the

---

1. Bruce, *Apostle of the Heart Set Free*, 75.

church in the Roman empire was an alternative society, based on the new freedom and fellowship that Jesus had announced: freedom to love God and to love and serve others (Mark 12:29–31). It must have taken Paul some time to process his new understanding about Jesus and the church. His sojourn in the Nabatean wilderness after his conversion, followed by a three year stay in Damascus, certainly provided him time to reflect and rethink his theology, but as far as he was concerned, it was on the Damascus road that the essential core of his faith as a Christian was first revealed to him.

While Paul's Damascus-road experience may be said to have contained within itself the totality of his apostolic message, that totality was not grasped by him immediately. The revelation he received on that occasion coincided with his call to preach Christ among the Gentiles, but not until he was fully launched in his evangelistic career could he understand what this call entailed. Justification by faith was certainly implicit in his conversion, but it would take a decade or more of ministry to flesh it out fully, as he does in his letters to the Galatians and to the Romans. Speaking of his Christian standing by contrast with his earlier situation, he describes himself as "not having a righteousness of my own that comes from the law, but one that comes through faith in Christ, the righteousness from God based on faith" (Phil. 3:9).

Over time, Paul came to see the death of Jesus as a sacrifice for the sins of others. The Jewish Law, with its requirement of animal sacrifices as atonement for sin, could no longer be the way to attain a right standing before God; Jesus' death was now the only way. Rather than continuing with the Pharisaic belief that Jews were to keep the Law more perfectly and Gentiles needed to start keeping the Law by being circumcised, Paul came to promote faith in Christ as the way of salvation. There could be no other way. Salvation was now available to all people, Jew and Gentile alike; all could belong to the people of God.

32. Paul, like Jesus, was an apocalyptic Jew, convinced that the world as he knew it was about to end.

Not only did Paul change his views about Jesus and the way to salvation, he also came to see the significance of Jesus' resurrection for the history of the world. As a Pharisee, Paul already believed in an apocalyptic form of Judaism. Apocalypticism maintained that there would be a resurrection of dead bodies at the end of the age, when all would come to face judgment. Jesus, however, had already been raised. In Paul's mind, this showed that the end had already begun. In his letters, Paul refers to Jesus as the "first-fruits" of the Resurrection (1 Cor. 15:23), meaning that the end of history had already begun. Therefore, the full resurrection would occur soon, within his lifetime (1 Thess. 4:13–18; note that in 4:15 Paul indicates that he and his fellow Christians will be among those who will be alive and remain when the resurrected Christ returns to inaugurate the kingdom on earth; see also 1 Cor. 15:51). As we saw in Jesus' ministry, the imminence of the kingdom explains, in part, the urgency of Paul's mission to spread the gospel throughout the world before the end arrived.

Throughout his letters, we find hints concerning what Paul said to potential converts. Because his audience consisted mainly of pagans, he first had to convince them that their worship was pointless, because the pagan gods were mere idols and had no real existence (1 Thess. 1:9–10). Furthermore, the one true God had sent his Son into the world to die for the sins of the world, of which every human being was guilty. The truth of this message was proven by the resurrection of Jesus from the dead. For people to have a right standing before God, therefore, and to be saved when the imminent day of judgment arrived, they needed to believe in the one true God and trust the death of his son, Jesus. For Paul, this was the fulfillment of the Jewish Law. It was no longer necessary to follow the requirements of the Jewish Law to attain salvation.

Nevertheless, throughout his writings Paul expressed concern that his converts live ethical, upright lives. He believed that Gentiles, like Jews, should strive to follow certain standards found in the Jewish scriptures, particularly the commandment found in Leviticus 19:18, that one should love one's neighbor as oneself (Rom. 13:8–10). Paul's fullest exposition of the love commandment comes in 1 Corinthians 13. In Paul's mind, another reason for behaving according to high ethical standards involved his deeply rooted apocalyptic conviction that the world as it was known was about to end. For this reason, he insisted that believers focus on the urgent tasks of the moment and not concern themselves with altering the social arrangements—such as slavery or marriage—in which they found themselves (1 Cor. 7:1–40).

33. Many of the letters attributed to Paul are disputed and, in fact, pseudonymous.

Thirteen of the twenty-seven books of the New Testament are letters attributed to Paul, who helped shape Christian belief, practice, and ethics and was instrumental in the spread of Christianity across the Mediterranean world. Scholars disagree over which letters were actually written by Paul, suggesting at least three categories: authentic, disputed, and pseudepigraphic. As a way of dealing with this classification, the following views of Pauline authorship have been proposed:

- *Radical Paul* (seven authentic letters): 1 Thessalonians, 1 and 2 Corinthians, Philippians, Galatians, Romans, Philemon
- *Conservative Paul* (three disputed letters; if not Pauline, they are Deutero-Pauline, that is, written by an admirer of Paul): 2 Thessalonians, Colossians, Ephesians
- *Reactionary Paul* (three letters, written by an anti-Paulinist, in order to make Christianity appear compatible with Roman values): 1 and 2 Timothy, Titus.

Paul's authentic letters typically follow epistolary correspondence common in the Greek-speaking world of the first century. Most of these letters are addressed to Christian communities in the northern Mediterranean world, churches Paul visited during his three missionary journeys. The author gives thanks for the people's faithfulness, chastises them for their failings, exhorts them to live as disciples of Jesus Christ, and clarifies his understanding of the meaning of the Christian gospel. Philemon is addressed to a friend of Paul. Three of the letters attributed to Paul but actually written to deradicalize Paul are 1 and 2 Timothy and Titus. Called the pastoral letters because of their concern with leadership in the Christian churches, their target audience is other Christian missionaries.

Like other New Testament documents, the Pauline letters are not arranged chronologically, that is, in the order in which they were written, but rather according to two criteria: length and audience. The first nine letters, written to churches, precede the last four, written to individuals; Romans, the longest letter written to a community, appears first, and Philemon, the shortest letter written to an individual, appears last.

The entire Pauline corpus, while varied and complex in content, has been classified thematically as follows:

- *Eschatology* (addressing the meaning and expected return of Christ): 1 and 2 Thessalonians

- *Soteriology* (addressing the way of salvation): Romans, Galatians, 1 and 2 Corinthians (all letters in this group are said to be authentically Pauline)

- *Christology* (addressing the doctrine of Christ): Ephesians, Colossians, Philippians, and Philemon

- *Ecclesiology* (addressing leadership for the local church): 1 and 2 Timothy, Titus.

34. When he wrote, Paul was not aware that his writings would become scripture.

Paul's letters are the earliest writings of the New Testament. Here we are in direct contact with living history. These letters sparkle with life and grow out of specific situations, the exact nature not always clear because we have too little knowledge of the background. From these letters we can see what early Christians believed, what they found difficult to believe, and where they were susceptible to aberration. What had been fluid in the period of oral tradition begins to crystalize into acceptable doctrine. However, the Christians had yet no Bible save the Hebrew scriptures. Paul's undisputed letters were "occasional" in nature. They were not systematic treatises but letters to specific churches, written to address actual concerns that arose in his churches. The last thing that Paul thought of in connection with his often hurriedly written letters was permanence. They were written for an immediate purpose, and once that purpose was fulfilled they might be expected to disappear. It was only accidental that some were preserved to become in due course sacred scripture.

When we read Paul's letters, we need to remember that he was not mindful that future generations would scrutinize his letters and seek to fit together every thought they contained. He had no idea, when he dictated his letters to an assistant, as was his custom, that centuries later Christians would be building theologies on thoughts and words uttered so precariously. At times his ideas rush so swiftly that they outstrip the flow of his words, and in those places the reader must leap over gaps so as to catch up on his thought. Repeatedly Paul starts a sentence that he does not complete, for a new thought strikes him and he turns aside to deal with that. His letters are sometimes filled with such lapses that when he returns to the original subject, he has forgotten the start of the sentence. Furthermore, as was the custom of dictation in antiquity, Paul must have given his assistants editorial power to write or complete final drafts of his letters, which explains the strange note found among the greetings at the end of Romans: "I, Tertius, the writer of this letter, greet you in the Lord" (Rom. 16:22).

While Paul had no idea he was writing scripture, there is no denying that he considered his writings to be invested with special authority, and furthermore, that he expected his readers generally to recognize this as factual (1 Cor. 2:16; 7:17; 14:37–38; cf. 2 Thess. 3:14).

The Paul we encounter in the letters is not a systematic theologian. Quite the opposite. He wrote his letters not to give a compendium of Christian doctrine, but rather to offer practical guidance. He came to herald Christ, not to rationalize him. He came to bring, not a system, but the living Christ. That was his apostle's call, his sole vocation and concern. He was a teacher first and a writer second. His religious position was hammered out, not in the study, but on the mission field. Even a letter as elaborate as Romans should not be construed as a theological treatise designed to set forth Paul's confession of Christian faith, for Romans, like all Paul's letters, is ultimately "not abstract but personal, not metaphysical but experimental."[2] What flows through the head originated in the heart.

Not surprisingly, Paul's phraseology is fluid, not rigid, and his terminology—faith, law, spirit—is complex and polyvalent (multi-layered in meaning). Faith can mean "belief" but also "trust;" Mosaic law can be "holy" but also a curse; and spirit, used to denote a person's inner life, can also mean the Spirit of Christ. Paul's readers must remain cautious about constructing theology from fragmentary ideas and restrained in demanding precision from a writer who thinks, as Paul often did, in pictures. As history shows, solitary proof texts create theological mayhem. For example, when Paul mentions predestination, as he does directly in Romans 8:29–30 and indirectly in 9:22–23, it is in the context of God's sovereign freedom and will to save, and we must be careful not to press the metaphor, as Augustine and Calvin and others have done, entangling it with ideas of reprobation and damnation.

Surprisingly, despite his obvious christocentrism, Paul rarely mentions any of the things that Jesus said or did during his lifetime. Rather,

---

2. Stewart, *Man in Christ*, 25.

his focus is on Jesus' death and resurrection (1 Cor. 2:2; 15:3–8). In this respect, it is important to remember that Paul was living and writing before the gospels were produced. Hence, we cannot assume that he knew what was going to be written in them. On rare occasions, he does cite Jesus as an authority for his views. It is certainly possible that Paul knew more about Jesus than he mentions. However, on the whole, his letters were occasional in nature, addressing specific concerns and problems and responding to specific questions. In such situations, information about Jesus would simply have been irrelevant for his mission.

Given their occasional nature, we cannot expect Paul's letters to cover every topic of importance to Paul. For example, he mentions the "Lord's Supper" in 1 Corinthians 11, but only because the Corinthians were not observing it properly. If their observance had been correct, we would never have known that Paul found its observance to be important.

Having completed our study of Jesus and Paul, the two most important figures of early Christianity, it might be useful to compare what we have discovered. An overarching question readers of the New Testament must ask is whether there was one early Christianity or several early Christianities, that is, whether early Christianity was one community adhering to normative teachings or a set of diverse communities.

As we might expect, there are a number of important similarities between the fundamental teachings of Jesus and Paul. Both men were first-century Jews who, like most Jews, believed in one God, creator of all, who had made a covenant with the people Israel and given them commandments to follow. Both were apocalypticists, who thought the end of history was imminent, to be accomplished in a cataclysmic judgment by a cosmic judge from heaven. Both taught that people needed to prepare for this coming climax of history, and both taught that the letter of the Law was not important regarding one's standing before God, and that the Law could be summed up in the command to love one's neighbor as oneself.

There are also numerous important differences between the two.[3]

1. The historical Jesus taught that the cosmic judge coming from heaven was someone that he called the Son of Man, and this personage was not Jesus. Paul, however, taught that the cosmic judge was Jesus.

---

3. The following points are adapted from Bart Ehrman's Great Courses lecture, "Paul, Jesus, and James," in *New Testament. Course Guidebook*, 112–13.

2. Jesus taught that to escape judgment, a person must keep the central teachings of the Jewish Law, primarily as interpreted by himself. Paul never mentioned Jesus' interpretation of the Law, but insisted that keeping the Law would never bring salvation. The only way to be saved was to trust Jesus' death and resurrection.

3. Jesus taught that people who repented and kept the Law would enter the kingdom. Paul taught that repentance and keeping the Law was not sufficient; salvation came only through Christ's death and resurrection.

4. Jesus saw his own importance as lying in his proclamation of the coming end and his interpretation of the Law. Paul saw Jesus' importance as lying exclusively in his death and resurrection for sins.

These changes have led some modern observers to speak of Paul as the second founder of Christianity. When we examine Matthew 25:31–46, a passage that, as we noted earlier, goes back to the historical Jesus, Jesus speaks of the coming cosmic judge not as himself but as a future heavenly Son of Man (25:31). Likewise, in this passage, salvation is said to come by loving others and doing good deeds, not through Jesus or belief in him. However, in both Romans 3 and Galatians 3, Paul says the opposite, that justification is through faith in Christ, not through works of the Law. The best explanation for these differences is that Paul represents a significant development of Jesus' teachings, that he altered the basic message in light of his experience of Jesus, making Jesus' death, rather than his teaching, the key to his message. According to this view, Paul transformed the religion *of* Jesus into a religion *about* Jesus. In this regard, it is striking that Paul rarely mentions anything that Jesus said or did.

Paul's understanding of salvation differs not only with that of Jesus, but also with that found in the epistle of James. This letter, traditionally attributed to Jesus' brother (known to history as James the Just, a leader of the Jerusalem church following the death of Jesus and himself martyred by King Herod Agrippa I; see Acts 12:2),[4] consists of a number of moral exhortations for believers, many sounding similar to Jesus' teachings in the Sermon on the Mount. One passage in particular, James 2:14–26, stands in stark contrast to what Paul teaches about salvation in Romans or Galatians. In James 2:24, the author indicates that a person "is justified

---

4. While some of the ideas in the letter of James might go back to the actual brother of Jesus, the letter itself, written by a well-educated Greek-speaking Christian, would hardly have been written by a lower-class Aramaic-speaking peasant.

by works and not by faith alone." This represents a contrast to Romans 3:28, where a person "is justified by faith apart from works prescribed by the law." Significantly, just as Paul in Romans uses Abraham as proof that justification comes by faith alone (Rom. 4:2, 22), James uses Abraham to show that a person is justified only by doing works (Jas. 2:21). Both even quote the same verse from the Old Testament, Genesis 15:6, to support their views.

This example highlights what by now should seem quite obvious, that there was a geat deal of diversity in early Christianity. The four gospels portray Jesus differently, and there appear to be discrepancies among them. Jesus himself preached a message that was altered before it was recorded in the gospels. Paul's message concerning the identity and role of Jesus also appears to differ from that of Jesus. As we continue our study of the New Testament, we discover additional diversity. Some of this diversity can be found in books that claim Paul as their author but that seem to present a different understanding of the gospel than his. That is the case with the Deutero-Pauline epistles (2 Thessalonians, Colossians, and Ephesians) and the pastoral epistles (1 and 2 Timothy and Titus). It also holds true for the General Epistles and the book of Revelation.

Assignment

Having read chapter 12, answer the following questions, writing the answers in your journal. [If you are in a study group, be prepared to share your views with others in the class.]

1. In your own words, explain how Paul's conversion impacted his thinking about God, Jesus, Christians, and God's plan for humanity.

2. In your estimation, which of Paul's contributions had the most lasting impact? Explain your answer.

3. In your estimation, did Paul understand Jesus and his message accurately? Explain your answer.

4. If you could meet Paul and ask him three questions, what would they be? What question would you ask first? Why?

5. What is the primary insight I/we gained from this chapter or session?

Chapter 13

Three Things to Know about the General Epistles

BESIDES THE LETTERS TRADITIONALLY ascribed to the apostle Paul, the New Testament contains eight letters written by five or six other leaders in the early Christian church. Most of them are addressed, not to a single Christian community, but to a cluster of congregations. They are less like personal letters than most of Paul's, and more like official letters or sermons from a bishop or elder to a group of churches.

In modern usage a distinction is often made between the terms "letter" and "epistle." Letters are generally private communications and deal with circumstances of the passing moment. Confidential and personal in nature, they are intended only for the person or persons to whom they are addressed. Epistles, on the other hand, are on a more sophisticated level of literary effort, and are written with the intention of being both public and more or less permanent. In brief, a letter is a slice of life, while the epistle is a product of literary art.

Furthermore, it should be noted that the literary form of a letter/epistle combines the advantages of a conversation and a treatise; in such a format it is possible to communicate teaching, not only abstractly, but in close relation to the personal circumstances of the recipients.

The New Testament combines features of both the letter and the epistle. The letters of Paul are all real letters, arising out of real situations in his life or the lives of those to whom he writes. At the same time, they are somewhat official letters rather than merely private letters, and their style is more formal than the ephemeral letters of antiquity. Some of the other letters in the New Testament resemble the form and style of a theological treatise (such as the letter to the Hebrews) or an edifying homily (1 Peter and 1 John). Even these, however, were not originally directed to all Christians but were intended for particular destinations, and were written, like the letters of Paul, in order to deal with urgent difficulties experienced by the recipients, such as persecution, heresy, and religious or moral laxity. Thus, the letters of the New Testament incorporate elements of the ongoing life of the churches, such as liturgical materials, moral guidelines, and religious instruction applicable to many believers besides the immediate recipients of the document.

35. Authorship and setting are essential for understanding the meaning and message of the General Epistles.

The various letters grouped under the category of General or Catholic Epistles can be divided into two overarching themes: three letters help readers understand the early church's Jewish heritage (James, Hebrews, and 1 Peter), and five with the peril of heresies (Jude, 2 Peter, and three epistles of John, in addition to the seven letters found in chapters 2–3 of the book of Revelation).

The Church and its Jewish Origins

As we have observed, one cannot understand Jesus, Paul, or Christianity without understanding their Jewish heritage. Judaism had always been deeply concerned with behavior. In the Roman world, Jewish people were often distinguished not so much by what they thought as by how they behaved. They circumcised their male children, kept the Sabbath day, and observed distinctive food laws. Additionally, they followed a distinct and comprehensive moral code. Many of the things that were taken for granted in a regular Hellenistic lifestyle were avoided by Jews, not simply because these practices were un-Jewish, but because they seemed to go against the Law of God. As Jewish people in different parts of the Roman empire explained their ancestral faith to other people, they found that Gentiles were often attracted by their moral standards. After the self-indulgence of much Greek and Roman culture, Gentiles found the Jewish way simple and disciplined. Many Gentiles attended Jewish synagogues, and some became full proselytes.

Jesus, it seems, valued the Jewish Law, and the letter of James continued this theme: it emphasizes that religious belief is worthless if it does not affect the way people live. What God considers to be pure and genuine religion is this: "to care for orphans and widows in their distress, and to keep oneself unstained by the world" (Jas. 1:27). The heart of real devotion to God is to love one's neighbor as oneself (2:1–13). Like Jesus, James uses illustrations to deliver his message, many from the familiar world of Palestinian agriculture. While the epistle of James, like Jesus' Sermon on the Mount, lacks any coherent argument as such, its message is not lost on its readers. People who endure suffering patiently, trusting in God for deliverance, will be vindicated in the end (Jas. 5:7–20).

The epistle to the Hebrews is not, as it seems, written to actual Jews, but appears to be a sermon delivered by an early Christian preacher to a congregation whose members were being attracted away from their Christian faith to Judaism. While the King James Version of the Bible originally included in its heading that Hebrews was "The Epistle of Paul the Apostle," this work is neither a letter nor a writing of Paul. Rather, it is anonymous, for it does not claim Paul as its author and appears unlike the actual letters we have from Paul, both in form and content. In addition to Paul, many other suggestions have been made about the author of the letter, including Barnabas, Apollos, Luke, Aquila, and Priscilla. There is no compelling proof for any of these, and the only sure conclusion about its authorship is that it was not written by Paul.

Despite the title of the book, the author's hearers were evidently not Jews but former pagans. In the sermon, the author provides numerous demonstrations that Jesus is in every way superior to anything that Judaism has to offer. The author makes three points to underscore the preeminence of Christ: (1) Jesus is greater than Old Testament prophets, included Moses the lawgiver and angels, who were connected by Jewish tradition with the giving of the Torah; (2) Jesus is greater than Aaron or the Jewish priesthood; and (3) Jesus' sacrifice is greater than the Old Testament Levitical sacrifices, in part because it is one sacrifice instead of many, and is undertaken by a free moral agent, who willingly offered himself on behalf of others. Salvation, for the author of Hebrews, requires faith, understood as commitment to God and God's will. All this, our author insists, is nothing new, but the natural outworking of the Jewish faith (Heb. 11:1–40).

The epistle to the Hebrews contains a forceful statement of the inferiority of Judaism to Christianity. Later, when the Roman empire became predominantly Christian, this ideology would be used to silence and punish Jews. This led to the nefarious acts of anti-Semitism that came down through the Middle Ages and resulted in such extreme and bizarre acts as the Nazi holocaust. How ironic, given the fact that the founder and the earliest Christian leaders were so thoroughly Jewish.

According to internal evidence, the audience addressed in Hebrews had recently experienced some type of hostility or persecution (10:32, 34), some being deprived of property and others put in prison. By the time Hebrews was written, the active persecution seems to have passed, but there was still ongoing tension and fear of future intensification. An exaggerated nostalgia or attraction for the Jewish roots of Christianity seems to be evident among the recipients of the letter. Specifically, the author believes some were putting too much value on the Israelite cultic heritage and not appreciating the enormous change brought about through Christ. Still others, it seems, were in danger of abandoning the advantages brought by faith in Christ, particularly in light of the imminent day of judgment (10:25).

Though some of the same themes appear in 1 Peter, they appear in a distinctive form. Abraham is mentioned only in passing, and in a different context altogether (3:6). Nevertheless, 1 Peter conveys the clear conviction that Gentile Christians have been incorporated as full members into the "people of God" whose history began with the covenants of the Old Testament (2:9–10). It also asserts that they have achieved this position as a result of their response in faith to what God has done for them (1:3–21).

Although 1 Peter claims to be written by the disciple of Jesus, Simon Peter, this is highly unlikely, given the fact that Peter was a lower-class Jewish fisherman from Galilee, whereas this book is written by a well-educated, rhetorically trained Greek-speaking Christian. Although it is possible that Peter wrote the book or dictated its contents to someone (perhaps the "Silvanus" mentioned in 5:12), who translated his words into Greek and provided them with a rhetorical flourish, it is more likely that the book was written pseudonymously in Peter's name, as were several other books that have come down to us from the second century, such as the gospel of Peter, three apocalypses attributed to Peter, several "Acts" of Peter, and other Petrine letters.

First Peter, it seems, is a kind of circular letter addressed to Christians scattered throughout several of the provinces of Asia Minor who are experiencing harsh forms of suffering through persecution. The author urges them not to suffer for any wrongdoing but only for doing what is right. In particular, they should willingly and fearlessly suffer, if suffer they must, for the sake of their Christian faith. Although written in the name of the apostle Peter, the letter was written c. 80 CE by one of his disciples in Rome. The letter lacks the kind of material one would expect from an eyewitness. Instead, the letter reflects much of the language and thought of the Pauline letters, and doubtless combines Petrine and Pauline traditions. By the end of the first century, the church at Rome found itself the heir of both Peter and Paul, and the custodian of the traditions associated with each. A late date for the letter is also suggested by the use of the term "Babylon" (5:13) as a designation for Rome, which became current only after 70 CE. Except for the first word, the letter makes no claim to authorship by an apostle, but specifically indicates that the author was an elder (5:1).

36. Early Christians suffered persecution, not for their beliefs, but for their exclusivism.

The believers addressed by 1 Peter were probably former pagans, who had removed themselves from the daily life of the larger community and adopted a stricter set of moral standards for themselves. There has been some kind of public outcry, apparently by those who felt abandoned by their former friends and companions (4:4). The turmoil may have reached the point of mob violence or governmental intervention, for the author speaks of the "fiery ordeal that is taking place among you" (4:12). He produces this letter both to console those in the community who are suffering and to urge them to maintain solidarity with one another.[1]

On the one hand, he explains that their suffering is natural and to be expected; they are, after all, followers of Christ, who was himself crucified (4:12-13). They should not behave in a way that offends outsiders but should be ready to explain what it is that makes them different (3:15-17). When outsiders realize how the Christians react to persecution, they too might repent (2:11; 3:13-15).

---

1. At one time scholars suggested that 1 Peter may have originated as a baptismal homily, based on the passage found in 3:18-22. However, this view is now largely rejected. Like the Pauline letters, 1 Peter was intended for reading in worship services. It was written, not for personal or group study, but to provide a message of hope to persecuted believers, encouraging them to hold fast to their faith until the end.

As we noted in chapter 9, Christianity was not "illegal" in the Roman empire. Christians were free to worship any god they chose in whatever way they desired, so long as they also were willing to worship the state gods. Christians, of course, would not do so, and this led to occasional persecution and eventually to empire-wide persecutions. Unlike Roman civil law, which was extremely complex and nuanced, Roman criminal law was, by our standards lax and haphazard. Criminal activities were not strictly defined and punishments were not prescribed by law. These were defined and carried out locally, under provincial governors, who were granted nearly absolute authority to achieve their objectives.

Christianity began as a sect within Judaism. Unlike other religions, including Judaism, Christianity was, from the outset, a religion that emphasized belief. It stressed that Jews, along with all other unbelievers, needed to believe that Jesus was the Messiah, God's long-awaited redeemer who would save believers from their sins. We see this belief in Jesus as Redeemer already in the earliest Christian sources, the letters of Paul, written between twenty to thirty years after Jesus' death, well before the appearance of the first gospels. In his letters, Paul indicates that Jesus is the fulfillment of the written scriptures of the Jews. For Paul, belief in Jesus is essential, the only way to be right with God.

From the beginning, then, Christianity was structured as a religion that emphasized proper belief and de-emphasized cultic acts such as sacrifice. Christians did not perform sacrifices to their God because they believed Jesus had already performed the perfect and complete sacrifice on the cross. Their religion was based on accepting the sacrifice of Jesus on their behalf, rather than on performing sacrifices on his behalf.

Moreover, unlike other religions of the Greek and Roman period, Christianity was exclusivistic. No other religion—perhaps excepting Judaism—insisted that to worship their god, you could not worship other gods. Ancient religions were inclusivistic, accepting one another. If someone decided to worship a new god, such as when one moved to a new town and wished to adopt its deity, that didn't require giving up one's former god or gods. Many gods were believed to exist, all desiring worship. Christianity, however, claimed that the only way to be right with God was through belief in Jesus. This teaching made other religions wrong, and Christianity right. Faith or belief in Jesus made Christianity unique in the ancient world, its missionary consciousness contributing to its expansion and widespread growth.

The earliest Christians were persecuted in a completely ad hoc and random fashion. It appears that persecution began at the grassroots level, as alienated family members or rebuffed friends took umbrage when Christians removed themselves from public religious observance. The problems were exacerbated when disasters occurred, because these were blamed on Christians, who steadfastly refused to worship the gods. If any acts of mob violence occurred, Roman governors might step in and round up the Christians. If Christians continued to flout authority by refusing to worship the gods, they could be punished or executed. This, it seems, is the background to 1 Peter and its exhortation to perseverance.

It was not for a couple of centuries that Christians grew large enough as a group to begin to worry the Roman administration in any serious way. At that time, in the middle of the third century, serious and systematic persecutions began.

The Peril of Heresies

One of the most influential factors in the changing pattern of life in the early church was the development of arguments about the nature of Christian belief, and in particular the emergence of various groups of people who, at a later period, came to be regarded as "heretics" by proto-orthodox Christians. In reality, those who were labeled "heterodox" were those who eventually lost the argument, while the "orthodox" were those who won. The New Testament as a whole warns of false teachers and enemies within, but by the end of the first century, various groups emerged that could be regarded as heretical by proto-orthodox Christians. It is no surprise that the last books of the New Testament to be written have as their main theme warnings and arguments against heretical teachings and practices. The letters found in Revelation 2–3 (written c. 95 CE), warn against the Nicolaitans (2:6), followers of the teachings of Balaam (2:14), and a woman named Jezebel (2:20). The same holds true in the three epistles of John (dated c. 100 CE), Jude (dated 90–100 CE), and 2 Peter (dated 100–125 CE). Whether by "heresies" we refer to moral or doctrinal deviancy, the opponents attacked in this group of letters all appear to be active in Asia Minor around the same time.

The gospel of John, a book attributed to the apostle John, the son of Zebedee, was written anonymously by a Jewish Christian of the late first century CE who served as theological mentor for a Jewish Christian community called the Johannine community. This community, a cluster of congregations in Asia Minor, was considerably different from other expressions of Christian faith in the first century. Yet even that one stream of early Christianity was not monolithic, but rather exhibited diverse understandings of faith and lifestyle.[2]

In addition to the gospel, four other books of the New Testament are associated with the name "John": three letters of John and the book of Revelation. Like the gospel, the three letters are anonymous documents; their attribution to John the apostle derived from the manuscript tradition of the early church. The book of Revelation, by contrast, identifies itself as written by "John" (Rev. 1:1, 4, 9; 22:8), though it is unlikely that this person is the author of the gospel or the Johannine epistles.

There appears to have been a school of Christian thought near the end of the first century organized around a man known as John the elder, who himself may have been a disciple of John, son of Zebedee, which opens up the possibility that the Johannine literature (the gospel, the three epistles, and the book of Revelation), are the products of different members of that Johannine school. If that is so, it would account for the similarities found in these works as well as for the obvious differences.

Although tradition labeled the epistles of John as having been written by the same author as the gospel, the internal evidence does not support that conclusion.[3] In 2 and 3 John, the author calls himself "the elder," but 1 John does not indicate the identity of the author. Based on internal evidence, the author of 1 John was a person of authority in the church (or churches), for this person presumes to guide the audience in matters of faith and life. While the term "elder" claims some authority, the title may not identify an established office. It may simply refer to an elderly person who by virtue of age and experience is respected by the community. With such scarce evidence, it is not surprising that the church took nearly three centuries to bring these writings together and to attribute them to the same author, the fourth evangelist.

The form of 1 John differs markedly from that of 2 and 3 John. The latter two are clearly letters, while 1 John lacks the usual features of a letter. The document appears to be an anthology of loosely related admonitions, possibly sermonic fragments, strung together into written form. Though the structure of 1 John remains obscure, its message revolves

2. Kysar, *Maverick Gospel*, 165.

3. The material below is adapted from Kysar, *Maverick Gospel*, 165–76.

around five themes: (1) the fleshly humanity of Christ (4:2); (2) the saving work of Christ (1:7, 9; 2:2; 3:5; 4:10); (3) the understanding of sin (1:8, 10; 3:4, 8, 9; 5:16–17); (4) the importance of moral living (1:7; 2:3, 4, 6, 24; 3:7, 14; 4:5, 6, 16), based upon the commandment to "love one another" (3:11, 23; 4:7, 11–12); and (5) the "last days" (2:18, 28; 3:2; 4:17, 18). Some of these themes appear in 2 and 3 John as well.

While we are limited in our knowledge of the setting out of which and for which 1 John was written, it seems clear that a group once within a church (or churches) has withdrawn, and its members—in the view of the Johannine author—were never full participants or even authentic Christians (2:19). The differences between the author of 1 John and the separatists seem to center on proper views of Christ, sin, and morality. It appears that 1 John was written to strengthen the confidence of the original Johannine churches. The author wants to solidify the readers into a coherent group around a single understanding of Christian life and belief. The readers have been shaken by trauma in the churches and need reassurance that their understanding of Christianity is true. According to the author, the dissidents do not practice love (2:9–11; 4:20–21); they deny the humanity of Christ (2:22; 4:2–3; 5:5–6); they are allied with forces at odds with the faith of the church (2:15–16; 4:5–6); they are weapons of evil (3:8) and even the antichrists of the last days (2:18–23) because they do not maintain the teachings of the community (4:6); they claim to know and love God and to practice their faith but in fact do not (1:6; 2:9); they are thereby guilty of "mortal sin" (5:16), even though they claim to be free of sin (1:6–10; 3:3–6); and they live without moral restrictions (3:4–10).

The author is clearly prejudiced in the assessment of these dissidents, a group that is difficult to characterize but presumably during the second century blended into groups of gnostic Christians. The separatists of 1 and 2 John seem to have been the precursors of gnostic groups that denied the humanity of Jesus in favor of a purely spiritual being and were inclined to think that their Christian faith freed them from traditional morality.

The setting for 1 John is related to that of 2 John, whose author urges the readers to lead moral lives, perhaps in contrast to the dissidents (verses 5–6). These dissenters are propagating their views in nearby congregations, and the "elder" is attempting to defuse their influence. First John also counsels a view of Christ as a fleshly being, against "deceivers" who teach otherwise (verse 7). Such false Christians should be denied hospitality when they arrive (verse 10).

Third John presents a different setting, a power struggle between rivals within a congregation. A certain Diotrephes has proven himself an irritant in the congregation of which Gaius (the recipient of the letter) is a leader. An isolationist who views himself a purist, Diotrephes refuses to recognize the authority of the elder and gossips about his leadership (verse 10). He has driven off those who disagree with him and is refusing even to welcome Christian visitors. The elder in this case tries to win the loyalty of Gaius and thereby strengthen the author's influence in the congregation.

These three documents are important in the New Testament for they present a Christian community struggling to maintain its unity and integrity. The Johannine epistles show us early Christian conflict between doctrinal and ethical purity on the one hand and tolerance on the other. The twin issues of orthodoxy and authority are paramount in the emergence of the church.

The influence of false teachers is also the subject of two of the most obscure books of the New Testament, Jude and 2 Peter. These books clearly belong together, for almost the whole of Jude (in slightly modified form) is contained in 2 Peter (compare 2:1–8 with Jude 4–16). Although the author of this letter calls himself "Simon Peter, a servant and apostle of Jesus Christ" (1:1), and makes reference to his being present at the transfiguration of Jesus (1:18), his style and contents have led modern scholars to regard it as the work of an unknown author of the early second century. Unlike the style of 1 Peter, which is written in fluent koine Greek, the style of 2 Peter has been described as "pseudo-literary"; its wording is unusual, artificial, and often obscure, and according to Bruce Metzger, is "the one book in the New Testament which gains by translation."[4]

Second Peter's style and content point to a date long after Peter's lifetime. Two passages point to a late date: 3:3–4 indicates that the apostolic age is over, and 3:16 indicates that the letters of Paul have been collected and are being referred to as "scripture," something that happened long after Paul's death. Both Jude and 2 Peter hit heresy hard, yielding no compromise. This emphasis points to a period of doctrinal struggle threatening the church's unity. It would take at least two centuries before orthodox Christianity achieved doctrinal and political authority. These

---

4. Metzger, *New Testament*, 258.

letters likely originated from a group of Peter's disciples, much like the Johannine letters originated from a "school" of John's disciples.

37. Pseudonymous authorship in scripture should not be regarded as dishonest, but as a way of honoring revered antecedents presumed to have been inspired by God.

As we have noted, some of the books of the Old Testament, such as the wisdom literature attributed to Solomon, or of the New Testament, such as the gospels and the book of Acts, were anonymously written. We simply do not know their authors. In addition, many of the letters, including some attributed to Paul and others found among the General Epistles, were pseudonymous, that is, falsely attributed.

The term pseudonym means "false name," meaning that such a writing is written under a name other than the author's. Pseudonymous writers were widely known in the ancient world. Writers forged documents in someone else's name for a variety of reasons, sometimes to honor a revered ancestor, but most commonly to gain an audience for their work. Even in Christian circles, this practice was common, as is the case for the vast apocryphal literature falsely attributed to apostles of Jesus or to their disciples. If people wanted their views heard and wrote a treatise using their own name, no one might read it, but if it was attributed to Plato or Paul, it might have a chance.

Forgery was relatively common practice in the ancient world, in part because there were no copyright laws. In addition, because books could not be mass produced, it was difficult for most people to compare a book in hand with other books by the same author to see whether they were similar in vocabulary and style. Furthermore, most people couldn't read, making forgery easy to go undetected. In secular society, people often forged writings in the name of famous authors for profit. If a new library needed original works by important authors, an underground market developed. In philosophical schools, advanced students often produced treatises in the name of a revered teacher, often as an act of homage. This, clearly, was widely practiced in religious circles as well.

To hide the traces of their forgery, forgers typically tried to imitate the style of the author they were claiming to be, using his vocabulary, and imitating some of his better known phraseology. The forger might also added biographical remarks, such as we find in 2 Timothy 4:13 or 2 Peter

1:18. We know that there were a number of forgeries of Paul's name, such as Third Corinthians and a forged correspondence between Paul and the most famous Roman philosopher of his day, Seneca, an advisor to the emperor Nero, in which Seneca praises Paul for being one of the greatest minds of his day. Many scholars are persuaded that the Deutero-Pauline epistles of 2 Thessalonians, Ephesians, and possibly Colossians, in addition to the pastoral epistles, are pseudonymous. Such judgments are principally based on questions of vocabulary, writing style, and theology. Of course, it is possible that Paul, Peter, or John simply adopted a different vocabulary, writing style, and theology when writing these letters, or that they dictated to scribes, in some cases giving them a free editorial hand, but that happened regularly with their authentic writings, and the results are negligible. In one case, Paul mentions explicitly that he has written the final greeting with his own hand, presumably as a guarantee of genuineness (1 Cor. 16:21), but even this device was subject to forgery, as Colossians 4:18 and 2 Thessalonians 3:17 attest. Near the close of Galatians Paul says to his readers, "See what large letters I make when I am writing in my own hand!" (6:11). Since the subject changes at this point, it is probable that here he has taken over the pen from his amanuensis. In Philemon (verse 19) Paul writes a personal note that is apparently different from the script in the rest of the letter. From this data we may conclude that Paul's usual practice was to dictate the bulk of a given letter to a scribe, occasionally adding notes in his own handwriting, and perhaps also correcting what the scribe had written.

We have already noted the comment in 1 Peter 5:12 regarding Silvanus, who the author supposedly used as a secretary. In the case of several other letters (both Pauline and General), it is now thought that a friend and follower of the apostle drew up the document in the name of the apostle, possibly after the death of the supposed author.

Assignment

Having read chapter 13, answer the following questions, writing the answers in your journal. [If you are in a study group, be prepared to share your views with others in the class.]

1. In your estimation, would the fact that a book is pseudonymous necessarily compromise its authority? That is to say, could it still convey true, important, or normative teaching? Explain your answer.

2. Choose several of the figures we have considered from the New Testament, such as Jesus, Matthew, Luke, Paul, or the author of Hebrews, and discuss ways in which they can be seen as both Jewish and anti-Jewish. Do you find anything in the New Testament that you would label "anti-Semitic"?

3. We have seen that pagan religions were mostly tolerant of one another, none making "exclusivistic" claims for itself. Christianity seems to be different. Do you think of Christianity as necessarily exclusivistic (that is, as claiming that it alone is "true" and "right")? Should Christians be tolerant or intolerant of other religions and views? Why or why not?

4. Given the enormous social, economic, and political power of Christianity in the modern world, what, in your opinion, is the ongoing relevance of writings such as 1 Peter today? Are Christians still a persecuted minority?

5. What is the primary insight I/we gained from this chapter or session?

Chapter 14

Three Things to Know about the Book of Revelation

THE BOOK OF REVELATION, also called the Apocalypse of John, is a fitting close to the Old and New Testament, for its final chapters depict the consummation toward which the entire biblical message is focused. Revelation may be described as an inspired picture-book that, by an accumulation of magnificent poetic imagery, makes a powerful appeal to the reader's imagination. Many of the details of its pictures are intended to contribute to the total impression, and are not to be isolated and interpreted with detached literalism.

> 38. *The book of Revelation, the most fascinating book of the New Testament, is also the most misunderstood.*

The book of Revelation barely made it into the New Testament. In antiquity, every great interpreter had difficulty with it. It was one of a number of apocalypses in circulation during the church's early centuries, and most if not all such writings were regarded with suspicion by church leaders. The reasons for this suspicion are obvious: apocalyptic literature conveyed a note of desperation and finality, its imagery was bizarre, its vocabulary extreme, its tone vindictive, and its God vengeful. The book itself seemed incongruous with the reconciling message of forgiveness found in the gospels and incompatible with the self-sacrificing love of God exemplified by Jesus. Even after its official acceptance into the canon, many Christians remained hesitant to include Revelation as a part of their Bible. The Protestant Reformers often sided with this hesitance. Martin Luther, for example, included the book in his Bible, but denied it functional status because he found its christology deficient. John Calvin passed over it in silence, writing commentaries on every other New Testament book. Among modern biblical scholars, Rudolf Bultmann, who wrote a famous commentary on John's gospel, relegated Revelation to the margin of the church's faith and life. To this day, Catholic and Protestant lectionaries include only minimal readings from Revelation, and the Greek Orthodox lectionary omits it altogether. On the other hand, Christian thinkers from Irenaeus to Augustine in early centuries to Walter Rauschenbush and Paul Minear in modern times have found Revelation to measure up to its canonical role of providing direction and sustenance for the church's life and mission, particularly in extraordinary times.

Having taught courses on Revelation for many years, I have always been impressed by the high level of interest and curiosity that college students have about this book. The teaching experience is rewarding because the class is always full, the level of sincerity is high, and the degree of interaction is intense. When I ask students their motivation for taking the course, their answers reflect both curiosity and apprehension. Many are curious about the book, having heard that it contains coded predictions about the end of the world, with current conflicts in the Middle East perhaps leading up to the great battle of Armageddon, which will end our known world. Some assume that Revelation provides clues to the identity of the figure known as the antichrist, whom they think will soon gain control of the global economy and dominate the whole world. Others are apprehensive, having been repelled by the views of religious groups that seem obsessed by the coming end of the world. Some assume that Revelation is a dangerous book understood only by experts. Many adults are repulsed by the book's intense imagery, feeling that exposure to this literature could add to the high level of violence already present in our society.

We are not alone in these assessments. Major historical figures were also drawn to the Apocalypse for different reasons. For example, the brilliant scientist and mathematician Sir Isaac Newton was absolutely fascinated by Revelation, spending as much time studying the Bible as he did math and science. In a book called *Observations upon the Prophecies of Daniel and the Apocalypse of Saint John*, Newton indicates his desire to decipher the mysteries of Revelation, much as he had been able to decipher the mysteries of the natural world. Having formulated the law of gravity and the laws of motion, he figured he could formulate the laws for interpreting apocalyptic writings. He thought that if his telescope could help people to see into the deep mysteries of space, then Revelation might help people look into the deep mysteries of time and history, accurately predicting specific future events. Using a chronological understanding of particular visions in Revelation, Newton thought that the mysteries of history were unfolding with a kind of mathematical precision. His scheme involved a great deal of guesswork, and his approach to Revelation was not well received. The reason is clear: he was not trained in theology or in biblical interpretation.

Another famous individual who had his own issues with Revelation was the British novelist D. H. Lawrence, author of such novels as *The Rainbow* and *Lady Chatterley's Lover*. Lawrence also had a kind of obsession with Revelation, not because he found it fascinating but because he found it appalling. Near the end of his life he wrote a book called *Apocalypse*, completed just two months before his death. In it he called Revelation unpoetic, ugly, and vindictive. He thought that the book was written by a second-rate mind for people with second-rate minds. He insisted that its violent imagery was the opposite of Jesus' message of love. He thought that Revelation was written by someone who could not wait for the world to end so that he could see cast into the eternal lake of fire all the people he didn't like.

As we conclude our study of the Bible with Revelation, we must recognize this book's extraordinary ability to generate both curiosity and confusion. And we need to set the record straight. The book is not as bizarre and vindictive as many have imagined. Furthermore, its message need not be viewed as incongruous with the biblical message of love, reconciliation, and forgiveness. While Revelation's method and theological conceptuality are relatively different from the rest of the New Testament, once they are appreciated in their own right, they contribute to make this book not only one of the finest literary works in the Christian canon, but also one of the greatest theological achievements of early Christianity.

39. Genre and historical context are essential for understanding the meaning and message of the book of Revelation.

Although parts of the book (for example, chapter 11) may have been written before the fall of Jerusalem in 70 CE, it is probable that the author, whose name is John, put the book in its present form toward the close of the reign of the emperor Domitian (81–96). It was then that Domitian began to demand that his subjects address him as "Lord and God" and worship his image. For refusing to do so, many Christians were executed (6:9; 13:15); others, like John (1:9), were exiled, and all were threatened. This book is a call to hope for the persecuted, assuring them that, despite the worst that the Roman empire could do, God reigns supreme, and Christ, who died and is alive forevermore (1:18), has the power to overcome all evil. Thus, John closes his book with the prayer, "Come, Lord Jesus!" (22:30).

Recognizing the genre of any piece of writing is important to its interpretation. The term "revelation" derives from a Latin word that is the equivalent of the Greek word "apocalypse," which means "an unveiling" or "a revealing." Apocalypse refers to a literary genre widely used by both Jews and Christians. Typically pseudonymous, apocalypses describe bizarre visions of a prophet, who is taken on a tour of heaven or told the fate of the earth (or both), in wildly symbolic language. Apocalypses are directed to people in the author's own context who are experiencing inordinate hardship and suffering. The books are designed to offer hope by showing that, contrary to all appearances, God is still sovereign over the world and will soon intervene to right its wrongs.

Apocalyptic literature is written for people who desire insight into the meaning of life. Such writings revolve around two mysteries posed by people everywhere, even by those who don't identify with any religious tradition: the problem of evil and the nature of hope. To be human is to consider such issues, and in so doing to recognize that one is not so much solving them as exploring mysteries. And the greatest mystery, which prompted the prophets of Israel and Judah as well as "the Prophet of Patmos," was the mystery of God. When John recounts his own vision of God, he weaves together images of the heavenly throne and the six-winged seraphs from the book of Isaiah (6:1–3) with a description of the crystal dome and the mysterious four creatures from the book of Ezekiel (chapters 1 and 10).

In order to better understand the apocalyptic worldview, how it originated and why it was so important in the ancient world, we need to understand how the Hebrew prophets dealt with themes of evil and hope.

When we think of the prophetic writings and the problem of evil, it is helpful to think in terms of three concentric circles:[1]

- At the center the prophets address the evils within the people of Israel (including violence, abuse of power, and other forms of social, political, and economic injustice);
- Beyond this inner circle we find a wider one, which takes into account the evils of other nations;
- Finally there is an outer circle of concern, where the prophets speak in cosmic terms of universal suffering and a curse that affects the inhabitants of earth and even earth itself.

Such prophetic themes helped shape the book of Revelation. Like the Old Testament prophets, John starts at the center. "He calls for repentance among his own people, the members of the Christian community, and he also gives them hope for life in the New Jerusalem. Then the author moves outward to the nations. He pictures a battle in which the nations are defeated, and yet he gives them hope for a place in God's city as well. And finally the author goes out still further and speaks of death being overcome and the heavens and earth being made new."[2] The contours of the expanding prophetic tradition have become John's.

While the themes of evil and hope in the prophetic writings were composed between the eighth and the fifth centuries BCE, the apocalyptic tradition emerged in Jewish circles during the centuries that followed. The two centuries before and after Christ can be described as a time of apocalyptic fervor across the Mediterranean world, during which period there appeared a considerable number of Jewish and Christian writings that belong to the category of apocalyptic literature. Though Jewish apocalyptic literature is said to begin with the book of Daniel, apocalyptic tendencies can be seen earlier, in passages such as Isaiah 24–27, Ezekiel 38–39, and Zechariah 9–14, which explains frequent references to the approaching "Day of the Lord." Important Jewish apocalyptic writings outside the Old Testament include the book of Enoch, the Apocalypse of Baruch, the Fourth Book of Ezra, the Ascension of Isaiah, the Apocalypse of Zephaniah, and parts of the Sibylline Oracles. The first-century Jewish community that wrote the Dead Sea Scrolls also composed and preserved apocalypses.

1. Koester, *Apocalypse*, 16, 27–29.
2. Koester, *Apocalypse*, 29–30.

One feature in particular distinguishes the apocalyptic tradition from the older prophetic tradition: a sharp dualistic contrast between the power of good and the power of evil, between people who side with goodness and those who side with wickedness. Apocalyptic thinking views history as consisting of two ages, the present, in which evil is operative, and the coming one, when only goodness will prevail. According to the apocalyptic mindset, evil is so great that humans cannot eliminate it; only God can do so. Divine intervention (often called the "Day of the Lord") is imminent, at which time the world will be judged, the righteous vindicated, and all things set right. While the prophetic tradition spoke of good and evil largely in human terms, the apocalyptic tradition viewed evil cosmically, as a demonic force operative in the world.

Christian Transformation of Apocalyptic

As we have seen, the New Testament writings are heavily influenced by apocalyptic thinking.

While the early Christians shared basic convictions with Jewish apocalyptic, one finds not only similarities but striking differences. For example, the New Testament has transformed the apocalyptic view by announcing that God has done something totally and radically new through the life, death, and resurrection of Jesus Christ. A "new creation" has begun to appear (2 Cor. 5:17). The New Testament portrays Jesus not merely as an apocalyptic visionary who announces the mystery of God's kingdom to a select few; rather, it considers him to be the sign of God's kingdom in the present historical age. Jesus' crucifixion, crowned with resurrection, signifies that Jesus is the victor in the long struggle with evil. The New Testament announces that the period of waiting is over, for the king has come and the dominion of God has already been inaugurated. In other words, the Christian gospel has altered the time scheme of apocalyptic, with its sharp separation of "the present evil age" from "the age to come," so that the old must pass away before the new can come. Rather the two ages are like overlapping circles, for already God has introduced the new age through Jesus Christ even while the old age persists. In the Christian reinterpretation of apocalyptic, the supreme sign of the new age is the resurrection of Christ from the dead. As Paul argues in 1 Corinthians 15, this end-time event has already occurred in the midst of the present age. So near and certain is God's triumph that Paul can go so far as to say that not everyone will die (1 Cor. 15:51).

To be sure, the Christian community lives in the tension of the "already" and the "not yet." Using the symbolic language of apocalyptic, the trumpet signaling God's final triumph has not yet sounded. There is still a period of waiting for the final consummation, the coming of God's kingdom fully on earth and the appearance of Jesus Christ in glory. But this waiting is not the expectation of counting the days or speculating on an apocalyptic timetable. For already God's triumph has been manifest in the resurrection of Christ.

Finally, "apocalyptic has given to the early Christian community a profound grasp of the meaning of God's triumph in Jesus Christ. God's victory is liberation from the power of sin through divine forgiveness, displayed in the vicarious and atoning death of Jesus. The apocalyptic perspective, however, pushes Christian interpreters to go beyond the prophetic message of sin and forgiveness and to proclaim God's triumph over all the powers of darkness, chaos, evil, and death."[3] Paul lists some of those powers in his great victory proclamation at the end of Romans 8, where he declares that through Christ we are "more than conquerors" (Rom. 8:37).

The call to conquer is fundamental to the structure and theme of the book of Revelation, the apocalypse that brings the Christian canon to a close. Everything that is said in the seven messages to the churches has this aim, expressed in the promise to the conquerors that concludes each (Rev. 2:7; 11, 17, 28; 3:5, 12, 21). Like Jesus, the real victors are the martyr-witnesses, those who are faithful to God even to the point of death. Conquering is not represented as something to which only some are called, but as the only way for Christians to reach their eschatological destiny. According to Revelation 21:7–8, there are only two options: to conquer and inherit the promises or to suffer the second death in the lake of fire. John's message in Revelation is a call for resistance against evil, not however, through violence but through kingdom living and witnessing.

The book of Revelation brings to a magnificent climax the biblical drama that opens in Genesis with Creation and the Garden. The whole historical drama is embraced within the redemptive timespan of the one who is "the Alpha and the Omega, the beginning and the end" (Rev. 21:6). True to the Christian faith, the author of Revelation affirms that

---

3. Anderson, *Contours of Old Testament Theology*, 335.

the kingdom of Christ has already broken into history. The divine victory, which in the present evil age can be discerned only by faith, ultimately will be openly manifest, for every creature will attest the triumph of God's redemptive love (Rev. 5:13). Thus the Lamb (Christ) that was slain is pictured imaginatively as the final conqueror who at the end will overthrow all forces of evil that had corrupted history. Christ's victory ushers in the "new heaven and the new earth" (Rev. 21:1).

40. *The book of Revelation was not written to provide a blueprint of future history.*

In order to understand the purpose of Revelation, the following guidelines are instructive. Revelation was written:

- to challenge the churches of Asia to greater faithfulness and to repent for past failure;
- to comfort and encourage those who were undergoing persecution and personal distress on account of their faith, and who were pondering the delay of Christ's promised return;
- to disclose the person and work of Christ and to remind believers that the future belongs to Jesus Christ and not to emperors or other temporal authorities;
- to critique and expose the absolutizing of political and military power embodied in the Roman imperial cult;
- to provide Christians with a philosophy or perspective (but not a chronology) of history.

While the first four principles seem largely self-explanatory, the fifth needs clarification. In a sense, Revelation is like great art. When viewers enter an art gallery, for example, they don't go to see the familiar world with conventional eyes. They wish to be guided by the perspective of the artist, to see aspects of the world in a new light. When Van Gogh painted the night sky, light did not merely shimmer; it exploded. He used colors in an extreme way—blue that was too intense, gold that was too bright—in order to provide a perspective on the night, so that one could see the familiar in new ways. When Picasso painted a person, it was as if he had created a picture of a person with eyes and ears, arms and legs, and then shattered the picture into a dozen pieces before reassembling them in a collage. All the pieces are there, but disjointed. We normally do not see people like that, but the artist has shown us a way of seeing the fragmentation we might otherwise have missed. Painting provides a new perspective, a new way of seeing; something like that is going on in Revelation.

If we are looking for something that merely describes the world, then we need to look elsewhere. However, if what we want is perspective, one that startles and challenges, then Revelation is very much what we want. The writer uses wild colors and fantastic images that shape the way we see the power of evil, the nature of hope, the character of God, and the character of the world. The scenes are unsettling and uplifting, disturbing and encouraging, sorrowful and joyous. And all of this allows the readers of Revelation to see with new eyes the world in which they live.

Since ancient times people have tried to turn Revelation into a roadmap for the end of the world, and thus far all of those expectations have been wrong. Others, thankfully, have learned from their mistakes and have come to realize that Revelation can best be read for what it might have to say about spiritual life in the present. The book opens up a transcendent world in which the presence of God is vivid and palpable, inviting people to consider what it means to live in God's presence and how that shapes a way of life.

Interpreting the Book of Revelation

While Revelation can be viewed in a number of ways, there are four traditional schools of interpretation.

1. *Preterist Approach.* This view, sometimes called the "contemporary-historical" approach because it emphasizes John and his contemporaries, stresses the importance of the original setting. This method is followed by practically every modern biblical scholar, of all theological persuasions. This approach applies the same historical method to Revelation that scholars use for the preceding books of the New Testament, attempting to determine the meaning of a text in its original historical context before determining its current meaning and application. This view assumes that John had a relevant message to the churches of his day, that they understood the message, and that the modern interpreter should not accept any interpretation of the book that its first readers would not have understood. It represents a corrective to unbridled futuristic speculation.

Early Christians were hoping for divine intervention that in their day would bring the anticipated kingdom of God to earth and end the hated Roman system of domination. However, this expectation resulted in frustrated hope, for the eternal kingdom did not come as expected. Over time, other schools of interpretation arose.

2. *Idealist Approach.* This view, also labeled "poetic," "spiritual," or "non-historical," represents the eternal conflict of good and evil. This approach underscores the general promise of God to be with his people always. The imagery is taken from apocalyptic views of the first century and from the general language of myth. The value of this approach is that it allows Revelation to speak symbolically to people in every time and place. It minimizes, however, the specific historical references known to the original audience and does not allow for concrete significance, thereby denying its character as a real letter.

3. *Historicist Approach.* This view, also called "church-historical," "world-historical," or "chronological," approaches the book as a symbolic presentation of the entire course of church history, from the first century to the end of history. Chapters 2–3 are regarded as addressing the church of John's own time, but the visions of chapters 4–22 are interpreted as predicting all future history. In practice this means that each interpreter saw John as predicting the course of history down to his or her own time, which was generally viewed to be the last period predicted by Revelation. Since this approach flourished in Europe, Revelation was understood to predict the course of European history, primarily church history. The value of this approach is that it emphasizes the prophetic nature of Revelation and allows for specific fulfillment. It also affirms God's activity throughout history and maintains God's sovereignty over history. But this view eliminates any real meaning for the first audience and is highly parochial. It also misunderstands prophecy by reducing it to prediction. In addition, it allegorizes Revelation, subjecting it to far-fetched spiritualization of historical events. Finally, the variety of interpretations produced by this method cancel each other out, thus invalidating the approach.

4. *Futurist Approach.* This view, also called "dispensationalist" and "premillennialist," considers Revelation to be predictive, but it differs from the preceding approach in two important ways: (a) the seven churches of chapters 2 and 3 are no longer real churches in first-century Asia but represent seven consecutive stages of church history, from the apostolic church (Ephesus) to the apostate church of the last days (Laodicea); (b)

the visions of chapters 4 through 22 are yet to be fulfilled. These events will take place in the last few years of world history, in the period immediately preceding the return of Christ. Advocates of this position see themselves as living in the eleventh hour of history, at the start of the final countdown.

This interpretation is correct insofar as it recognizes that Revelation deals with God's activity throughout history. Among its major problems is that it transfers the context of Revelation from the first century to that of the interpreter's lifetime, thus making the book meaningless to its original audience. It takes a hyperliteralistic approach to Revelation, misconstruing the nature of prophecy and the imagery of apocalyptic literature in general, and it generally supports a sectarian understanding of Christianity.

This view is the most recent of the four types of interpretation, having been devised by a group of fundamentalist ministers during the late nineteenth century, notably John Nelson Darby in England, and then popularized by the American lawyer Charles Ingersoll Scofield in his Scofield Reference Bible. Despite lacking a theological education, Scofield founded in Dallas, Texas a nondenominational Bible School that continued after his death as Dallas Theological Seminary, which became a major center for the dissemination of this dispensational view.[4] This interpretation has become quite popular in the media and among evangelicals today. It is a dangerous approach, however, particularly when it is associated with current events and tied in to America's role in the Middle East, since it often advocates the necessity of a nuclear war as part of God's plan "predicted" in Revelation.

The following principles are important in interpreting the book of Revelation.

1. *Keep in mind the historical context.* If we want to understand Revelation, we must recognize that it was not written to us. As a letter, Revelation contains a particular message to a particular situation and not a collection of "general principles" or "universal ideas." It must be read in terms of the original hearer-readers and their situation.

2. *Do not read Revelation as encoded message.* It has sometimes been suggested that in view of the political situation under which Revelation was written, John wrote his message in code so that Christians but not

---

4. Dispensationalists have developed various schemes to support their belief that God relates to humans in different ways during history. This system of interpretation divides biblical history into a series of covenants known as "dispensations."

the Roman authorities could understand it. This view is untenable on various counts: (a) Only a fraction of the visionary material deals with Rome, yet all the visions are expressed in symbolic language; (b) the references to Rome are transparent (e.g. 17:9, 18), so that only the dullest Romans would be fooled; (c) there are many undisguised statements that could be taken as subversive by the Romans—including references to God or Christ as king (11:15) as well as references to Christians having a kingdom (1:6); (d) unlike a code, John's symbols are traditional and widespread. John used symbols in order to communicate what could not be expressed in any other way, not to conceal things that could be said more directly.[5] Encoded language is a kind of literal language; all one needs is the key. Revelation is not code language. It does not so much conceal meaning as provide perspective.

3. *Always look beyond the literal approach.* Revelation's language, akin to poetry, is pictorial and polyvalent—expressive and evocative. It does not appeal to logic but to the emotions, using symbols that are tensive, not referential. Attempts to express Revelation's images and metaphors in factual language rob them of their power of persuasion.

The distinction between "steno symbols" and "tensive symbols," made popular by Philip Wheelwright, or between "sign" and "symbol," suggested by Paul Tillich, is helpful. "Sign" language, in our culture, is represented, for example, by traffic signs, which convey precise information. When a traffic light is red, the meaning is straightforward and unambiguous. Traffic lights function as "steno symbols" in that they do not produce any tension in the mind. Tensive symbols, on the other hand, create tension in the mind. John's language is not the language of signs but of symbols, which are evocative. Unlike "signs," John's symbols are polyvalent: they *increase* tension, suggesting images and overtones of meaning that cannot be reduced to one level of meaning. As a mythopoetic work, Revelation is "not like a window to the world but is more like an onion or a rose with layers and layers of meaning . . . One could liken Revelation's symbolic narrative function to a prism refracting rich meaning in different and multiple ways."[6]

Much that is contained in Revelation is best perceived by the ear and the imagination. The book is unique in appealing primarily to our imagination—not, however, a loose or reckless imagination, but a

---

5. Boring, *Revelation*, 54–55.
6. Schüsler Fiorenza, *Revelation*, 19.

disciplined one. The book contains a series of word pictures that convey an overall impression. Many of the details of these pictures are intended to contribute to that total impression, and are not to be allegorized or interpreted literally.

Ecstatic experience of various kinds is generally an aspect of human religion, and "visions and revelations" seem to have been quite common among the prophetic figures in the early church, as Paul and Acts note (1 Cor. 14; 2 Cor. 12:1–10; Acts 10:1–23; 22:17; 27:21–26). While John was one of those early Christian prophets who experienced visions and revelations, we should not take this to mean that Revelation is simply the "reporting" of what he "saw" or "heard" in his visions. As Eugene Boring states in his commentary on Revelation: "The images from the Scripture and John's religious tradition that resided in his imagination were already active in the revelatory experience itself, providing the raw materials that were reshaped by his visionary experience. In later reflection and composition he used all the resources of his tradition and his creative literary imagination to express the visions to his hearer-readers, painting them in colors drawn from the rich palate already prepared in the Bible and other prophetic and apocalyptic tradition. In their present form the visions are literary compositions based on John's visionary experience, not merely descriptive reports of what he 'actually' saw and heard."[7]

4. *Be aware of hyperbole.* John's symbolic language includes a tendency toward hyperbole, a feature of prophetic discourse in general and of apocalyptic literature in particular. Jesus, along with his Jewish contemporaries, delighted in sharp contrasts and extreme statements. Teachings about a log in someone's eye (Matt. 7:3–5) or about hating one's family in order to follow Jesus (Luke 14:26) must be seen in the light of the Near-Eastern characteristic of exaggeration and are not intended to be taken literally. Like his Semitic counterparts, John combines contextual specificity with eschatological hyperbole. For example, in speaking about the power, dominion, and worship of the beast in chapter 13 or about the mission and witness of the church, he consistently uses universal language. The church is drawn from *every* nation (5:9) and constitutes an *innumerable* multitude (7:9); its witness, symbolized by the angel's proclamation of the eternal gospel, goes out to *all* nations (14:6); the expected period of trial under the rule of the beast is coming on the *whole* world (3:10); the beast has authority over *every* nation and

---

7. Boring, *Revelation*, 27.

is worshipped by *all* the inhabitants of the earth (13:7–8); the second beast enforces his worship by a system of totalitarian control of economic life (13:12–17), which far exceeds the realities or possibilities of the first century; the dragon, the beast, and the false prophet assemble the kings of the *whole* world for the final battle (16:14); and Babylon deceives *all* the nations (14:8; 18:3, 23). These references depict the impending conflict between the church and the beast in terms that are eschatologically universal rather than historically realistic.

This does not mean that John predicts, in some distant future, a universal, totalitarian, anti-Christian state. The hyperbole is of the same kind as when John writes *as though* all Christians are to suffer martyrdom (cf. 6:9–11; 7:14; 11:7–10; 12:11; 14:1–5). This is how Christians conquer in Revelation, through faithful witness unto death, viewed as the continuation of Christ's sacrificial work by his followers. Those who follow the Lamb resemble the one they follow "wherever he goes" (14:4). The hyperbole makes clear what is at stake in the conflict between the church and the evil empire. The beast (Babylon) represents, in a thousand other historical forms, any society that usurps ultimate power before the coming of God's eschatological reign. Hyperbole gives these symbols intrinsic power to reach as far as the End. Thus Revelation, in its predictive element, found fulfillment in its own immediate future and also finds a continuing relevance that transcends its original context.

5. *Read Revelation as a pastoral letter.* John's letter should be read as a pastoral letter, not as a theological treatise. In a treatise or book the author is a particular person, but the readers are unknown to the author or to one another. The distinctive aspect about a real letter is that both the author and the readers are particular persons. A real letter presupposes the particular situation of the readers and addresses it specifically. Revelation is a letter to Christians John knew and for whom he felt a pastoral responsibility. The letter was intended to be read by a worship leader to a community gathered for praise and prayer.

The imagery of Revelation, which seems bizarre by modern standards, is mostly taken from the tradition of images familiar to first-century Christians who heard the Bible read in worship services, much like the tradition of Jewish worshippers who gathered in synagogues to hear their scriptures read during worship. In keeping with this tradition, contemporary students of Revelation might wish to gather in church, sing a hymn of praise, join in prayer, and then listen as a liturgist reads the book of Revelation in its entirety. Better yet, members of one congregation might wish to read Revelation from the perspective of Christians in other cultures and with people who have been marginalized and have found hope in this book.

6. *Embrace the message of hope instead of fear.* In Revelation, the outcome of history is assured: Jesus has already won the victory through his death and resurrection. Because God reigns, hope is always near. This letter was not written to terrify people but to encourage first-century believers to be faithful despite personal suffering and believers of all ages to persevere in hope, despite uncertainty and adverse conditions. God is in control, not evil or capricious fate. Hope is the most important message of Revelation. Readers must always take into consideration the goal in 21:5, which acts as a compass pointing to the book's "true north": "I am making all things new." In Revelation, these are the *only* words spoken directly by the one sitting on the throne. This is where the Bible's storyline is headed, and it is incumbent upon people of faith to discern that the arc of history is bent toward hope.

7. *Read Revelation canonically.* Though the Bible is a "library of books," with a variety of theologies and conflicting points of view, it contains a unified story. Biblical theologians see the Bible as a narrative drama, with God as the main character. As noted earlier, the following headings adequately describe the plot: Creation, Covenant, Christ, Church, and Consummation. The book of Revelation brings the Christian canon to a close, figuratively and literarily, since its place in the Bible and its message is associated with the consummation of history: "The kingdom of the world has become the kingdom of our Lord and of his Christ, and he shall reign for ever and ever" (11:15). In vivid pictures the book of Revelation establishes God's just rule throughout history, depicting the triumphant finale of the biblical drama with scenes of the last battle and the last judgment.

Revelation, however, is more than simply the concluding act in the biblical drama. The book should be viewed, not merely as a dramatic finale or a bizarre appendix to the biblical narrative, but as an appropriate capstone to scripture, in harmony with key biblical themes and encompassing each of the Bible's principal headings. In this sense, Revelation may be described as a Bible in miniature.

Assignment

Having read chapter 14, answer the following questions, writing the answers in your journal. [If you are in a study group, be prepared to share your views with others in the class.]

1. In what ways is the apocalyptic worldview found in the book of Revelation similar to and different from the apocalyptic views of Old Testament prophets? Of Jesus? Of Paul?

2. Many Christians over the centuries have read the book of Revelation as a blueprint for events that were soon to come and thus to see it as a source of hope. Were they wrong in so doing? If you read the book historically, as addressed to Christians suffering in the days of Rome and not as a descriptive account of things yet to take place, can you still find its message inspired by hope?

3. Read Revelation 21–22. What do these chapters teach you about "a new heaven and a new earth"? About heaven and eternal life?

4. In your estimation, does the image of the New Jerusalem represent a reality at the end of history or something else entirely? Does John's depiction of the New Jerusalem as coming down out of heaven imply that heaven and earth are ultimately different perspectives of the same reality, or do you view heaven and earth as eternally separate realities? Explain your answer.

5. What is the primary insight I/we gained from this chapter or session?

Chapter 15

The Application of Scripture

As we noted in chapter 2, reading and interpreting scripture involves three processes: understanding, exposition, and application. Understanding and exposition lead to application. It seems obvious that understanding and exposition are needed in reading any book, but application seems unique to reading the Bible or, at least, to religious literature. It is, after all, possible to read a book with merely "academic" interest, that is, without any concern to apply its message to one's own life.

There are, of course, other kinds of writing than simply religious literature where application is important. Laws, for example, exist principally to be applied, and much of the biblical (certainly the Jewish) literature relates to ethical life. But quite apart from this narrow sense of the word "application," all reading of texts is in a broader sense as concerned with application as with understanding and exposition. We read books because we expect to "get something out" of them; we expect to benefit in some way from what we read.

In the case of the Bible, exposition tends to pass naturally into application. When we expound the text in a way that takes account of our own concerns as well as those of its authors, we are trying to find ways of making it as fruitful in our own context as it was in its original context. Most scholars who have written on the theology of the Bible have had as a further aim to make the Bible come alive in the present by showing that what was true then can still be true now.

Because the Bible is the foundation document for both Judaism and Christianity, people will have quite varied ways of finding spiritual value in it, and if some of these are not strictly ways of applying the Bible itself but ways of applying insights reached by studying the Bible, that only demonstrates how inspirational the Bible is. Like other great classics of literature and religion, the study of the Bible can stimulate an endless diversity of new thoughts and ideas. Application, in this sense, is not a form of slavish imitation, but of expansive possibility.

We conclude this study of scripture with questions, for that is how students approach the Bible. If we want to understand a biblical text, bombard it with questions. The Bible demands questions because it demands honesty. It might not answer all of our questions, but we need to ask them to determine if they can be answered. The answers to our questions will come from understanding and exposition. That is why the more time we spend in the descriptive and dialogical process, the more authentic and practical will be our results.

As we examine the meaning of biblical texts in our contemporary world, we are guided by two questions: (a) what does this passage mean to me? (in other words, what does it say to me, how does it work in my life?), and (b) what implications does this passage have for others? In application, we begin with ourselves. If something doesn't work in my life, then what authority do I have to share it with someone else?

Assignment

Having read chapter 15, answer the following questions, writing the answers in your journal. [If you are in a study group, be prepared to share your views with others in the class.]

The following nine questions are helpful to ask whenever you read a passage of scripture. To start, consider applying them to Luke 14:25–17:10. Here Jesus gives a series of parables and instructions. Using the skills of understanding, exposition, and application, answer the nine questions, based on the passage from Luke:[1]

1. Is there an example for me to follow?
2. Is there a sin to avoid?
3. Is there a condition to meet?
4. Is there a promise to claim?
5. Is there a prayer to repeat?

---

1. These questions are taken from Hendricks, *Living by the Book*, 338–42.

6. Is there a command to obey?
7. Is there a belief to challenge?
8. Is there a challenge to face?
9. Is there a verse to memorize?

Bibliography

Achtemeier, Paul J. *The Inspiration of Scripture: Problems and Proposals*. Philadelphia: Westminster, 1980.
Anders, Max. *30 Days to Understanding the Bible*. Expanded edition. Nashville, TN: Thomas Nelson, 2011.
Anderson, Bernhard W. *Contours of Old Testament Theology*. Minneapolis: Fortress, 1999.
———. *Understanding the Old Testament*. 5th ed. Upper Saddle River, NJ: Pearson Prentice Hall, 2007.
———. *The Unfolding Drama of the Bible*. 4th ed. Minneapolis: Fortress, 2006.
Archer, Gleason. *A Survey of Old Testament Introduction*. Rev. ed. Chicago: Moody, 1979.
Borg, Marcus J. *The God We Never Knew*. New York: HarperSanFrancisco, 1998.
———. *The Heart of Christianity*. New York: HarperSanFrancisco, 2004.
———. *Meeting Jesus Again for the First Time*. New York: HarperSanFrancisco, 1994.
———. *Reading the Bible Again for the First Time*. New York: HarperSanFrancisco, 2001.
Borg, Marcus J. and John Dominic Crossan. *The First Paul*. New York: HarperOne, 2009.
Borg, Marcus J., and N. T. Wright. *The Meaning of Jesus: Two Visions*. New York: HarperSanFrancisco, 1999.
Boring, M. Eugene. *Revelation*. Interpretation: A Bible Commentary for Teaching and Preaching. Louisville: John Knox, 1989.
Brown, Raymond E. *An Introduction to the New Testament*. New York: Doubleday, 1997.
Brown, Raymond E., et al. *The New Jerome Biblical Commentary*. Upper Saddle River, NJ: Prentice Hall, 1990.
Bruce, F. F. *The New Testament Development of Old Testament Themes*. Grand Rapids, Eerdmans, 1968.
———. *Paul, Apostle of the Heart Set Free*. Grand Rapids: Eerdmans, 1991.
Brueggemann, Walter. *Genesis*. Interpretation: A Bible Commentary for Teaching and Preaching. Atlanta: John Knox, 1982.
———. *Theology of the Old Testament*. Minneapolis: Fortress, 1997.
Burridge, Kenelm. *New Heaven, New Earth*. New York: Schocken, 1969.
Cadbury, Henry J. *The Making of Luke–Acts*. London: SPCK, 1958 (1927).
Caird, George B. *Revelation of St. John the Divine*. Harper's New Testament Commentary. New York: Harper & Row, 1966.

Bibliography

Caird, G. B., and L. D. Hurst. *New Testament Theology*. Oxford: Clarendon, 1994.
Cassidy, Richard J. *Jesus, Politics, and Society: A Study of Luke's Gospel*. Maryknoll, NY: Orbis, 1978.
Chadwick, Nora K. *Poetry and Prophecy*. Cambridge: Cambridge University Press, 1942.
Childs, Brevard, *Biblical Theology in Crisis*. Philadelphia: Westminster, 1970.
———. *Biblical Theology of the Old and New Testaments*. Minneapolis: Fortress, 1977.
———. *Introduction to the Old Testament as Scripture*. Philadelphia: Fortress, 1979.
Clifford, Richard J. *The Wisdom Literature*. Nashville: Abingdon, 1998.
Conzelmann, Hans. *The Theology of St. Luke*. 2nd ed. Translated by Geoffrey Buswell. Philadelphia: Fortress, 1982.
Coogan, Michael D. *A Brief Introduction to the Old Testament*. New York: Oxford University Press, 2009.
Cory, Catherine. *A Voyage through the New Testament*. Upper Saddle River, NJ: Pearson Prentice Hall, 2008.
Countryman, L. William. *Biblical Authority or Biblical Tyranny? Scripture and the Christian Pilgrimage*. Valley Forge: PA: Trinity International, 1994.
Crenshaw, James L. *Ecclesiastes*. Old Testament Library. Philadelphia: Westminster, 1988.
———. *Old Testament Wisdom: An Introduction*. Atlanta: John Knox, 1981.
Cross, Frank Moore. *Canaanite Myth and Hebrew Epic: Essays in the History of the Religion of Israel*. Cambridge, MA: Harvard University Press, 1973.
Drane, John. *Introducing the New Testament*. Revised and Updated. Minneapolis: Fortress, 2001.
Dunn, J. D. G. *The Acts of the Apostles*. Valley Forge, PA: Trinity, 1996.
Duvall, J. Scott, and J. Daniel Hays. *Grasping God's Word*. 3rd ed. Grand Rapids, MI: Zondervan, 2012.
Ehrman, Bart D. *A Brief Introduction to the New Testament*. 3rd ed. New York: Oxford University Press, 2013.
———. *The Historical Jesus. Course Guidebook*. Chantilly, VA: The Great Courses, 2000.
———. *Jesus: Apocalyptic Prophet of the New Millennium*. New York: Oxford University Press, 1999.
———. *The New Testament: A Historical Introduction to the Early Christian Writings*. 7th ed. New York: Oxford University Press, 2020.
———. *The New Testament. Course Guidebook*. Chantilly, Virginia: Teaching Company, 2000.
Eichrodt, Walther. *Theology of the Old Testament*. Vol. 1. Philadelphia: Westminster, 1961.
Friedman, Richard Elliott. *Who Wrote the Bible?* New York: HarperSanFrancisco, 1997.
Gordis, Robert. *The Book of God and Man: A Study of Job*. Chicago: The University of Chicago Press, 1965.
———. *Koheleth—The Man and His World: A Study of Ecclesiastes*. 3rd. ed. New York: Schocken, 1968.
Guthrie, Donald. *New Testament Theology*. Downers Grove, IL: Inter-Varsity, 1981.
Harrison, R. K. *Introduction to the Old Testament*. Grand Rapids, MI: Eerdmans, 1969.
Hendricks, Howard G. and William D. *Living by the Book: The Art and Science of Reading the Bible*. Chicago: Moody, 2007.

Hillers, Delbert R. *Covenant: The History of a Biblical Idea*. Baltimore: Johns Hopkins Press, 1969.
Klein, William W., et al. *Introduction to Biblical Interpretation*. Rev. ed. Nashville, TN: Thomas Nelson, 2004.
Koester, Craig. R. *The Apocalypse: Controversies and Meaning in Western History*. Transcript of 24 lectures. Chantilly, VA: The Great Courses, 2011.
———. *Revelation and the End of All Things*. Grand Rapids, MI: Eerdmans, 2001.
Koterski, Joseph W. *Biblical Wisdom Literature*. Lecture Transcript of 36 Lectures. Chantilly, VA: The Great Courses. 2009.
Knight, George W., III. *The Pastoral Epistles*. The New International Greek Testament Commentary. Grand Rapids, MI: Eerdmans, 1999.
Kysar, Robert. *John: The Maverick Gospel*. 3rd ed. Louisville: Westminster John Knox, 2007.
Ladd, George Eldon. *A Theology of the New Testament*. Grand Rapids, MI: Eerdmans, 1974.
Maddox, Robert. *The Purpose of Luke-Acts*. Edinburgh: T & T Clark, 1982.
Marshall, I. H. *Luke: Historian and Theologian*. Grand Rapids: Zondervan, 1970.
McGrath, Alister E. *Christian Theology: An Introduction*. 5th. ed. Malden, MA: Wiley-Blackwell 2011.
McLaren, Brian D. *A Generous Orthodoxy*. Grand Rapids, MI: Zondervan, 2004.
———. *A New Kind of Christian: A Tale of Two Friends on a Spiritual Journey*. San Francisco: Jossey-Bass, 2001.
———. *A New Kind of Christianity: Ten Questions That Are Transforming the Faith*. New York: HarperCollins, 2010.
Metzger, Bruce M. *The New Testament: Its Background, Growth, and Content*. Nashville: TN, 1965.
Murphy, Roland E. *The Tree of Life: An Exploration of Biblical Wisdom Literature*. 3rd ed. Grand Rapids, MI: Eerdmans, 2002.
Neill, Stephen. *Jesus Through Many Eyes: Introduction to the Theology of the New Testament*. Philadelphia: Fortress, 1976.
O'Connor, Kathleen M. *The Wisdom Literature*. Collegeville, MN: Liturgical, 1990.
Richardson, Alan. *Genesis I–XI*. Torch Commentary. London: SCM, 1953.
———. *An Introduction to the Theology of the New Testament*. New York: Harper, 1958.
Schüssler Fiorenza, Elisabeth. *Revelation: Vision of a Just World*. Rev. ed. Minneapolis: Fortress, 1998.
Spong, John Shelby. *Liberating the Gospels: Reading the Bible with Jewish Eyes*. San Francisco: HarperSanFrancisco, 1996.
———. *Rescuing the Bible from Fundamentalism*. New York: HarperSanFrancisco, 1991.
———. *Why Christianity Must Change or Die*. New York: HarperOne, 1999.
Stewart, James S. *A Man in Christ: The Vital Elements of St. Paul's Religion*. New York: Harper & Row, 1963 (1935).
Talbert, Charles H. *Literary Patterns, Theological Themes and the Genre of Luke-Acts*. Society of Biblical Literature Monograph Series 20. Missoula, MT: Scholars, 1974.
———. *Perspectives on Luke-Acts*. Edinburgh: Clark, 1978.
———. *Reading Acts: A Literary and Theological Commentary on the Acts of the Apostles*. New York: Crossroad, 1997.

Valantasis, Richard, et al. *The Gospels and Christian Life in History and Practice.* Lanham, MD: Rowman & Littlefield, 2009.

Vande Kappelle. Robert P. *Beyond Belief: Faith, Science, and the Value of Unknowing.* Eugene: OR: Wipf & Stock, 2012.

———. *Dark Splendor: Spiritual Fitness for the Second Half of Life.* Eugene: OR: Wipf & Stock, 2015.

———. *Refined by Fire: Rethinking Essential Teachings in Scripture.* Eugene, OR: Wipf & Stock, 2018.

———. *Securing Life: The Enduring Message of the Bible.* Eugene, OR: Wipf & Stock, 2016.

Virkler, Henry A. and Karelynne Gerber Ayayo. *Hermeneutics: Principles and Processes of Biblical Interpretation.* 2nd ed. Grand Rapids, MI: Baker, 2007.

Weber, Max. *The Sociology of Religion.* Boston: Beacon, 1963.

Willimon, William H. *Acts.* Interpretation: A Bible Commentary for Teaching and Preaching. Louisville: John Knox, 1988.

Witherington, Ben, III. *The Acts of the Apostles: A Socio-Rhetorical Commentary.* Grand Rapids, MI: Eerdmans, 1998.

———. *Jesus the Sage: The Pilgrimage of Wisdom.* Minneapolis: Fortress, 1994.

Index

Abraham, 5, 10, 46, 47, 48, 50, 54, 57, 95, 96, 159
　See also covenant, with Abraham
Acts, book of, 7, 8, 12, 30, 88, 91, 106, 110, 113, 121, 131, 133–47, 150, 151, 158, 170, 185
afterlife, doctrine of, 82
Alexander the Great, 109
Amos, book of, 86, 88, 97
apocalypse, apocalypticism, 6, 8, 85, 86, 99–103, 106, 123–31, 157, 173, 175–80, 183, 185
　definition of, 176
　See also Jesus Christ, as apocalyptic Jew, resurrection of; Paul (apostle), as apocalyptic Jew
Apocrypha, 3
apocryphal, deuterocanonical, 4, 6, 33, 53, 170
Astruc, Jean, 46
Athanasius (bishop), 108
Augustine (bishop), 149, 156, 174

Babylonian Exile, 5, 6, 57, 61, 62, 71, 73, 74, 84, 88, 93, 94, 99, 101
Beard, Charles A., 74
Bible, the, 1–10, 82, 86, 155, 187
　application of, vii, 20, 189–90
　definition of, 2, 37
　contextual reading of, 24, 123
　historical material in, 35–37, 53–63
　　See also Historical Books
　inspiration of, 21–30

　interpretation of, 11–20, 109, 189–90
　literal reading of, 13–14, 17, 24, 26, 147, 183
　literary genres in, 12, 13, 37, 67, 147, 176
　method for studying, 19–20
　sacredness of, 1–2, 17, 93
Borg, Marcus, 17
Boring, Eugene, 185
Brown, Raymond, 141
Bultmann, Rudolph, 174
Burridge, Kenelm, 90. 91

Cadbury, Henry, 143
Calvin, John, 149, 156, 174
canon, Christian, 2, 10, 26, 40–41, 173
canon, Jewish, 6, 40–41
canonical process, 106–8
Cassidy, Richard, 143
Chadwick, Nora, 90
Christianity, 1, 8, 17, 18, 27, 72, 82, 88, 104, 106, 110, 118, 165, 189
　growth of, 137–44
Chronicler's History, 6, 55, 59–63
Chronicles, books of, 3, 6, 27, 37, 54, 59–63, 85
Colossians, letter to, 82, 133, 148, 154, 159, 171
Columbus, Christopher, 1
Constantine (emperor), 109, 112
Conzelmann, Hans, 143

197

Corinthians, First, 14, 82, 88, 90, 109, 130, 137, 145, 146, 148, 151, 153, 156, 157, 171, 178–79, 185
Corinthians, Second, 82, 104, 130, 131, 145, 146, 151, 178, 185
Countryman, William, 24
covenant, vii, 9, 35, 50, 56, 95–96, 101, 104, 157
   new, 9
   with Abraham, 28, 46, 50, 57, 95, 101
   with David, 57, 63–65, 95, 101
   with Moses, 5, 50, 95, 97, 104
   with Noah, 50, 95
covenant lawsuit, 96–97, 98
creation, doctrine of, vii, 5, 9, 18, 46, 47, 48, 101, 102, 130, 157
   new, vii, 99, 131, 178
Cullmann, Oscar, 131

Daniel, book of, 6, 8, 9, 34, 48, 73, 86, 99, 100, 130, 177
Darby, John Nelson, 183
David (king), 5, 35, 47, 55, 58, 60, 62, 63–64, 68–69, 71, 76, 88
   See also covenant, with David
Day of the Lord, 99, 100, 131, 177, 178
Dead Sea Scrolls, 39, 125, 177
Deuteronomistic History, 5, 43, 54, 55–59, 61, 62, 64, 93
Deuteronomy, book of, 5, 29, 43, 49, 50, 51, 55, 56, 58, 89, 150
dispensationalism, 182–83
Documentary Hypothesis, 43–46, 54

Easter, 51, 131
Ecclesiastes, book of, 6, 67, 73, 75, 76, 78, 79, 80, 82, 83, 84
Eichhorn, John, 46
Elohist (E writer), 43
Ephesians, letter to, 90, 148, 149, 154, 159, 171
epistle
   definition of, 160
eschaton, the, 131
Esther, book of, 4, 6, 33, 55, 61
evil (cosmic), 102–3, 123–24, 126, 176–77, 178, 179, 180, 182

Exodus, book of, 5, 22, 27, 36, 40, 46, 50, 51, 52, 67, 71, 89, 91, 102, 142
Exodus, the, 5, 36, 48, 50–51, 60, 98, 102, 130
Ezekiel (prophet), 88, 94, 95
Ezekiel, book of, 28, 37, 86, 93, 99, 100, 176, 177
Ezra (scribe), 61, 69, 77
Ezra, book of, 6, 34, 59, 61, 62

faith, 18, 29, 35, 40, 51, 56, 71, 83, 101, 113, 114, 116, 120, 126, 142, 152, 156, 159, 162, 163, 165, 180
Five Scrolls, 6
form criticism, 39
Former Prophets, 4, 5, 6, 85

Galatians, letter to, 10, 105, 137, 140, 145, 146, 148, 149, 150, 151, 152, 158, 171
General Epistles, 7, 8, 113, 159, 160–71
Genesis, book of, 5, 9, 35–36, 39, 45, 47, 48, 83, 95, 159, 179
genre. *See* Bible, the, literary genre in
gospels, 7, 8, 13, 18, 22, 28, 39, 106, 113, 114, 116–29, 133, 159, 170
   synoptic, 7, 116, 117, 119, 120
Greco-Roman world, 109–12

Habbakuk, book of, 86, 88
Haggai, book of, 86, 88
Hebrew Bible. *See* Old Testament (Tanakh)
Hebrews, book of, 8, 82, 104, 136, 161, 162–63
heresy, 166–70
hermeneutics, 12, 20
Herodotus, 35
Historical Books, 5, 53–65
Hobbes, Thomas, 45
Holy Spirit, 18, 23, 26, 91, 138, 140, 149, 156
hope, 9, 34, 65, 176, 177, 181, 187
Hosea, book of, 48, 86, 88, 95, 98

Intertestamental Period, 95, 99

Irwin, James, 1
Isaiah, book of, 9, 28, 37, 39, 86, 88, 91, 92, 93, 99, 100, 102, 176, 177
Israel, kingdom of, 5, 57, 59, 65, 68, 70, 71, 87, 88

James, letter of, 8, 82, 107, 158, 159, 162
Jeremiah (prophet), 37, 61, 88, 93, 94, 95, 99, 104
Jeremiah, book of, 9, 29, 34, 37, 39, 86, 93, 95, 97, 98, 104
Jesus Christ, 7, 8, 10, 30, 82, 88, 104, 105, 106, 110, 112–14, 116, 117, 130, 138, 141, 143, 144, 148, 151, 162, 165, 178, 180, 185
    as apocalyptic Jew, 121–29, 157
    ethical teachings of, 127–28
    as Messiah, 7, 112, 116, 120, 128, 149, 150, 151, 165
    resurrection of, 130–31
    as wisdom, 82
Job, book of, 6, 67, 73, 75, 78, 80, 81, 82, 84
Joel, book of, 86, 88, 91, 99
John, gospel of, 7, 76, 82, 107, 109, 114, 116–20, 121, 123, 124, 125, 126, 133, 166, 167
John, letters of, 8, 107, 161, 167, 167–69
John the Baptist, 88, 122, 124, 125
Jonah, book of, 86, 88
Joseph, 36, 83
Josephus, 85, 125, 140
Joshua, book of, 5, 40, 54, 56, 58
Judah, kingdom of, 5, 27, 57, 58, 65, 71, 88
Judaism, 7, 71, 72, 75, 82, 88, 90, 104, 123, 128, 140, 149, 152, 161, 165, 189
    and Christianity, 7, 140, 162, 165
Judas Iscariot, 128–29
Jude, letter of, 8, 107, 108, 113, 166, 169
Judges, book of, 5, 27, 54, 56, 58, 76, 91

kingdom of God, 6, 34, 99, 102, 123–29, 130, 151, 153, 158, 178, 179, 180, 182, 184, 187

Kings, books of, 5, 27, 37, 50, 54, 55, 57, 58, 59, 60, 61, 62, 89, 91, 93

Lamentations, book of, 6
Latter Prophets, 4, 6
Law, the. *See* Torah
Lawrence, D. H., 175
Leviticus, book of, 5, 40, 50, 153
Lightfoot, J. B., 141
Lindbergh, Charles, 1
Luke (author), 133–47
    as historian, 138–44
    portrayal of Paul, 141, 144–47
Luke, gospel of, 7, 28, 30, 90, 106, 107, 114, 116–29, 133, 138, 139, 140, 141, 142, 143, 144, 185
Luther, Martin, 149, 174

Malachi, book of, 86, 88
Mark, gospel of, 7, 28, 30, 106, 116–29, 152
Marshall, I. H., 140–41
Masoretic Text, 39
Matthew, gospel of, 3, 7, 28, 30, 82, 90, 105, 107, 109, 110, 116–28, 130, 131, 135, 158, 185
McLaren, Brian, 15
Messiah, the, 65, 69, 93, 101, 103, 112, 116, 120, 122, 128, 129, 149, 150, 151
Metzger, Bruce, 169
Micah, book of, 86, 88, 98
Minear, Paul, 174
Minor Prophets, 4, 6, 38, 86, 94
Moses, 5, 9, 22, 42, 43, 44, 45, 46, 47, 48, 50, 52, 56, 57, 59, 77, 89, 162

Nahum, book of, 86
Napoleon Bonaparte, 112
Nehemiah, book of, 6, 59, 61, 62, 91
New Jerusalem, 102, 177
New Testament, 2, 3, 7–9, 10, 19, 29, 32, 69, 82, 90, 108, 109, 113, 114, 120, 130, 160, 166, 173, 175, 178, 181
Newton, Isaac, 174–75
Numbers, book of, 5, 40, 43, 50, 56, 87

Obadiah, book of, 86
Old Testament (Tanakh), 1, 2, 4–7, 9,
    29, 32–41, 95, 96, 99, 104, 107,
    117, 173
  as Hebrew scripture, 2, 3
  relation to New Testament, 105–6
orality, 38, 49, 93, 94, 113

paganism, 111, 191
Passover, 2, 51, 119
pastoral epistles, 113, 136–37, 154,
    159, 171
patience, 83–84
Paul (apostle) 8, 29, 90, 104, 105, 107,
    126, 130, 133, 134, 135, 136,
    137, 138, 140, 148–52, 170, 171
  as apocalyptic Jew, 152–53, 157,
    178–79
  epistles of, 7, 8, 12, 107, 110, 113,
    140, 148–59, 160, 162, 165,
    169, 170
  ethical teachings of, 153
  and Jesus, 151–52, 156–58
  and justification by faith, 134, 152,
    158, 159
  See also Luke (author), portrayal
    of Paul
Pentateuch, 3, 4, 5, 39, 53, 56, 72, 95
  compositional history of, 42–52, 54
persecution (religious), 110–12, 163,
    163–66, 176, 180
Peter (apostle), 8, 30, 108, 163, 169
Peter, letters of, 8, 23, 51, 52, 107, 108,
    135, 149, 161, 163–64, 166,
    169, 170–71
Philemon, letter to, 8, 154, 171
Philippians, letter to, 145, 150, 152
Philo, 75, 90
Picasso, Pablo, 180
Plato (philosopher), 90
poetic parallelism, 68
poetry, 71
Priestly writer (P), 43–44, 62, 69
prophecy, 3, 36, 74, 85, 87, 88, 89, 95
  and apocalypticism, 99–103, 183
prophet(s), 6, 57, 58, 59, 64, 65, 75, 85,
    89, 92–94, 99
  and covenant, 95–99

definition of, 89
role of, 86–87, 89–91
women as, 91
Prophets, the, 3, 4, 53, 74, 85–103
Proverbs, book of, 6, 39, 67, 73, 75, 76,
    77–78, 79, 80, 81, 82, 84
Psalms, book of, 1, 4, 6, 12, 39, 49, 65,
    67–72
pseudepigrapha, pseudepigraphic, 77,
    137
pseudonymous authorship, 170–71

"Q" source, 120, 121, 122, 124, 126
Qoheleth, 80, 82, 84

rabbi, 95
Ramsay, W. M., 141
Rauschenbush, Walter, 174
redaction criticism, 40
Renan, Ernst, 112
Revelation, book of, 7, 8, 10, 13, 85,
    103, 106, 107, 109, 113, 159,
    161, 166, 167, 173–81
  interpretation of, 181–87
Romans, letter to, 8, 10, 29, 104, 105,
    137, 145, 146, 148, 149, 152,
    153, 154, 156, 158, 159, 179
Royal Theology, 64–65
Ruth, book of, 4, 6, 33, 53

Sabbath, 22, 51, 52, 131, 161
Samuel, books of, 5, 37, 40, 54, 57, 58,
    60, 62, 63–65, 67, 73, 76, 87, 89
Schweitzer, Albert, 124
Scofield, Charles I., 183
scripture. *See* Bible
Second Isaiah, 9, 86, 88, 93, 100–101,
    102
Seneca (philosopher), 171
Septuagint, 3, 32, 39, 62, 74, 78, 86
Sermon on the Mount, 127, 158, 162
Solomon (king), 5, 28, 47, 55, 58, 60,
    64, 71, 76–77, 170
Son of Man, 9, 124, 125, 126, 127, 128,
    129, 130, 157
Song of Solomon, book of, 4, 6, 28,
    33, 76
Spinoza, Baruch, 45

suffering, 81–82, 83, 102, 163, 164, 176, 177, 187
  See also persecution
Suffering Servant, 9, 93

Ten Commandments, 22, 56
Thessalonians, First, 126, 149, 153, 154
Thessalonians, Second, 154, 156, 159, 171
Third Isaiah, 86, 93, 99, 100, 101, 102
Thomas, gospel of, 121, 122, 123, 125, 126
Tillich, Paul, 184
Timothy, letters to, 15, 23, 136, 137, 154, 155, 159, 170
Titus, letter to, 136, 154, 155, 159
Torah, 3, 4, 9, 33, 42, 46, 50, 52, 53, 70, 73, 74, 75, 157, 158, 162
  See also Pentateuch

Van Gogh, Vincent, 180

Weber, Max, 91
Wells, H. G., 112
Wheelwright, Philip, 184
Wisdom Books, 4, 67, 72–84
wise women, 76
Witherington, Ben, 80
Writings, the, 3, 4, 6, 53, 74, 86

Yahwist (J writer), 35, 43, 47–48, 49, 56

Zechariah, book of, 28, 86, 88, 99, 177
Zephaniah, book of, 86, 88

www.ingramcontent.com/pod-product-compliance
Lightning Source LLC
Chambersburg PA
CBHW051738230426
43670CB00012B/2072